AN OKANAGAN HISTORY

The Diaries of Roger John Sugars

1905 – 1919

Bob– Enjoy! — John
July 16/05

Sugars Publishing

AN OKANAGAN HISTORY
THE DIARIES OF ROGER JOHN SUGARS
1905 - 1919

Copyright 2005 Sugars Publishing

John A. Sugars, Editor

Published by: Sugars Publishing
3804 Brown Road
Westbank, BC V4T 2J3
(250) 707-1551
e-mail: jasugars@telus.net

Distributed by: Sandhill Book Marketing
#99 - 1270 Ellis Street
Kelowna, BC V1Y 1Z4 250-763-1406
E-mail: info@sandhillbooks.com

Layout and cover design: Jennifer Grover (Sugars)

Photographs in this publication are contributed from the collection of Roger J. Sugars.

ISBN: 0-9738153-0-2

ACKNOWLEDGEMENTS

The Sugars family, as publishers, would like to thank the following individuals for their help in launching *"An Okanagan History: The Diaries of Roger John Sugars, 1905-1919."*

"Friends of Fintry" for their generous financial assistance and constant encouragement.

"Central Okanagan Regional District" for their financial support.

The Kelowna Heritage Foundation for their generous financial support in enabling *"An Okanagan History"* to be shared by the entire Okanagan Valley and beyond.

Mike Roberts, CHBC TV, for his support and assistance with this project over a ten-year-plus period.

Dorothy Brotherton, *Westside Weekly*, for her publicity that started the ball rolling.

Judy Steeves, *Kelowna Capital News*, for her publicity and support of the diaries.

Wayne Wilson, Executive Director, Kelowna Museum, for holding the book launch for his never-ending support of the project.

Dave Preston, Publisher, *The Peachland View*, for his publicity and support.

The Okanagan Historical Society for their support and encouragement.

For transcribing the diaries from handwritten to print:
Jo Jones - Desktop Publishing, Vernon, BC
Linda Wills, Vernon Museum

Dorothy Zoellner for her final editing and proof-reading.

Jennifer Grover (Sugars) for her work on the computer doing layout and design.

Thank you all and any we may have missed.

John A. Sugars, Publisher

A WORD FROM THE AUTHOR

By Roger Sugars, October 1968 (Age 71)

Roger, Vancouver Street Photo, 1948

It all began a way back when!

My father was the youngest of four brothers and two sisters born in Lancashire of almost pure English origin. He graduated from Oxford as an MA in Classics - a mild and modest man with a vast knowledge of languages and literature. He married young and moved to London where his work was. He was not ambitious but never lazy. He had a comfortable living in London and was content with that.

My mother was very different; born in Cheshire of English, French and German origin with a touch of American from Virginia somewhere. Her mother's name was Greenbank, while her father wore the unpleasant name of Helberger. She had only one sister and no brothers.

We lived in London where I was born in a comfortable flat in Clapham until I was about eight years old. Next door to our apartment building was a Catholic college and not being bigoted about Catholics, my parents sent me to school there because it was so convenient. That was where I learned the "3 Rs" - The cassocked "brothers" were very good and didn't try to convert me.

While I was there one boy died and a collection was taken to say masses for his soul. I threw in a three penny bit! I was afterwards told that this would excuse me from several hundred days in purgatory! I remember, even at that early age, thinking how ridiculous it was that sins could be bought off with money.

Meanwhile my father was doing quite well as a private tutor - mainly coaching boys and young men for Oxford and Cambridge. He loved this work and took a keen interest in all the different types of students - some Chinese and Siamese from highly cultured families.

However, my mother grew more restless and the great thing in those days (1904-05) was a to go out to the colonies, Canada in particular.

Everything was uprooted, and in April 1905 we embarked from the port of London on a converted cattle boat, the S.S. "Sarmatian," destined for Montreal. A small group of "first class" passengers and numerous emigrants (or immigrants?) up forward. The voyage took three weeks, the first week was stormy, the second week fog and icebergs, the remainder grinding through floe ice from the St. Lawrence breaking a channel for 3 or 4 other ships not so sturdy. To me, as a little boy, it looked like the Arctic Regions.

We stayed 3 or 4 days in Montreal in the "Baths" hotel - and went up Mount Royal and to Lachine - then onto Toronto where we only spent about 2 days. My father had a friend who was to meet us in Winnipeg. Apparently they had no definite plans as to where to go: this was to be decided in Winnipeg. At that time the west was just emerging from the pioneer period. Alberta and Saskatchewan were still "territories" but B.C. offered terrific opportunities, especially in the fabulous Okanagan Valley. If you could get a piece of land - any land - you just planted it to fruit trees and went fishing or hunting for a few years when the trees would be bearing and your fortune was made!

So we went to Vernon, stayed in the Coldstream Hotel for a week or so then went camping on the shores of Long (Kalamalka) Lake among the rattlesnakes for most of the summer of 1905. My father and his friend cruised around the country and finally, as fall was approaching, bought a "preemption" from the original settler for a few hundred sterling. It was 140 acres of wild land with 1/2 a mile of lakeshore; nothing on it but a tent and an old log cabin. It was near Shorts' Point (later called Fintry) where the sternwheelers "Aberdeen" and later "Okanagan" and "Sicamous" called and were the only communication with the outside world except the original Hudson Bay Fur Brigade Trail, which traversed the entire west side of the lake and on to Kamloops and the Cariboo.

We stayed in a tent and then the log cabin and just before winter set, we had a small frame house completed (the coldest I've ever lived in!). My poor mother soon realized this was not the Mecca she had dreamed of. It was a daily round of hardship and hard work; no conveniences of any kind, coal oil lamps, no plumbing, carrying water from a well, bucking wood to keep the fires going, mail once a week, a small general store four miles away, walk ride or row. Nearest neighbour 2 miles; only one other woman in over 20 miles.

My father, on the other hand, took it all very philosophically and never complained, though he was utterly unadapted to pioneer life.

I think he rather enjoyed it. I know I did! - Although there were no other children anywhere near, it was all highly romantic and exciting; cowboys and Indians frequently passed back and forth on that Hudson Bay Trail. I learned to ride and row and sail and hunt and shoot and to be proficient with woods tools. As the years went on, more people came into the area, many of them fine types mainly of English or Scottish origin. As I grew up I went to work on the fruit ranches and in the logging camps.

I decided the woods were my dish and planned to be a Forest Ranger. World War I changed all this. I spent a couple of years in the Forestry Corps on the Aisne Front in France working in the woods under shell fire.

When I came back my parents had moved to Salmon Arm, having sold the old homestead for a paltry $1000 to J.C. Dun-Waters (nicknamed "The Laird of Fintry"). I had to do something in a hurry - rehabilitation grants not being what they were in World War II.

I took a farm under the S.S.B. and made a home for my parents - worked like a fiend for about 8 years growing fruit and hay, driving horses and milking cows, and in the winter hacking ties, hauling cordwood and railroad ties with horses and sleighs.

I was getting nowhere financially so went into the hardware business in Salmon Arm. The Depression came along and fixed that!

In the meantime my mother had died at the early age of 50, worn out with life in this land of promise! Such a shame because she was a well educated woman and an accomplished pianist; many of my favourite Chopin, Schubert, Beethoven and Liszt records are numbers she used to play. (My father died in 1936 at the age of 67).

Shortly after her death I married Margaret Hooper in June 1923. She was one of a large family of English and Scottish parentage.

In desperation I went to work for Beatty Bros. out of Vernon B.C. and sold pumps and farm equipment all over the Interior. This job lasted 11 years! Anyway it carried me through the Depression.

By now I had 4 children - 2 boys and 2 girls. About 1942 Beatty Bros. sold their B.C. interests to Mc & Mc (*McLennan, McFeely and Prior - a hardware chain*) and our sales staff was disbanded. That summer and fall my wife and I worked in the orchards in Kelowna. I had inherited a few dollars in a legacy and we built a house at 1953 Water Street Kelowna and lived there for over 20 years.

In '43 I joined the staff of Carruthers & Son Insurance and was with them over 20 years. Ted Carruthers was a grand old man and I thought the world of him. When he went (at 84) his son-in-law Maurice Meikle took over and it became "Carruthers and Meikle."

I never cared too much for Maurice and in June '64 I went to DeMara & Sons Insurance as a commission salesman and have done very well with them.

In 1954 my wife purchased the land that I now live on - 23 acres of unimproved open grass and sagebrush overlooking the Lake near Westbank - for $1600. This was known as Indian Reserve cutoff land. Some 200 acres in all - the Federal Government surveyed it into parcels from 17 to 27 acres in size and sold it by auction. We sold about 13 acres for $17,000 and proceeded to develop it - built roads and put in domestic water - all very costly and extremely frustrating; thwarted with red tape at every move.

Then we sold the house at 1953 Water Street in Kelowna for $12,500 (this was my contribution to the effort) and proceeded to build a new house, which, when completed, cost over $20,000. Nearly all of the remaining land has been sold since and I now have the house with a clear title on about 1/2 an acre of land. There is still about 2 1/2 acres of somewhat rough land. It can sit and wait for a purchaser.

This was my wife's dream and ambition and her faith in the project never faltered. But fate decided that she was not to enjoy it. She gradually became ill with an obscure and terrible disease (cause and cure unknown), diagnosed as Pseudo Bulbar Palsy or motor neuron disease - a progressive paralysis which first took her voice and then the use of her arms and later her life - a terrible thing to watch. It took her life in about a year (at 67).

We spent much money seeking relief or cure without avail. Doctors assured us nothing could be done.

I would prefer not to dwell on this subject any further. I am getting used to the more or less solitary life and have little time to get lonely. The various families visit me from time to time and I visit them (even to Nova Scotia).

I was 71 last January 25 and still enjoy good health.

AUTHOR'S HANDWRITTEN NOTES

Oct   1968

an away back when !

My father was the youngest of 4 brothers & 2
sisters born in Lancashire of almost pure
English origin.   He graduated from Oxford as
an M/A in Classics   A mild & modest man
with a vast knowledge of languages & literature.
He married young & moved to London where
his work was. He was not ambitious but never
lazy He had a comfortable living in London & was
content with that

My mother was very different, born in Cheshire
of English French & German origin with a Touch
of American from Virginia Somewhere
Her mothers name was Greegank while
her father wore the unpleasant name of Helberger
She had only one sister & no brothers.

We lived in London, where I was born, in a comfortable flat
in Clapham until I was about 8 years old
next door to our apartment building was a
Catholic College & not being bigoted about
Catholics, my parents sent me to school there
because it was so convenient   There was
where I learned The "3 Rs"   The cassocked
"brothers" were very good & didn't try to convert me
        was there one boy died & a collection
was taken to say masses for his soul. I threw
in a Three penny bit !   I was afterwards Told
that this would excuse me from Several hundred

AUTHOR'S HANDWRITTEN NOTES

days in purgatory! I remember, even at that early age, thinking how ridiculous it was that sins could be bought off with money

Meanwhile my father was doing quite well as a private tutor — mainly coaching boys & young men for Oxford & Cambridge.

He loved this work & took a keen interest in all the different types of students — Some Chinese & Siamese from highly cultured families.

However, my mother grew more restless & the great thing in those days (1904 05) was to go out to the Colonies, Canada in particular

Everything was uprooted & in April 1905 we embarked from the port of London on a converted cattle boat destined for Montreal. S.S. "Sarmatian" A small group of "first class" passengers & numerous emigrants (or immigrants?) up forward   the voyage took 3 weeks; the first week was stormy, the second week fog & icebergs, the remainder grinding through floe ice from the St. Lawrence breaking a channel for 3 or 4 other ships not so sturdy. To me, as a little boy it looked like the Arctic Regions —

We stayed 3 or 4 days in Montreal in the "Bath" Hotel & went up Mt. Royal & to Lachine —

Then on to Toronto where we only spent about 2 days

Library and Archives Canada Cataloguing in
Publication

Sugars, Roger John, 1897-1981
   An Okanagan history : the diaries of Roger John
Sugars, 1905-1919 /
Roger John Sugars ; editor: John A. Sugars.

ISBN 0-9738153-0-2

1. Sugars, Roger John, 1897-1981 .   2. Okanagan
Valley (B.C. : Region)-
Biography.   I. Sugars, John A. (John Allan), 1929- .
II. Title.

FC3845.O4Z49 2005   971.1'5
C2005-904008-4

An Okanagan History

The Diaries of Roger John Sugars

Contents

FOREWORD

By Lilian Sugars

Roger Sugars, 1901 England

John Edward Sugars, who had earned a Masters Degree in English at Oxford, made his living as a private tutor to young people needing to pass the rigid exams that would get them into Eton, Oxford, or Cambridge.

John Edward, a gentle and amiable gentleman, married Lily Helberger, a restless and adventuresome young lady, who was an accomplished pianist [*Lily had studied with noted pianist Sir Edward German*]. On January 25, 1897, Lily bore a son, Roger John. As Roger grew and took less and less of Lily's time, she became more and more restless.

Lily dreamed of becoming a pioneer in the wilderness of Canada. A.K. Menzies (pronounced Ming-eez), a handsome young adventurer and family friend, had been to Canada and filled her head with romantic tales of life in Western Canada.

Lily had little trouble convincing John Edward that they should emigrate to Canada, and, in 1905 they packed up their most treasured possessions, sold the rest, and booked passage to Montreal. They agreed to meet A.K., who had gone on ahead to scout out possible places to settle, in Winnipeg.

By this time Roger was eight years old.

On March 24, 1905, the little family set sail in the S.S. Sarmatian (a sturdy, converted cattle boat of the Allan Line) for Montreal. After days of dense fog and icebergs off Newfoundland and grinding at dead slow through ice floes, the Sarmatian docked in Montreal. A three day stop there to get their land legs, and a brief stop in Toronto, then the C.P.R. deposited them in Winnipeg where they rendezvoused with A.K. (We never did find out his full name).

A.K., who was practically broke, raved about the beauties of the Okanagan Valley of British Columbia, "a veritable land of promise". He had never actually been there, but had met some adventurers who had. The family spent five days in Winnipeg.

Roger, about 1912
"Coureur de bois!"

Roger wrote in the Okanagan Historical Society's 39th Report: "While in Winnipeg, my father presented me with a "Daisy" air rifle. From the second floor balcony of the Winnipeg Hotel I was tempted to test my skill as a marksman with my new air rifle. I was watching the traffic going by on Portage Avenue and there on the opposite side of the street (Portage is quite wide) was a farmer perched on the box seat of his wagon, wearing a jaunty bowler hat---it was too good a target to miss I guess; anyway I drew a bead on that bowler hat and to my amazement I heard the BB pellet go "pop" when it struck the hard crown.

The farmer immediately drew his team to the curb. He then came straight over to the hotel and up to the second floor where I

*aptain T. D. Shorts, "a very likeable man, always genial nd friendly." Nothing bothered him, except possibly one rip when his cargo included several kegs of whiskey owned y a farmer. The farmer came aboard carrying a sheaf of vheat, promptly bored a hole in one of the kegs and with straw plucked from his sheaf, sampled the contents. All ands reached their destination safely, although the farmer vas somewhat unsteady.
aptain Shorts rowed Okanagan Lake for three years, mak-g $6,000 which he lost when he ventured into steam.*

The Sugars bought their land from Captain T.D. Shorts' - Courtesy Okanagan Archives

was huddled in mortal fear. My father had no trouble in appeasing his anger with a five dollar bill, and that was the end of my first adventure in the Wild West."

Following that incident, they travelled west by C.P.R. and on April 29th 1905, the party of four arrived in Vernon. There John Edward paid $500.00 for a 160 acre Preemption at Shorts' Point, on the west side of Okanagan Lake, sight unseen. That 160 acres turned out to be 140 acres of land and 20 acres of water, a cove in Okanagan Lake!

A.K remained with the family. He had no money to buy land of his own.

Roger remained at the homestead until 1917 when he went Overseas with the Army in W.W.I. While he was away, his parents sold the preemption to Dun-waters of Fintry for $1,000 and moved to Salmon Arm.

Mr. Menzies moved with them to Salmon Arm, and after several tries to earn a living at various jobs, became a successful insurance agent. He married and had a daughter, Hillary.

After the war Roger settled in Salmon Arm on a farm purchased with the help of the Soldiers' Settlement Board. In

Salmon Arm he met Margaret Charlotte Hooper. They were married on June 2, 1923. They produced four children, Edmund in April, 1924, Lilian in May, 1926, John in August, 1929, and Madeleine in September, 1932.

John Edward had a cabin built on a part of the "Ranch" as the farm was called. There he could be independent and still be close to Roger and his family. Lily had passed away in Kamloops Hospital in 1922 before Roger was married.

Roger, as well as attempting to run a successful fruit farm, had a half interest in the Sugars

Roger, Kelowna, May 1917

Greenwood Hardware Store in Salmon Arm.

The Great Depression forced changes. In 1933 the Sugars family moved to Kelowna which was the central point in the territory Roger covered as a travelling salesman for Beatty Bros., peddling washing machines and farm equipment. He worked there until 1939 when Beatty Bros. sold out to McLennan, McFeely and Prior, a hardware chain that closed down Beatty Bros. After a brief stint as Fruit Inspector, Roger began selling Insurance for first, Carruthers and Meikle and later for De Mara and Sons.

Margaret passed away in 1967 at the age of 67. Roger remarried in 1969 to a widow, Marjorie Foulkes.

Roger continued to work until he was 75 in 1972. He passed

away in 1981 at the age of 84.

When Roger left England as a boy, he promised his aunts that he would write to them. Instead of letters, he chose to keep diaries. When a book was full, he sent it to his Aunt Bessie. After she made sure that all interested parties had read it, she sent the book back. Some of the books managed to be returned, but several were either lost in transit or mislaid before they could be

Roger Sugars 1923

sent. However, those that were returned are worth reading for both their historic content and the excellent English of a young pioneer lad.

We, the four offspring of Roger and Margaret Sugars, are often amazed at the way our father moved from one phase of his life to the next. We would have known nothing of his life before marrying our mother had it not been for the diaries, and some stories he wrote for the Okanagan Historical Society.

According to his diaries, he was a fine woodsman, a hunter, a horseman, and a builder. He was capable of inventing useful articles and doing a hard day's manual labour. He brought none of those skills to his married life. His ability to run a farm and a store were left in Salmon Arm. His army experiences were never discussed with us but were recorded in his diary.

We knew our father as a top notch salesman, a perfect gentleman with impeccable dress, a well-liked friend to many with a marvelous sense of humour, a soft-hearted dad and a total loss at fixing anything whatever in our home.

The following diary entries gave us much insight into the young Roger Sugars and life on the West side of Okanagan Lake in the early 1900's.

****

1911

FRIDAY JUNE 2, 1911

Before I start on this diary, I will record things in general, that have happened since I finished my last diary. [*This (or these) diaries was lost in the transfer back and forth to England.*]

The winter after Christmas was severe until well on in February.

In January we had a spell of zero weather, about a week, the average temperature being about zero, the lowest 13° f below. The rest of the winter was cold with no thaws; there was about an average of a foot of snow on the ground all winter, which was perfectly dry & powdery. The depth of snow up the hill (not more than a mile or two) was about 2 to 3 feet right into March. [*Note: all temperatures are in Fahrenheit (F°)]*

On the night of the 6th of Jan. there was a bad storm, terrific squalls of wind & hail (hail stones as big as 5 cent pieces – or about the size of a three penny bit) and also – a thing I've never seen or heard of, in winter in this country before, there were two flashes of lightning, & a peal of thunder. After this the real winter weather set in.

First sign of winter, about 1909

We saw the Aurora Borealis twice during the winter.

The snow melted very gradually so we did not have the usual sudden slush & mud, in fact this has been the best spring since we have been here (6 years). From the latter part of March to the end of April we had lovely spring weather, warm & balmy. May was inclined to be showery but very warm. The last 3 or 4 days have been very hot and dry, the highest temperature 82° in the shade.

All the glorious blaze of spring flowers are over now.

That is an account of the weather.

Now for some news.

I got, last fall, a book called "*Forest Trees of The Pacific Slope*" (*of America*) by G.B. Sudworth. It is most interesting & in the early spring (after I had identified every other tree here) I got what I took to be a spruce cone & compared it with the book, but could find nothing resembling it, so sent it to Mr. G.B. Sudworth, to be identified. I got a reply from him saying it was Picea Canadensis (white Spruce) & the thing I had mistaken for a cone was caused by a gallfly. It was wonderfully like a true cone, only instead of being, composed of thin scales like a true spruce cone, it was covered with sharp spines. The other day I looked carefully, and found the true cones.

Then I looked at the book, & the distribution of this tree was said to be at its Southern limit, the Stikine River B.C. As this river is several hundreds of miles north of Okanagan Lake, I again wrote to Mr. Sudworth, who thanked me very much for the information, saying it (Picea Canadensis) had previously been unknown, south of Stikine River. I also discovered by the aid of this book that what I had before taken for a stunted form of the ordinary Juniper Tree (Juniperus occidentalis) was a different species (J. communis) It is usually called "ground juniper". It grows in low flat-topped shrubs about 4 to 8 feet across, whereas the J. occidentalis grows as a twisted & knarled tree from 10 to 30 feet high.

As I mentioned in the last diary the spruce above-mentioned grows only along with Jack pines (Pinus Contorta) & tamaracks (Larix occidentalis) that is on the higher hills & mountains – never near the lake.

Two horrible things occurred this spring. A fellow called Jack O'Mahoney was living nearly all winter in a deserted shack, south of Kennards (Nahun) & we used to see him nearly every mail day at Kennards, & we got to know him more than we had done before.

In the early spring he went over to a ranch on

Loggers 1909

Woods Lake [*Woods Lake is a continuation of Long Lake, separated by an ancient beaver dam. South of this is a small lake (Duck Lake) which is separate from Long & Woods Lake. All this chain of lakes (altogether about 20 miles long) lies parallel with Okanagan Lake, about 3 miles east with a range of hills between. [Woods Lake is now called Wood Lake. Ed.]*
In the middle of the spring we heard the horrible news that after his being on a spree, he had got melancholy, and shot himself!

The other incident was this:

Two years ago when the loggers were logging on our place, we got to know among the other "lumberjacks" who worked here, a very nice little half breed Indian fellow called Billy Smithson. He lived at Westbank (opposite Kelowna, 20 miles South and he used to work at Cowpunching & horse breaking, mostly.

Well the other day we heard that he had gone up on the range at Whiteman's Creek (10 miles North of here.) to catch or break a cayuse & sometime after he was found lying dead on the road, with his head smashed, evidently had got bucked off. We were awfully sorry about it.

To return to a little less tragic news. About a month ago MacNair sold out & has gone up north to the Queen Charlotte Islands. The man he had sold to is a Mr. Durant – a very nice fellow, but is unable to speak of anything but fish, fishing, & fishing tackle, which is rather trying.

A.K. & Deana [*Deana was my father John's nickname.*] have been working all spring at the Point & are still doing so.

I have put in a garden of onions, radishes & carrots, which seem to be doing alright.

During the spring I had several letters from Colin Haddon, saying he was coming out here, and asked all kinds of questions which I answered to the best of my ability.

He arrived yesterday, & we were very pleased to see him. He & his brother Geoffrey had been my best chums in England. *[or rather Geoffrey was. I was never very keen on Colin.]* He is going to stay here till he gets a job on a ranch. He has altered a good bit since we last saw him – 6 years or more ago – he is now 18. When I said he

Durant's House Summer 1914

arrived yesterday I meant the 3rd of June, I am writing on this Sunday the 4th..

In this diary I shall not record every day, only days when something interesting has happened. I shall leave out mail days, as they are nearly always the same – going to Kennard's for the mail every Monday & Friday.

There was rather an extraordinary thing happened, a week or two ago that I forgot to mention. It was getting dusk, & I was reading in bed when suddenly I heard a loud flapping of wings at the window, so I jumped out of bed & went & looked, but could see nothing, so concluded it must have been a bat come in & gone out again. About 20 minutes after this. Deana went outside, & found under the bedroom window a dead grouse. It must have been flying at a terrific pace & struck itself on the house.

We cooked it for dinner the next day..

This afternoon (June 4th) Colin & I went to Shorts' Creek to see if we could get any brown trout in the creek (Brown trout are mountain trout, rather scarce & only in the creeks) we had no luck, below the falls so went up & looked at the falls - they are now simply grand as the creek is in flood. The creek runs through a canyon for about half a mile above the falls & then pitches itself over a sheer cliff about 200 feet high into a deeper canyon below which is about a 100 yards long & then ends abruptly, & the creek flows out over Shorts' Point flat, & so into the lake.

I mentioned just now that the canyon goes about 1/2 a mile, above

Shorts' Creek Falls, 1910

the falls, after that it runs in the bottom of a deep gulch, the sides of which are covered thickly with bullpine (Pinus ponderosa) & fir (Pseudotsuga taxifolia), & right on the edge of the creek with cottonwoods & birches. It is like this all the way up to Attenborough's ranch (a distance of about 3 or more miles from the mouth of the creek) where it broadens out to a wide flat heavily timbered (except of course where Attenborough has cleared it) lying between steep heavily wooded mountains. It goes up from this point several miles back into the mountains through canyons gulches etc.

Colin & I got home about 4 o'clock.

TUE. 6TH.

Colin & I went hunting up the hill, for an hour or two but had no luck. In the afternoon we went fishing but caught nothing but an old sucker (allied I believe to Chub) which we threw back, as they are not much good to eat.

WED. 7.

We had our census taken today. The most amusing entertainment I have had for a long time. It was done by an elderly & very uneducated Canadian. He said to Mother, when he asked her name (which is rather a long one) "Don't choke a feller" & I had to correct him for putting down my sex as female. Among other questions there were, how much cultivated land; land in fruit trees etc. He asked Deana how many acres we had of turnips "taties" etc (meaning in his very official language <u>potatoes</u>). We had to spell N-a-h-u-n, 4 times before he grasped it. After many difficulties he managed to get through with it, & went on his way.

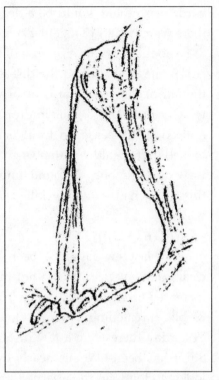

Roger's drawing of Shorts' Creek Falls

THUR. 8.

Today was hot & calm, with clouds banked on the horizon. Colin & I fished nearly all day, & had most abominable luck. We got a fine trout (about 4 or 5 lbs. it looked at least) right up to the boat, & [were] just lifting it in when it got off. 2 other smaller ones also got off shortly afterwards, & finally we landed a sucker which we killed & threw back.

We noticed a strange thing today in the fact that, every 50

yards or so there would be a dead trout, belly up. In some places there were two to 12 together or near each other. They all appeared to be about the same size – small trout of about 6 to 8 inches long.

Some of them had the disease that the Kikkaninny's have in the fall of the year, that is a sort of white fungus on their scales, which causes fins & tails to drop off before they die. I have never noticed this disease on trout before. Others that we saw today looked quite healthy with no sign of the fungus on their bodies, but we examined one, & found under its gills, a slight sign of the fungus. It had evidently killed them before it spread over their bodies.

TUE. 13.

The last few days have been, on the whole, fine. North wind & clear sunny sky, & not too hot in the mornings. The heat usually increased till it was very sultry, in the afternoon, the wind dropped, & big threatening looking clouds would rise from the west. Yesterday there were a few distant rumbles of thunder. Since the 8th it has been like this nearly every day, but in spite of the bad looking clouds in the afternoon, we only got one shower usually the big clouds would pass over by the evening.

The mosquitoes during the last day or two have been rather bad, worse than they have been for years.

Mosquitoes are not really thick here - sometimes summers go by without being troubled with them at all, hardly. This summer they seem rather bad, but not by any means very bad. We never have such experiences, as one reads about in other parts of British Columbia such as, closing a book, & opening it again to find the pages black with squashed mosquitoes!

During the morning, Colin & I walked up to Attenborough's, for the purpose of seeing if Mr. Attenborough could give him (Colin) a job, in which he succeeded in getting a job for a month. He is going to start on the 15th.

Yesterday we caught 5 fish which, altogether weighed about 8 lbs. these we sold to the Godwins at the Point. [Shorts' Point - Ed.]

This evening we caught 2 more one about a foot & a half long

& one about a foot. Got 2 others on, but they got off. Had first bathe of this spring. Water cold!

WED. 14.

Fished all the morning with Colin & caught 3 fish, 1, 6 lbs & 2 about 1 lb, each, these & the ones we got last night we sold at the Point. The six-pounder was a beauty about 2 feet long or more.

All the fish we have caught during the last day or two have brought in for us altogether $.1.85 at 12 cents a lb. They are trout of course, as they are the only marketable fish in this lake. In the afternoon we got more fish. Colin & I bathed again. The water is getting warmer, although usually at this time of year it is warmer but this year the snow in the mountains, was very late to melt, the creeks are still high with snow water, & there are a few small patches of snow left on Terrace Mountain, which is decidedly unusual, snow seldom staying there later than May.

Little Cold Mountain *[Editor's note: I believe this to be "Little White Mountain"]* is still covered entirely (that is the peak itself) & it looks very fine away in the distance to the South, gleaming white against big black thunder clouds. Today has been very hot, but no thunder threatening, the sky being clear all day, & a fresh North wind off & on.

I forgot to mention before, that during the spring months , we saw several immense flights of geese, & sand hill cranes, flying on the Northward migration at a great height. Of course these migrations are seen every spring, but this spring there were a good many more flocks than usual. I have also noticed several large flocks of Martins, which I think must have been migrating.

It might be interesting to make a note of the fact, that Mr. Ewing (at Ewing's Landing) put down some pheasants I think last fall; they have been seen as far away from Ewing's Landing as Shorts' Point, & the Andrews tell me that they are nesting near their place. (The Andrews live close to Ewing's Landing.) These are the first imported birds ever put down on this part of the Lake.

Andrews family, 1910

THUR. 15.

Another hot, clear day. Colin & I bathed twice. The water is getting warmer every day.

At four o'clock in the afternoon, Colin & I started for Attenboroughs, & got there in an hour. I left him, & one of the fellows working there, making a bunk to sleep in. Hope he will like the job up there. I walked home alone.

Most of his work, I believe will be riding the range, & tending horse, although he has worked for two years on an English farm, he is quite green to that sort of work & specially, of course, to Western Methods & rough range riding, on uncertain horses, In fact it will be turning an English farm boy, into a Western Cowpuncher which I suppose he will find hard.

SAT. 17.

Early this morning a bunch of 28 cayuses were driven north along the trail, 2 cowboys after them. I believe they came from a ranch across the line in the States.

Did a lot of fishing, but caught nothing.

SUN. 18.

Fine, hot & clear day. Colin came down from Attenborough's on a horse, & had dinner, stayed the afternoon, and left at six o'clock.

We fished most of the afternoon but got nothing but a large sucker.

MON. 19.

For the last week, A.K. & Deana have been at home. They now have a contract at the Point for clearing some acres of light Cotton wood & Willow bush. A.K. started on this today. But Deana has some work with Durant which will take about two days, when he has finished it, he is going to join A.K. at the clearing. When Deana & A.K. are working at the Point or near home they always come home for supper, & the night.

Their wages are as follows:

for any kind of work paid by the day. $2.80

for Cordwood – per cord. 2.00

for Clearing bush - per acre. 25.00

for fruit-picking - per day. 2.00

Last winter was very bad for people who grew peaches in this valley Nearly all the peach orchard in the country were ruined by the frost.

It seems peach growing is going to be given up in this valley, people will plant nothing but apples now, as they and a few other tree fruits, will stand a lot of frost, far more than peaches.

I believe the peach crop this year, will be practically nil.

Today was fine, & clear, with a north wind, & much cooler than usual, indeed when we got up at five o'clock. before the sun had risen, it was so cold that I shivered with it.   (The usual summer costume here is suited to the usual heat of summer, being as a rule, a shirt with all its buttons undone, cotton trousers or "overalls" and boots, & no underclothing whatsoever, & on top some kind of wide-brimmed hat).

An amusing feature of overalls worn in this country, are their large cotton labels firmly stitched to the waist band at the back, giving the the size you happen to wear, & the brand of the overalls such as "Pride of the West", & "Bighorn Brand."

TUE. 20.

Hot day as usual, no clouds but a thick blue haze of smoke hanging over the Mountains & Lake In the afternoon the smoke cleared off & we could get a clearer view of the more distant hills, & saw the source of the haze, away down to the South East, across the Lake, & beyond the distant, & heavily wooded hills east of Woods Lake [*now called Wood Lake*], we saw a great column of

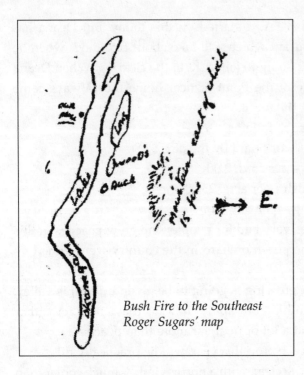

*Bush Fire to the Southeast
Roger Sugars' map*

rolling smoke, evidently from a bushfire, the Mountains behind which the smoke was coming, are at least, I should say 20 miles to the Southeast. On this page is a diagram showing the direction of the fire.

Mother & I went to Andrews today.

WED. 21.

Coolish day. Cloudy & very smokey, & with the two combined it was very dull all day.

The sunrise was very weird, & beautiful the sun shining through the smoke was deep red, as though shining through red-stained glass. For the rest of the day it was obscured in clouds & smoke. There was a distant & almost continual rumble of thunder, throughout the afternoon, & there was a shower of rain.

THUR. 22.

Thundered, lightninged, & rained, most of the night. It rained heavily for more than half the morning. In spite of the rain the smoke was still hanging thickly along the Lake.

At about midday it cleared up, & the sun came out. The afternoon was dull, with a short shower of rain. Today is Coronation Day - a holiday – so Colin came down from Attenborough's for the day.

There are two new steamers on the Lake, quite small ones called the "Kaleden" & the "Castle Gower." The "Kaleden" was built

The Kaleden 1911 - Courtesy Kelowna Museum

about a year ago, but the "Castle Gower", has only been running for a month or two.

When we first came here there were only two steamers, the "Aberdeen" & the "York" the latter is not much bigger than a fair sized steam launch, but the former is about twice as big. When we had been here two years the "Okanagan" was built, it is about 1/4 bigger than the "Aberdeen".

So now altogether there are five steamers on the Lake. All except the "Castlegar" & the "York" are stern wheelers and flat bottomed, drawing only a very few feet of water. They are run by

The S.S. Sicamous 1914 - Courtesy Kelowna Museum

The Okanagan 1907

the Canadian Pacific Railway Company.

I am reading "Macbeth" & find it extremely hard to understand. As Deana tells me I have absolutely no taste for poetry, it is far harder to understand, is unnatural, & not, I think, to be compared with prose.

SAT. 24

The latter part of yesterday afternoon, & last night it rained heavily.

Today has been fairly clear, & sunny with a steady South wind.

I saw for the first time today (Deana has seen it once) a beautiful little bird which I think was a Lazuli Bunting (Cyanospiza amoena). it was about six inches long & had a bright blue head & back, brownish wing coverts & a whitish looking breast. These birds seem rare here.

I forgot to mention on Thursday an extraordinary thing which happened at the Point. That night it thundered & lightninged a good bit, & a large tree at the Point was struck: at the foot of the tree there was a kennel, with a dog chained in it, the lightning ran up the steel chain & killed the dog. I have noticed plenty of trees in this Country that have been struck, but have never heard of an animal or man getting struck.

The York 1907

Thunder storms are few here, sometimes a summer will go by with only one slight one, sometimes it threatens thunder. Very frequently but does not come to anything.

Usually there is one bad thunder

The Aberdeen 1907

storm in a summer, what others there may be are usually slight.

We have only felt one earthquake shock here, & that was on New Year 1906 (at or about the same time as the San Francisco earthquake). [Ed. Note: Our mother, Margaret (Hooper) Sugars lived in Ventura, a suburb of San Jose, California. All birth records were held in San Francisco, and were lost. The Hooper family had to rely on their family Bible records to verify their existence.]

It shook the house (which is a small four-roomed structure of unpainted boards) violently, & rattled all the doors & windows. One of the steamers which was fastened to the wharf at Penticton (at the foot of the Lake) broke its moorings & drifted out on the Lake. It was, I believe travelling from North to South (the 'quake, not the steamer).

Third from right, front: Roger Sugars Second from left: Lily

On June 19th, I mentioned that it was very cold in the early morning.

Mrs. FitzGerald, told us, the other day, that on the night previous to June 19th, the thermometer at the Point dropped within 16 degrees of freezing point - 32°.

To my knowledge it has never dropped so low in June, since we have been here, certainly a most extraordinary country this, for sudden changes of climate. And only the day before, it was very hot, & then again the day after, it was very hot too. An almost frosty night, dropped into the midst of hot June weather!

WED. 28.

Today has been fine & fairly clear, with a strong Chinook Wind. It rained nearly all the 26th & yesterday it cleared up.

I was watching a blue mason wasp in our bedroom this morning. It has a masonry nest on the Roof just over the bed, plastered half onto the roof & half onto one of the beams. It is made of neatly constructed cells, & looks like grey stone with dull coloured lichens on it, but is really I suppose different coloured muds or masonry. This nest has been in the bedroom for a year or more. This morning I watched it going to one of the cells with a paralysed spider grasped in its "arms", it rammed this poor beast well into the cell, then the wasp pulled its head out of the cell & wiped its antennae thoroughly & then plunged its head into the cell again for a final prod at the spider, to make quite sure it was firmly wedged into the cell, & then flew off in search of more spiders. They do, I believe put one spider in the bottom of the cell, & an egg on top of that again enough spiders to fill it then the cell is cemented up.

THUR. 29.

A fairly fine day with a some what cloudy sky, & Chinook Wind. I measured myself today, & am 5 feet 1 inch & my chest measure is 28_ inches. (I was 14 on the 25th of January 1911)

FRID. 30.

A dull close day, with showers. Finished reading "Macbeth". I must say it improves as you read it. I found it interesting enough to keep me going but did not get at all enthusiastic. This damp weather is very bad for Mosquitoes. I said the other day that Mosquitoes were never really bad there, I meant in the ordinary country, (open forest, of pines & firs & quite dry) Mosquitoes are fearful on low flats where the ground is moist. & the bush is close, willows birches & other swampy trees.

Colin & Rilands from Attenborough's rode South today, after a bunch of horses. Ginger is with that bunch & they will bring him to us if they find the bunch. Attenborough's men, when they happen to get in a bunch & Ginger is with it, bring him down for us every year.

JULY 1911

DOMINION DAY

A fairish day, brighter than yesterday. In the evening Colin came down with Ginger. I'm very glad as there will be not so much walking & rowing to do.

During the summer the feed on the range is very good – bunchgrass chiefly , & as we cannot afford to keep Ginger in the winter, (when he would require oats & hay if he were kept in off the

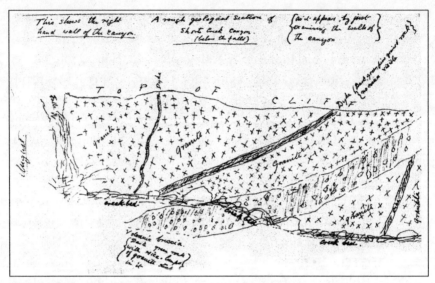

Roger's drawing of canyon

range) we only have him in the summer, when we picket him out to trees with a long rope where the feed is good, changing the picketing place 3 times a day. In the winter horses have a hard time "rustling" for food on the range, on account of the depth of snow, many dying on bad years.

These range "cayuses" are used to it though. Ten years ago this valley was purely a great horse & cattle range, now there are very few big stock ranches. Attenborough's is one of these & he only has about 80 head of Cayuses, several broodmares, & 2 Hackney Stallions, *[Another mistake: one is a Hackney and the other a thoroughbred.]* which he brought out from England two years ago. These horses range over the mountains for miles around his ranch.

Colin spent the night with us.

SUN. 2.

Colin spent the day. A fairish day again with one shower, & a strong Chinook wind. Colin & I had some fun with Ginger, he (Ginger) being fresh off the range is a bit frisky, & when either of us got on bareback & lashed him, he would buck in a mild way, but he failed in unseating either of us, except once, when he was prancing & pitching full-on for the barbed wire fence, & as I was afraid of getting thrown on the wire, I slid off & fell.

MON. 3.

Nice Chinook again. Cloudy but no rain. Mother & I rowed to Kennard's.

The Steamer (Okanagan) when she came in with the mail, forgot to slow up as she came in, & piled onto the beach Her bow was driven into the gravel & her stern low in the deep water at the other end. She nearly knocked the wharf down (the wharf is about 70 feet long, by 20 feet wide, made of log piles & covered with boards) smashing two piles & causing the whole thing to sway & crash. She took half an hour to get off again. *[At Nahun - Ed.]*

On the way home we saw from the boat as we rowed along about 60 yards from the shore, a deer on the bank. It stood perfectly still & watched us <u>out of sight.</u>

I forgot to mention that about two weeks ago, the Potatoes at Armstrong were frozen to their roots. Armstrong is about 10 miles North of Vernon, & as Vernon is about 15 miles North of here, Armstrong will be 25 (probably more) miles.

The principal rock here seems to be granite. In any place such as bluffs, canyon walls etc, where the bedrock is exposed, it is nearly all grey granite, sometimes pink. Whitish, vertical quartz dykes are very common. Another rock which is nearly as common as granite is a dark greenish grey rock, & fine grained, which I think is diorite. All this interior of Southern B.C. is I believe an eroded (very much eroded) plateau of igneous rock. Lime stone & sandstone & other stratified rocks seem scarce, I have only seen what I think are these in pebble form on beaches of the Lake. Fossils seem entirely absent. I have been told that up Shorts' Creek there are some bluffs composed of Limestone.

I have also seen, in the hills, stratified-looking boulders, mingled with the granite & diorite boulders (which when separate from the bed rock, seem to be all worn to a more or less round shape, by, I suppose, glacial action.) but they (the stratified- looking rocks) are very few.

Besides the quartzy-looking dykes, other dykes are common of a rock which looks like porphyry or else diorite. In both kinds of dyke side branches, frequently stretch out horizontally from the main vertical dyke. Probably the white dykes which look like quartz are white porphyry.

Kennard (who prospected in these parts about 10 years ago) tells me that there is gold in many places, but nowhere enough to pay. It occurs chiefly, I believe on the long alluvial flats on points, which project out into the Lake, at the mouths of creeks. Shorts' Point is a good example, & at the mouth of nearly every creek which flows into this lake there is such a point or flat – a moist, low, & sometimes gravelly flat .

SAT. 8.

Since Monday the weather has been much the same; sometimes fine, but all the time <u>inclined</u> to be showery & wet.

The latter part of the spring & so far into this summer, it has

H.B. Kennard had a post office and store at Nahun

been wetter than, we have ever had it before, with the exception of last fall. I have noticed that each year has become moister, the first summer we were here (1905) was very dry indeed (as a matter of fact the summers have been dry each year, but I am speaking, now, more of the winter, spring, & autumn.) The winter of 1905 was practically snowless, each winter seems to have increased in quantity of snow since then. Last winter the snow lay longer than it had ever done before, & deeper. The latter part of

1910 & the first 7 months (up till now) of 1911, have been the moistest, since we have been here. The moisture of each year decreasing, back to 1905 (the year we came out, before that of course, I don't know what it was like).

Shorts' Creek Canyon

I saw three groundhogs this week. Groundhogs are animals allied to the marmot, about 18 inches long, very fat, & of a sandy fawn colour, with tails about 5 inches long, & rather bushy. Groundhogs are numerous on dry knolls canyon walls, rock slides, & rock bluffs. anywhere, as long as it is dry, sunny & rocky, & usually a slope or cliff. Their scientific name is Arctomys Caligatus.

SUN. 9.

Showery as usual. Colin spent the day here as usual. We (Colin & I.) spent all the afternoon, on the uncleared thick bushy parts of the Point , where hundreds of wild raspberries grow. On these we fed.

MON. 10.

Mother & I went to Leney's (about a mile beyond Kennard's). We took Ginger & took turns at riding. We picked up our mail at Kennard's on the way home. Shortly after we left Leney's we saw Toby (one of Leney's dogs) being chased by a grouse, - which evidently had chicks - Toby was running, with the grouse flying & running after him.

Grouse are wonderfully plucky when they have chicks. Once about 4 years ago I saw a grouse which put up the usual bluff of having a wounded wing, & running along the ground whining, So as to lead you after it, & away from the chicks. So I went in the opposite direction, & found a little ball of yellow fluff – a Chick before I knew where I was, Mother Grouse was back on me, fluffed up her feathers & rushed at my legs, & tried to peck them.

Two kinds of grouse are common on this part of the lake; the Ruffed Grouse (Bonasa umbellus) & the Blue Grouse (Dendrogapus obscurus). Another species, less common is the Franklin Grouse, "Fool hen" (Canchites franklinii) I believe there is also one called the Prairie Chicken.

The Ruffed Grouse is common in moist bushy swamps etc., keeping almost entirely on the ground. Blue Grouse is much larger & flies more, & is chiefly on the higher parts, open hillsides, & never in swamps.I don't know anything about the Fool hen, or the Prairie Chicken. All these birds are very good eating.

Ruffed, Blue Grouse & Fool hen sometimes will sit on trees & have stones & sticks thrown at them, without moving. I have almost caught Ruffed grouse in my hands. At other times they will be very wild, & fly before you can hardly see them. There seems to be no fixed season for these strange habits but they just do it when it enters their heads, at any time of year.

THUR. 13.

The weather seems to have settled. Since Sunday 9th it has been fine, & hot: clear, cloudless, hot days, with a continual North wind; typical summer weather of this country.

I have noticed the North wind here is nearly always accompanied with fine weather; in winter it brings, bright cold, & frosty days, & dry snow; & in summer the sort of dry weather we have had since Monday.

On the other hand the South wind or "Chinook" *[pronounced Shinook]* wind brings, in winter wet snow, rain, & thaw; & in summer rain, & thunder & general "mugginess" Of course the weather which these winds bring is not invariably like that mentioned above, but usually so.

There is never a real east wind here; And the West [wind]is only in tremendous blustery gusts on summer evenings. This gusty evening wind blows down more trees than any other wind here. I think the reason that the regular winds always come from the North or South, is, that the valleys & mountain ranges all tend in a North & South direction, which of course impedes east & westerly winds & induces North & South winds.

The North wind does not often make the Lake very rough, but the South, or Chinook wind, nearly always makes the Lake rough. Sometimes fearfully rough. In dull weather with a South wind, it is very impressing, the Lake looks very angry, & of a forbidding steel grey colour, flecked with whitecaps.

The general appearance of this lake, is somewhat like a river, being about 3 miles wide, for its entire length – about 80 miles. On each side rise ranges of high wooded hills, mostly round-topped hills, all covered with a thick growth of the usual firs, & pines, making them at a distance appear blue-black in colour. In some parts there are lone, yellow-brown hills, with next to no growth but withered bunch-grass & sagebrush; but it is generally wooded. Sometimes you can get glimpses of distant mountains which have perpetual snow on them.

The following is a list of the towns on the Lake:

	population
Vernon	about 3,000
Kelowna *	2,000
Okanagan Centre *	few hundred
Peachland	700
Summerland	1,800
Penticton	1,000

Kelowna: Indian for Big Bear.
Okanagan Centre has only been in existence for about 4 years.
Later Okanagan Centre had 3 hotels! One eventually burned down.

They say in future years there is going to be a railroad from Hope (on the Fraser River) to Penticton.

Besides these towns there are post offices and wharves, scattered along the Lake front at intervals of, from 3 to 10 or more miles apart, practically all the settlement, is along near the Lake, & the hills (especially on the west Side) are quite wild & uninhabited until the Nicola Valley (to the West) is reached, across the divide; this valley is 50 or 60 miles West of this lake.

The only railway in the country is a branch of the main C.P.R. This branch runs down from Sicamous Junction (about 50 miles North of Vernon) – to Vernon - & Okanagan Landing, at the Head of the Lake. All around the Lake there are rough wagon roads. The only place where the old Hudson Bay trail is left is between Nahun & Ewing's Landing.

In the mountains there are nothing but old hunting & cattle trails, (except near the towns, where there are roads Going in all directions, but not far into the mountains.) Most of the towns have Electric Lights & telephones.

The nearest thing which approaches a town on this part of the Lake is Ewing's Landing, which has a store (built this spring) a post office & a pile of boards, which some day is to be a "church-room" A parson from Okanagan Centre holds services there once a month.

The Ewing's Landing "Colony" extends over about 2 miles of Lakefront, with houses (little painted wooden affairs) quite close together each with its little fruit orchard.

All along the Lake except at Ewing's the ranches are usually about a mile apart.

Today (Thur. 13) I rode over to the Ewing's Landing Store, reached there about 10 a.m. (it is about 5 miles north of our place.) It is a very "tony" looking outfit, a Union Jack flying over it. It all looks very smart, & very new. Billy Rylands, from Attenborough's was there, & one or two other people I knew among them Willie Andrews, & Pattie Kenyon (the Kenyons are some of the Ewing's Landing "colonists" and Pattie is the 13 year old daughter.)

I have forgotten to mention that the Okanagan Lake lies in Latitude 50° (at least that latitude crosses the Lake about midway.) & Longitude 119° 30'. (about)

FRID. 14.

Very hot, & clear. Got a letter in the mail from Geoffrey Haddon.

SAT. 15.

Very hot again. Rode up to Attenborough's in the morning, with some mail for Colin, as he is not coming down here tomorrow.

Wrote to Geoffrey in the afternoon.

The Saskatoon berries, are now in their prime The Saskatoon bush (Amelanchier Alnifolia) grows chiefly on dry, sunny hillsides or flats. It is a very large lanky shrub, composed of several stems (usually about 2 inches thick) growing in a clump, & usually about 15 feet high, sometimes 20 or 30 feet. In the early spring it has a beautiful white blossom on every branch, – masses of it – finer than cherry blossom. The fruit is ripe in July, it is a purple-red black berry about as large as a big black currant & grows in pendulous clusters. It is very good flavoured & juicy, is very nice eaten either raw, or cooked.

The following is a list of wild fruits that grow here: – (edible fruits)

Raspberry – in moist, swampy parts

Black Raspberry in rocky & gravelly places – scarce

Wild Strawberry – on dry hillsides.

Wild Gooseberry – in swamps, chiefly.

Saskatoon, or "Olally"

Salmon berry – small bush, very large leaves, fruit resembling large Raspberry, grows in swamps.

Elderberry – on small trees, in moist places

Oregon Grape – fruit like tiny grapes & very sour, grows on small bush with leaves like holly.

Choke cherry. (Prunus demisoa) – dark red fruit like small cherries , but in clusters, a small tree growing in moist places. The fruit is sweet, but too astringent to be very pleasant to eat.

I have also heard that there are blueberries on the higher mountains but have never seen them.

SUN. 16.

Fearfully hot again, clear sky with a scorching sun. As a matter of fact it is not so very hot, but feels so, the temperature for the last few days has been about 90° in the shade, & I have been told that it is usually at this time about 96° to 98° sometimes up to 104° in the shade. The highest temperature I have ever heard of in these parts, was in the year 1908, when it went up to 113° in the shade, but this I think was on the East side of the Lake, which is much barer & hotter than this side. I think the highest temperature on this side of the Lake for the last 5 summers at least, was when it went up to 104°, in 1908. The lowest it has ever been here, (since we have been here) was about 16° below zero, but ten miles north it frequently drops to 20° below, & last winter at Whiteman's Creek it went to 22° below. Last winter the lowest (the lowest right here,) was 13° below. But the temperatures always vary here, for every few miles, & a very slight difference in altitude will cause a considerable difference in temperature.

This lake never freezes properly. on cold winters (such as last winter) it freezes for several miles at each end, but never the entire length.

Nearly every spring in March & April (the Lake is coldest during these months) when there are fairly hard frosts at night & when the lake is calm, it freezes right over with a skim of ice, usually about 1/4 to an inch thick. I have known it to do this for many mornings in succession. It freezes over night, & often the ice will stay on the lake till as late as 9 a.m. By that time the sun has enough power to melt it. Small fragments of ice, sometimes remain floating all day.

TUE. 18.

Yesterday & today have been clear & sunny, but not so fearfully hot, as before.

Durant, said, the other day, that he saw a beaver at his spring near the Lake. He said he was sure it was a beaver, as it. Certainly was not an otter or a muskrat, what could it have been?

Years ago there were plenty of beavers in this country, even now I believe there are some in small & remote lakes in the mountains. Beavers were nearly all exterminated by trappers. Fortunately what are left, are now protected, & they are I believe on the increase.

I do hope Durant was not mistaken.

WED. 19.

Very hot as usual. In the afternoon Mrs. Fitzgerald came over, & she told us that the other day, (Sunday she thought) it was 98° in the shade.

Our place was surveyed two years ago, & it is 140 acres, and only just now we are taking out the Crown grant (that is buying it out from the Government) before that it was a pre-emption. Most of the places along here are Crown granted, but there are also quite a number of preemptions .

There is very little land (no lakefront at all) left now which can be preempted, I suppose there is plenty back in the mountains but what good is that country (a mountainous & heavily wooded wilderness) to anybody? Probably there are hundreds of square miles, in the mountains, which will remain wilderness for many years.

The chief export from here is, I suppose fruit, most of the temperate country fruits, vegetables are scarce. Most of the grain is grown around Armstrong & Enderby (North of Vernon) quite a lot of tobacco is grown at Kelowna, which is manufactured into cigars on the spot.

In the Similkameen & South Okanagan Country (about 100 miles south) there is quite a lot of mining. There is plenty of good lumber all over the country. There are several sawmills on the lake & logging-camps are always shifting about (there has been a logging-camp above Ewing's for two years)

Most of the lumber there is used for local purposes. The best tree is the Yellow or Blue pine (Pinus ponderosa) & next Douglas Fir (Pseudotsuga taxifolia).

These are the only trees used for lumber here.

Bullpine grows to a very fine tree: the average diameter is about 2-1/2 feet, but they often grow to 3 & 4 feet, sometimes 5 & 6 feet (there are several on Shorts' Point that are six feet thick at the butt.) They also grow to a great height, 150 to 200 feet. A forest of them looks very fine, with their great tall & straight, cinnamon-red trunks Douglas fir grows very large sometimes (at the Coast of B.C. it grows nearly as big as the California Redwoods – the largest trees in the world, but here the fir is much smaller) Its average size here is about 2-1/2 feet for a good tree, but the diameter sometimes gets as large as 3 & 4 & sometimes 5 feet. It also grows very tall & usually straight. Both Bull pine & Douglas fir are the commonest trees in the country growing nearly everywhere.

Cedars (Thija plicata) are common in swamps & sloughs & creek sides, they grow nearly as big, very often, as Douglas fir, but they are not used for anything except fence posts telephone poles etc, (that is the ones that grow here – on this Lake)

Tamaracks are plentiful on the mountains, but they are not often very large, & usually are inaccessible for timber. The species is Larix occidentalis.

The principal timber of the high mountains is spruce (Picea canadensis) & Jack pine (Picea contorta). Spruce usually is about 6 inches to 1 foot thick, tall & shapely, with spire-like tops & blue-green drooping boughs.

Jack pine is also tall & slender but with more of its foliage at the top. All the higher mountains & flats are covered with these trees, forming a very dark & gloomy forest. Up high too, these trees are always festooned with black or dar moss, which hangs in brownish black hair-like streamers from the branches. on the flats in the mountains, there are often sloughs, - i.e. flat marshes covered with sloughgrass, & fringed with cottonwoods & willows.

Nearer the lake the scenery is not so wild & gloomy, the hillsides are there covered with bull pines & firs which grow some distance apart, so it appears quite high & open. The largest deciduous tree here is the cottonwood (Populus trichocarpa) which grows anywhere, so long as it is wet, or swampy. It sometimes reaches 3 feet in diameter.

I said above that all the mountains were timbered, I meant usually. In some parts there are great, steep, & bare mountain sides, also rockslides or screes are common at the foot of cliffs.

THUR. 20.

Hot as usual. In the afternoon we were surprised to see Colin. He wanted to stay with us for a few days as he had unfortunately cut his leg with an axe, & would be unable to work, So of course he is going to stay down here till it is better. It was a nasty clean-cut gash, just below the knee, & about an inch long & it looked nearly an inch deep. Blood-poisoning is very common in this country, & I hope he will be better soon.

FRID. 21.

Smoky & hazy in the morning & dull & windy with a slight shower in the afternoon. Mother rode over to the Redsulls' (Old Mr. Redsull & Mrs. Brixton alias Miss Redsull) for the day. Deana & A.K. of course were working at the Point as usual.

So Colin & I went fishing for the day - he can get about all right on his leg but I did nearly all the rowing. We left home at about 9 a.m. & went to Ewing's Landing, which we reached in about 1-1/2 hours, we fished off the wharf there, till 2 p.m. & caught about 25 squawfish, with grasshoppers, bread & artificial flies for bait. The squawfish were in hundreds all round the wharf, they were all about 6 inches long. These fish are not much good for eating, but we managed to sell them at the Point for 5 cents a pound instead of 12 (the average price for trout). We also caught one trout – about 2 lbs. We got home from Ewing's at about 4 p.m. & had a stiff pull against the evening western gusts (which came extra-early.)

MON. 24.

The weather has been much as usual, though Saturday was rather cloudy & cooler. Since Friday Colin & I have fished a good bit every day but have caught nothing. Rode to Leney's to take some photos that they had asked me for. (I charge 60 cents a dozen for photos size 2-1/2 x 3-1/2, but as I can seldom sell any, I don't make much at it) Got home about 6 p.m. Had supper. Colin told me that he had caught some fish during the day, so we rowed round to the Point in the evening, caught a little trout on the way, & sold the lot at the Point. It was dusk when we started home, & we got caught in the evening breezes, & had to put in and walk. Reached home at about 9 p.m. when it was dark.

WED. 26.

Last night it was very smoky from some bushfire. Today has been hot as usual & very windy.

FRID. 28.

Rode to Kennard's on Ginger. Not much mail. Evidently one of the booms of logs at the other side of the Point has broken, because today there were several hundred logs, scattered about the Lake.

The logs are sawn usually in winter. They are then conveyed to the top of the chute on big sledges drawn by heavy teams of horses. The chute is a sort of flume about 6 feet wide, made of logs laid lengthwise. The chute between Ewing's & the Point is about 200 yards long & very steep. The logs go down it at a great speed, & plunge into the lake with a huge splash. A boom of logs chained together surrounds & prevents the loose logs (from escaping) – When the boom is full (it contains several hundred logs & a great many 1000 feet of lumber) it is towed away, by a steam lumber tug to the sawmill.

Today has been very hot, & this evening it was very smoky.

SAT. 29.

Clear in the morning, but dull & smoky, & very sultry in the afternoon.

Rode up to Attenborough's to tell them that I had seen one of their cows with foul in one of its hind feet, this wretch was on the range, & could hardly move to feed itself, & was fearfully thin. Tom Attenborough & one of his men rode down in the afternoon & got the cow, & drove it home.

I noticed particularly today the difference in the atmosphere, down by the lake & up on the bench. It is nearly always in the summer very relaxing & sultry down by the lake & what wind there may be (except in the early morning) is warm. But go back up the hill half a mile & there is nearly always a cool breeze, which tempers the heat of the sun.

I saw about 1/2 a dozen grouse today, about 3/4 grown, all blue grouse.

SUN. 30.

A beautiful clear day with a fresh north wind during the morning. The afternoon was extremely hot. Leneys are going to leave their place for 2 weeks to go camping, & they wanted somebody to see that their place was alright while they were away, & as it is a nice quiet job for a bad leg, Colin has taken it on for $10.00.

MON. 31.

A dullish day & cooler than usual. A strong north wind during the day, which changed to a tearing Chinook in the evening, this brought heavy black clouds & some heavy rain in the evenings for some hours.

The fence laws here are made for cattle country – not for sheep - & therefore 4 wires (barbed on a fence is legal & if cattle & particularly sheep get through there – sheep can walk through with perfect ease - the owner of the stock is liable to be sued for damages. The Point people keep sheep loose on the range & nearly every other day this week they have been along here, & last year they simply devastated our garden.

But as we do not wish to complain to the Point people, we use an other remedy, namely, I get on Ginger bare back & drive them right back to the Point, hard & through the gate. Another very objectionable thing about sheep is that they crop the grass clean up, in fact eat every thing before them, & leave little for horses.

I had to ride after these beastly Sheep this morning. Saw the blue grouse again.

AUGUST 1911

TUE. 1

Fairly bright, with heavy clouds in most parts of the sky. Grumbles of thunder most of the afternoon.

WED. 2.

Fine day , & hot. Mother & I went to Andrews, & were going to get some stuff at the Ewing's Landing Store. But when we got there, they told us that the store had been burnt down last night. I rode along & saw the ruins. It was a lumber building about 30 x 15 feet in size, & two storeys high. All that was left was a heap of still warm cinders & ash. Also dozens of blackened cans which had contained various groceries. It was a great pity. I was told that the fellows who ran it (Fox & Colquhoun) are sickened but are going to put up another store & start again.

THUR. 3.

A fine day, though hot as usual. North wind. A man called Casorso from Kelowna came here today. He is looking out for a place for a friend of his, & perhaps he will get the friend to buy our place, & he seemed to have ideas for himself – but we must await results, & I hope that either he or his friend will buy us out – our price is $3500.00.

Mr. Casorso seemed very nice, he stayed for dinner & left about three o'clock (he had ridden up from West bank – about 25 miles South – & opposite Kelowna – & was going to take the ferry launch to Kelowna, from there.)

SUN. 6.

An unusually wet day rained from about 4 a.m. to 3 p.m. The rest of the afternoon & evening was very dull, with a misty leaden sky.

Mrs. Durant came over for about an hour in the afternoon.

MON. 7.

It evidently rained all last night & it also rained more than half today. Had a wet ride to the mail.

WED. 9.

Yesterday was showery, but today has been splendid.

As we are short of provisions, some what, I rode to Ewing's Landing in the morning, to see if I could buy some eggs & potatoes from anybody. Did not succeed, but if I go to Jimmy Bruce's * on Saturday, I can get some potatoes.

I saw the "church" in progress of being built, it is like a lumber-built barn about 40 feet long by 20 wide, & has a little cross at one end, made of 4 inch by 4 inch beams, all perfectly planed like an ordinary stable or store house. I should think it will be finished in about 3 or 4 days.

THUR. 10.

Another fine day. Colin returned from his job at Leneys. is going away from this county (Yale) to some friends of his in Kaslo, Kootenay Lake. They have offered him a good job. He is leaving in 3 or 4 days.

This afternoon Colin & I went into the canyon above the Point (the part of the canyon below the falls) This part of the canyon is a great cleft over a hundred yards long, with the falls dropping over the cliff at one end (the upper end of course) on each side there are sheer cliffs, from 50 to a 100 feet high, & in most parts overhanging, these cliffs are not smooth, but are cracked in many places & have projections & ledges everywhere. The creek bed is strewn with great water-worn boulders amongst which the stream runs. In one part there is a deep & narrow pool, with a sheer cliff on one side & a steep slope of smooth rock on the other.

The creek is now in low water, & today we got as far as this pool easily by jumping from stone to stone, but we found it difficult to get past this pool, without sliding into it, on the smooth rock. However we managed it & got up into the rocky basin at the extreme foot of the falls. There was not much water coming over the falls, & all we felt was a little cold wind & spray.

In this "basin" to my great delight, I discovered a dead <u>beaver</u> lodged between the stones in the creek. It smelt fairly strong but was not decayed. It was a very large beast, about 2 1/2 feet from the nose to the end of the tail, it was also very fat. The great flat scaly tail was nearly a foot long, & about 3 inches wide. The fur was practically all gone.

I think this rare animal must have got washed down the creek from the mountains away back where I suppose there are quite a lot of beaver.

It is of course impossible to reach the foot of the falls, as we did to day, in the Spring when the creek is in flood. The easiest time to get up is when the creek is frozen.

FRID. 11.

In the map I marked the stretch from Nahun to Ewing's Ldg. as the only piece of HudsonBay trail left near the Lake. I drew it on August 8th, & probably by the end of August or sometime in September, even this old bit of trail will be converted into a rough wagon road as A gang of men have already started to work on the road, at Nahun.

So I suppose my sketch map will be out of date in about 2 months. It will help to sell our place, but for the look of the country I shall be extremely sorry, to see the road.

Four years ago it was trail from about Bear Creek to Ewing's Landing.

Anyhow there will be still the old trails in the mountains, probably for many years – 30 years at least, I should think.

SUN. 13.

Clear in the morning, but dull in the afternoon.

In the afternoon I went up the creek, fishing. As I said, the canyon extends for about half a mile above the falls of Shorts' Creek. This part of the canyon (or cañon) is much the same as the part below the falls, but of course much longer. Also there are several pretty cascades about 20 to 30 feet high.

Today I managed to find one spot where I could scramble down into the canyon, when I got down, I jumped from stone to stone along the creek bed, with high over-hanging cliffs on each side of me, I went about 50 feet & rounded a corner of rock, & came upon a lovely big, deep, dark pool, at each side of which there were

Shorts' Creek Canyon 1914

dark over-hanging cliffs, & at the upper end of the pool was a beautiful cascade about 20 feet high, which roared down into the pool. I cast my fly into this pool & at once got a lively little brown trout about 8 inches long,

I stayed about half an hour & caught nine of them, & lost about 4 others besides. They were all about 8 inches long.

I got home just in time to cook them for tea.

Mr. Durant came over & partook of them.

TUE. 15.

A fairly fine day, but hot. Colin went off to the Kootenays today. I went to Kennard's in the morning & saw him off. I believe he will reach his destination tomorrow or the next day.

SAT. 19.

Nothing of any particular interest has happened since Tuesday. The weather has been fine up till today, Each day being bright & sunny. This afternoon, we had quite a heavy thunderstorm, with extremely heavy rain & some hail.

SUN. 20.

Dullish day with one shower. In the afternoon I went up to the canyon again, & fished in the same pool that I went to last Sunday, Aug.13, the fish were not biting so well, & I only caught six. I think that probably I am the first person that ever fished in this pool I only know of about 3 people that ever fished up the creek anywhere.

I expect that is the reason, the fish bite so readily. After a time I expect they will get "hook wise".

I turned Ginger out to day.

MON. 21.

A delightful day, bright & sunny but almost cold in the shade. Got a long interesting letter from Bessie in the mail.

I also got the Game Laws of B.C. (which I sent for the other day). It also said that in an <u>unorganised</u> district, it is legal for residents to shoot game for <u>food</u> at any time of year, but I am not sure, unfortunately, whether this is an unorganised district, or not. *(This is an organised district: Note 1912)*

I saw for the first time, two Boy Scouts on the steamer, when she came into Kennard's today, with the mail. The Boy Scouts certainly have spread, for they already have corps of them at each little town on the Lake.

WED. 23.

A glorious day, very chilly in the early morning before the sun rose. At about 5 o'clock this morning we heard a coyote howling. (Coyotes howl a great deal in winter but it is rather unusual for them to do so in summer, they are quite plentiful about here but one doesn't often see them, as they travel mostly at night, & are very cunning: their howl is a sort of: yap yap yap yo-o-ow.)

THUR. 24.

A fine clear day. Like last year I have got a job at fruit picking at Shorts' Point. So, was at it all today (picking crabs) I am doing 9 hours & shall ask $1.50 a day. Deana & A.K. are getting for the same work $2.00 or $2.50. *[Crab apples - Roger at age 14 - Ed.]*

Apple picking at Fintry: John Edward on ladder; Roger Sugars on ground

FRID. 25

No clouds, though smoky.

Had the day off from fruit-picking, to go to Kennard's for the mail.

I found out today that I had made another mistake in saying there was no trail except between Ewing's Landing & Nahun. There is another portion left on the east side between K e l o w n a (outskirts) & Naramata (a tiny place opposite Summerland.) A distance of about 18 or 20 miles. I have never been on that part of the Lake so I do not know this for certain but that is what I was told today.

TUE. 29.

It has been fine since Friday but today (excepted) was slightly wet. Was fruit picking on Sat. & Mon. We have finished for a time now.

They have been doing a great deal of rock blasting, on the road at Kennard's lately.

The Diaries of Roger John Sugars

The start of the original Westside Road. J.E. and Roger pick-axed here.

SEPTEMBER 1911

THUR. 7.

Since the 29th it has been fairly fine; Sunday & Monday were wet.

Was fruit-picking on Tuesday & Wednesday & today. The deer season opened on the 1st. *[The open season for shooting grouse & deer is from the 1st Sept. to 15th Dec, but these laws are not very rigidly obeyed.]*

Saw a flight of Martins today; think they were on the Southward migration.

The last few days have been very chilly in early hours.

Got a long letter from Geoffrey Haddon on Friday.

FRI. 8.

No rain, but a very threatening sky most of the day.

Went to Kennard's with Mother for the mail.

The gang that were working on the road at Kennard's bluffs

have gone, so the road will not be completed this year.

All that is done now, is round the bluffs – about 150 yards. The work has been nearly all blasting & drilling rock. on the outer side of the road it is nearly a sheer drop of about 60 feet to deep water on the upper a steep rocky hillside - almost a precipice.

It will be easier walking round these bluffs in winter, on a wagon-road, instead of a narrow trail, as before.

When we first came here, the Bighorn Flats were a wild & absolutely uninhabited valley, with nothing but the old HudsonBay Trail, running through it. Now there are several pre-emptions & good log cabins, & the fellows up there are clearing & putting up some log-fences. Also a wagon-road is expected to be put through there next spring!

The country is gradually changing.

I made a map today of the Okanagan Valley. It is copied from a government map & is quite inaccurate, as all maps of this valley are. I have never seen two maps of this Lake exactly alike. There is a survey of the mountain watersheds going on at present, & I suppose will do for some years. When this is completed the maps should be much more accurate.

SUN. 10.

A beautiful day. Was fruit-picking all yesterday.

A.K. went a long way up the mountains this morning, & shot 2 deer, one of which unfortunately fell over a precipice, where he could not get at it.

The other, however he succeeded in bringing home alright, except that he got onto a wasps' nest & got badly stung all over the head.

WED. 13.

A lot of bright green sheet lightning last night & a few grumbles of distant thunder.

Rained all this morning. Cloudy but dry in the afternoon, & a very strong Chinook wind in the afternoon & most of the morning.

Fresh snow fell on Little Cold Mountain.

I think I will give a brief account of the general weather here, though I have written a little about it before.

The winters are not severe as a rule, frosts start in October, the first snow falls usually about the end of November Up till about New Year the weather is uncertain, usually with snows, & thaws & some rain.

About New Year we nearly always have a "cold snap" which lasts usually about a week, sometimes a fortnight or more. During this time the snow is deep & dry, the temperature goes down to, from 2° to 12° or more below zero, at night, & usually rises to about 20° in the warmest part of the day. In very cold winters it drops sometimes to 16° below & at Vernon to 40° below zero.

During the "cold snap" the wind is always in the North. At the end of the cold snap it usually goes to the South & there is a thaw.

After that there are various heavy snowfalls, cold snaps, & thaws till about the end of February. During March the weather breaks up & the spring thaw sets in.
Some winters – (such as last winter) the snow lies deep all winter without a single thaw.

In the spring of 1907 the leaves of shrubs were not out till the beginning of May.

The spring is windy, slushy, muddy, showery & sunny alternately, as a rule. This spring was delightfully & exceptionally pleasant.

In May, it quietens down & everything is gloriously fresh & green, & the wild flowers are gorgeous. June, July, & August are usually very hot & dry; practically all the wildflowers are over by the end of June, & sometimes the leaves begin to shrivel on the trees.

Frequently weeks go by without a drop of rain, & barely a cloud in the sky. [*The average annual rainfall (including snow) seems to be about 12 inches.*]

During this kind of weather the air is often very thick & hazy with smoke from forest fires.

As I think I remarked before this summer has been extra wet & cool. I also said that thunderstorms were few on this Lake.

Roger hiking or hunting

The worst thunderstorms I have seen were over on Long Lake in the summer of 1905. They were very frequent & nearly always at night; they were accompanied with terrific winds & a great deal of greenish-blue lightning, & tremendous rain. We were camping at the time & we had a tent blown down once with one of these awful storms; & we also had to hold the tent poles steady, until the worst of the wind was over on each occasion

The fall is the best time of year in my opinion. Often in this season many days go by which are perfectly cloudless, at night frosts which whiten the ground; warm & sunny in the day; snow on the higher mountains; & all the deciduous trees fringing the Lake shore & the creek beds & moist hollows & "sloughs" in the hills, are turning gold & red. Away back on the hills speckled about among the dark evergreen spruce & pine trees are Tamaracks or larches, all bright yellow. It is a fascinating time of year partly I think because of the strange look of sadness over the mountains & trees.

THUR. 14.

Sunny most of the morning. Clouded over with a Chinook wind, at about two o'clock in the afternoon, & rained the rest of the day & evening.

FRID. 15

Last night was very wild & boisterous, what with thunder lightning, tearing wind, & torrents of rain. It seems rather extraordinary to me, having so much thunder, on such a cool, damp summer.

SUN. 17

Dull most of the day with no rain. At a quarter to nine this morning I went up the mountains, hunting. I went SouthWest along the upper trail for about 2 miles & then struck straight up the mountain to a fair height: it was a fearfully steep climb up a very rough rocky hillside covered with dead logs & brush. When I had got up about half a mile I went North along the mountain for 2 or 3 miles.

This mountain side was fearfully steep, & covered with boulders, rocky knolls burnt trees & logs, stubs & half dead & young trees. All the branches of the trees, both dead & green, were festooned With brown hair like black-moss. In some parts there were broad belts covered with quite young firs, but growing so close together that I could hardly squeeze through them.

Most of the trees were fir, pine & tamarack, in some places groves of very pretty whitebarked aspens, willows & birches.

After scrambling through this kind of country for some way & through an extra thick patch of young firs I suddenly came to the foot of a high, rocky crag about 60 or 70 feet high. I climbed round the back of it & got right on top, & lay down gasping for [a] few minutes. At this point I got a glorious view: to East lay the Lake far below extending some way to the South & North, I could nearly see Okanagan Landing, & I could see right up the Siwash Arm. Beyond the Lake, to the east were range after range of wooded plateaux.

To West, North & South were mountains of various shapes & heights. To the North West was a fine view of a great, bare mountain, called the Sheep bluffs. Terrace & Goat mountain were out of view for a wooded ridge close to me. The crag I was on is known to us by the name of "the White Rock" from the white streak on its face.

When I was down at the foot of the White Rock, I put up five grouse which flew straight into the thick fir scrub, so I did not bother about them.

I got home at a quarter to one p.m., pretty tired.

I then fished off a rock in the Lake for about half an hour & caught 3 trout, the largest of which weighed about a pound & a half. The fly I used was a "bucktail" made of the hairs of a deer tail. I saw one solitary goose flying South, this afternoon.

TUE. 19

A fairly fine day; North wind. Shot a ruffed grouse.

FRID. 22.

The last few days have been very cool, dull & windy; the nights very cold, almost frost I think.

Saw some geese flying over; also in the evening there were hundreds of Martins flying about in all directions at a considerable height, evidently preparing for the Southward migration. Heard a Horned Owl hooting in the evening.

The Big horned owl (Bubo Virginianus) is a very fine bird. It measures about 3 feet from tip to tip of the wings. It has beautiful soft downy feathers, of a greyish-brown colour. It has the usual owl shaped head, only with a tuft of feathers on each ear.

I suppose it is a nocturnal bird, but I have seen quite a lot, in the daytime. It hoots only in the spring & fall.

There is a $2.00 bounty on this bird also $3.00 on Golden Eagles (which are scarce), & $3.00 on Coyotes.

SUN. 24

A perfect day. Very cool, out of the sun, & absolutely cloudless. The Lake was sparkling in the sun with a fresh North wind most of the day. I was out in the boat this afternoon, & when I was coming back in a lazy sort of way, near the shore, a muskrat swam close past the boat & climbed out on cedar snag, sat up & went through an elaborate cleaning, wiping its face with its paws & scratching: all this within about 15 feet of the boat. When it had finished this pretty performance it jumped in & swam away, perfectly regardless of me!

MON. 25.

Another day similar to yesterday though colder. There was no frost here, but 7° Fahr. at the Point.

On an ordinary dry summer here, the Saskatoon leaves (unlike the leaves of other trees) are dried up & brown, & falling off, by August.

This year (on account of the damp I suppose) they are only beginning to fall now, & instead of turning a dull brownish colour as on other summers they are all a beautiful orange- gold. On steep hillsides facing the sun, there are scattered about among the dark firs & pines, glorious patches of the low sumac shrub all a deep crimson; & the saskatoon. But the best autumn colours are to come, for the cottonwoods, birches, maples, Aspens etc. fringing the Lake, have by means turned to their fullest brilliancy.

The tamaracks on the higher mountains are now beginning to show up yellow against the dark pine & spruce forest of the higher country.

OCTOBER 1911

SUN. 1

A fairish day. The weather is gradually getting colder though we have had no frost at our place yet. On looking back in this diary, it appears that there has been no rain since the 15th of September, this fall so far, seems to be improving on the summer for fine weather. *[This was a mistake as there was a little rain about a week ago.]*

Went fishing up the cañon this afternoon, only got five trout. Am reading "Captain Singleton".

WED. 4

A cloudyish day with no rain: since Sunday it has been much like this with no rain.

The Kikkaninnies (an Indian word spelt as you like) are now running.

The Kikkaninny is, I believe a true land-locked salmon.

It much resembles the other trout of the Lake and it is chiefly seen in deep water. The great difference between it & the trout is that in the fall (about now, or usually earlier) it runs in shoals of hundreds along in the shallows near the shore, & up creeks a short distance. It does this, I suppose for the purpose of spawning. At other times of the year it is of a bright silvery colour, but in the spawning season it turns red with a green head. It then gradually becomes more & more diseased & finally dies off & their belly-up bodies float about in the Lake for some time.

During the spawning season they are caught in hundreds with nets or gaff-hooks on the end of sticks. In spite of their being in a diseased state, people seem to like to eat them, especially the Indians. This fish never seems to be larger than about a foot long.

A.K. found, at the Point (Shorts' Point) today a very fine Indian pestle made of the same sort of volcanic stone. It was 8 inches long & very heavy. Arrow & spear-heads are often found here – I have found about seven – They are nearly all of a jet-black & very hard stone [*Occasionally of white quartz*]. Many of them are unfinished but the complete ones are usually of this sort of shape: & varying from about half an inch to 4 or 5 inches long.

Roger's Indian Arrowhead

The method of working them was, I have been told, by heating the stone & then applying a blade of wet grass which split small chips off. The Indians substituted guns for these, I suppose about 60 or 70 years ago.

The Siwashes [*Siwash: From Sauvage*] here are a somewhat poor looking lot, being rather short & inclined to broad noses.

They are confined to reservations. Their dress is nearly always that of the cowboy – the only true Indian part of the dress left seems to be mocassins They always travel either in boats (they no longer use canoes) or on horses & they take great pride in their saddles & bridles. How they scrape along for a living is a mystery for they never seem to do anything but ride about the country after horses, hunt, fish, or else do nothing at all. They understand a good

Local Indians 1905

bit of English but speak to white men mostly in Chinook – a jargon invented by the early fur-traders. Among themselves they speak their own languages which few whitemen seem to understand. The Siwashes round here consist of two tribes – the Shushwaps & Okanagans – & I should not think there are more than 200 or there abouts. They are all Roman Catholics & have been for a good many years.

They are all named by the priests (who are mostly French-Canadians).

They are very superstitious & believe in various kinds of "skookums" (Ghosts or devils) which live in the mountains.

I believe, in the old days they were always pretty peaceful with whitemen , though there are various stories abouts fights between different tribes – Shorts' Point was a battle-ground on one occasion. There seem to be more "breeds" than full-blooded Indians now.

I think there are 4 reservations on this Lake – one all around the shores of the Siwash Arm, another at the Mission (south of Kelowna. At Trout Creek, & a large one west of Penticton & Dog Lake.

I might add that the chief of the Shushwaps (who often rides along the trail) is a very old copper-coloured man with a white goatee beard, & wears an old tail-coat & a brown bowler hat, feeling, I suppose, that he is above the common cowboy dress, being chief.

A man who owns a ranch up the Coldstream Valley, employs among other Indians, in the fall, for hop-picking, the entire tribe (about 300) of the Nez Percès who come all the way from their reservation in Idaho or Washington. Up till about 2 years ago they used to come up the HudsonBay trail on the west side of the Lake. They all came – men, women, & children, all riding, & with hundreds of pack horses.

They came through about the middle of September & went back about a month later. These Nez Percès are a much finer tribe than the Siwashes, though classed among coast Indians, they are

Westbank Natives (McDougalls?)

regular plains Indians, being far different from the more Northern & Western Siwash. They were as fierce & warlike as any of the other plains Indians in the early days.

They are mostly tall & good looking.

Their costume is much the same as that of the Siwashes, though more picturesque. They have mocassins , gloves & gun scabards, very beautifully bead-worked, & some wear the cloth or buckskin leggings, a few wear buckskin shirts, but most wear overalls or "chaps" (chaparejoes) & ordinary shirts. Most of them use the usual big Mexican spurs.

They are very fond of brilliant coloured handkerchiefs & scarfs . They all wear wide brimmed, high-crowned felt hat of black or fawn, with leather, silk, bead work or metal bands. Most of them ride Mexican saddles with gorgeous saddle blankets. The squaws wear a sort of semi civilised dress of bright cotton, with vivid coloured handkerchiefs tied round their heads. Occasionally the "papooses" are carried in queer sort of cradles made of a board with cloth or buckskin laced across, & very gorgeously ornamented . When in camp the men wrap themselves from head to foot in bright coloured blankets.

THUR. 5

A day much the same as yesterday. At Shorts' Point the ground was white with frost, & some potatoes which had been left out on the ground all night, were frozen right through.

SUN. 8

A decent fine day with an early but glorious sunrise.

I arranged yesterday with Durant, that we should go out hunting today. I got up at a quarter to five (about dawn) & walked, to Durants, which took one about 20 minutes. Had breakfast by lamplight with Durant; & at six we set out. We covered much the same country, that I did on the 17th of September, but instead of walking all the way along the mountain side, we got right on top, which caused travelling over "flat" country (that is to say instead of climbing a steep, continuous hill we were scrambling down hollows, ridges, over rocks, all covered closely with scrubby firs, pines, tamaracks, willows, birches & cottonwoods; dead, & green, big & small, and dead falls, (fallen trees & logs all jumbled across each other) We walked through this kind of thing for several miles & then came round & down to "my White Rock" then sat & admired the view (which I think is unrivalled for a good many miles around)

We saw right up North, a glimpse of distant snow-capped peaks, which showed up very small & indistinctly in a gap in the mountains up the Siwash Arm. The peaks I think must have been the Selkirk mountains which are about 150 miles North of here. I went back with Durant & Lunched with him, we reached his place at ten o'clock, having had no luck.

THUR. 12

Both yesterday & today have been beautifully fine.

Two flights of geese went South yesterday & I saw one today. The trees along the lake-shore & in swamps are turning to their brightest golds & reds, & the higher mountains are thickly speckled with tamaracks or larches turned bright yellow.

FRID. 13

Birds are very numerous now. they are mostly robins, magpies, woodpeckers, Black-headed Jays & Juncoes. In the spring & early summer, birds are very plentiful, in July & August birds seem scarce, then again in the fall they are numerous again. I think this proves that most of the migrating birds do not remain here for the summer, but go considerably farther North – Their spring visit is when they are passing to the North & Vice Versâ in the fall.

Of course there are quite a number of birds which remain here & nest & also ones which stay the year round. This afternoon was wet.

SUN. 15

A very nice day except for a very strong Chinook wind. At half past nine I went out hunting, I went straight up the hill & crossed the creek about half way to Attenborough's, & climbed a mountain on the North side of the creek. This mountain went up gradually with little plateaux & benches. It was nice open country all the way, thinly covered with beautiful large pines. It took me about an hour to reach the top, when I was rewarded with a beautiful view. Behind me, to the east was the Lake which I could not see much of, but in front of me, was a great broad gulch, which looked over a mile wide. At the bottom of this gulch, far below me, ran Shorts' Creek.

The mountain I was on sloped away right from beneath my feet, tremendously steeply, to the creek. Far up beyond the other side of the gulch to the South west rose Terrace Mtn. (the highest mountain in this district. The summit is formed of two or three mighty cliffs or terraces one above the other. It is about 7000 feet above sea level) And directly opposite me was a huge, bare mountain – side covered with rock slides & fallen burnt trees. It terminates at the top in a great crag – (Goat Peak) then, several miles away to the North West were the Sheep Bluffs which stood out very boldly against the sky. This mountain is really an immense precipice with an absolutely bare face which rises up nearly sheer for at least, I should think, a thousand feet.

To the South of Terrace, were more mountains in the South Fork region, all very heavily timbered.

After a few minutes rest I descended the mountain & came up with a rush almost in the Creek

At this point I was I think about half way between Love's & Attenborough's. The creek-bottom is thickly timbered with straight, tall cottonwoods, birches, spruce, Jack-pine, fir etc. They are mostly large trees & I saw a cottonwood about 4 feet in diameter & a birch, about a foot & a half (the largest birch I have ever seen) I shot two grouse in this place. I then walked down the creek for about a mile or more, passed Attenborough's ranch house, struck the trail from his place down the North side of the creek to Shorts' Point.

When I was within about half a mile of the cañon (above the Point) I saw about 50 yards ahead of me on the trail, a Coyote eating the carcass of a sheep.

I flopped down on my stomach, & fired at him, & I think I missed, he then ran up the hillside, & then turned round & looked at me; I fired at him again evidently wounding him, for he made a bound into the air, & trotted over the hill. I suppose the 22 calibre is not powerful enough to kill an animal as large as a Coyote, at a range of 50 yards.

Anyhow I cussed my luck, for missing a $3.00 bounty & a decent hide, & walked on & reached home at a quarter past two.

TUE. 17

Yesterday & today have been fine. Was fruit (apple) picking at the Point, both yesterday & today.

Shot a grouse coming home from the Point this evening. Durant caught a 17 lb. trout yesterday morning.

WED. 18.

Slight frost here last night. A beautiful day.

Shot another grouse, going to the Apple picking this morning.

FRID. 20

A fine day, & a frost last night.

SAT. 21

quite a hard frost last night. Another fine day.

MON. 23

Dull, with a strong North wind. Mr. Durant is most awfully nice to us – in fact he is one of the best neighbors we have ever had – When Mother & I, or when I am alone, Walking to the mail, he always insists on rowing us back as far as his place (which is only about a mile away) & often all the way home.

He comes over nearly every Sunday & is always giving us trout.

TUE. 24

A.K. took the steamer from the Point & left us for Victoria, where he intends to remain & find a good position, & look out for one for Deana, because we all intend to follow him in a few months time, as life out here in the bush, though it is free & easy, does not seem to pay.

For my own part I hate towns, & hope in the future to get into the Forestry Service of this Province which is well paid, & of course as the name implies it is mostly work in the forest, & before I can enter this I shall have to put in a certain length of time in an Agricultural College in one of the towns (Vancouver I expect)

Last night it rained heavily, today was fine.

SUN. 29

Every morning now the ground is white with frost & there are icicles hanging from our water-flume. Every day since Tuesday was perfect with a constant North wind & cloudless sky.

I have got a job to herd the Shorts' Point sheep. I have to walk to the Point in the morning, catch a cayuse out of the meadow, take it up to the stable & saddle it, then turn the sheep out of the corral & count them (there are 76) then drive them along & leave them on the hill above our place for several hours (during which time the horse is tied up at our place)

In the late afternoon I round them up & drive them back & corral them, unsaddle, put the cayuse in the meadow & walk home when it is nearly dark.

I do not know what I shall be paid for this, but I imagine about 50 ¢ a day. I have been doing it since Wednesday.

MON. 30

Fine as usual. Hard frost. At about 5 a.m. I saw the latest comet (Brooks')

It looks like a faint star of the 3rd magnitude, with an almost imperceptible tail going up vertically from the nucleus. At the time above mentioned it is about due east, & it fades rapidly with the dawn

This comet looks extremely poor & small compared with Venus which is shining beautifully large as a morning star just above the Comet.

TUE. 31

When I was riding out on the range this afternoon after the sheep I saw a coyote trotting through the trees about 150 yards away.

I suspect he had scented the sheep.

NOVEMBER 1911

WED. 1

Every day is fine now, freezing all day in the shade.

The wind is constantly from the North. When the sun sets, the creek at the Point at once starts to freeze lightly in quiet parts.

SAT. 4

The weather has changed, yesterday & today were wet. A.K. returned today, & unfortunately he had had no luck in Victoria.

MON. 6

Rained all Saturday night all Sunday & all this afternoon.

Not far up the mountains the snow is considerable.

The sheep stray several miles in the afternoon, & this afternoon when I rounded them up & drove them home to the Point, through the rain & wet bush, I & the saddle were in a soaked condition. I finally got home, wet & bedraggled about an hour after dark.

TUE. 7

Rained all last night. About a hundred yards up the hill there was about 2 inches of wet snow & just a sprinkle round the house. Drizzled most of the day.

Since Friday 3rd the wind has been in the South, which has evidently caused all the rain.

WED. 8

Wind changed to the North last night. All the mud & puddles frozen hard & tight. The Point thermometer registered 12° of frost. Saw 2 hen-pheasants near our North east corner post, this morning.

THUR. 9

About half an inch of fine dry snow fell last night.

Today has been bitterly cold, with a fearful North wind tearing down the Lake. There was nearly 20° of frost at the Point, & continued so all day. Riding after the sheep is fearfully cold work, & I could not get on enough clothes. The sheep wander so far that I have to ride out almost right after dinner to hunt for them, & usually find them about 1/2 or an hour's riding, it then takes about 2 hours to drive them home this means a good bit of cold riding, & the only time during the middle of the day, that I have at home is from about 10 a.m. when I get in, to half past one or 2 p.m. when I go out again.

When I went out to the meadow for the horse this morning, there was a tremendous icy wind, whistling across the Point, & I felt fully as cold as have done in zero weather. I am wearing woollen underclothing, 2 pairs of overalls, a flannel shirt a sweater & a coat lined with Mackinaw, with a huge sheep collar, & yet with these & lined leather mitts I am not nearly warm enough riding.

FRID. 10

Colder than yesterday. Only 5° above zero, & 4° below up on the Bighorn Flats.

The same North Wind all day. People who have been here ten & twelve years say they have never known such cold weather in November before.

I have quit the sheep-herding on account of the cold.

SAT. 11

Cold as yesterday, though with less wind. 3° above zero last night.

SUN. 12

Several inches of soft, dry snow fell during the night, & it has snowed all today, result, about 9 inches of snow, the boughs of the trees are pretty heavily laden and everything looks unusually white & wintry for so early in the season.

We have had as much snow, & as early before, but it has always thawed, almost at once, today it never stopped freezing.

There was a slight North wind during the afternoon. I went out hunting for a couple of hours up the hill this morning, in hopes of seeing a deer *[Deer frequently come down from the high mountains, after a fall of snow.]* I saw a few tracks, 3 or 4 hours old, & the fresh 15 foot jumps of a deer that I had evidently "jumped" without seeing it.

MON. 13

Snowed nearly all day & there is now about a foot of snow. Slight North wind all day.

TUE. 14

Dull with a little snow in the morning; a little breeze sprang up from the South & the sun came out, I thought this meant a change of weather, but the wind shortly went back to the North, & the sky clouded again.

WED. 15

A dull cold day, with a slight North wind. The grey leaden clouds were down almost level with the lake. The snow is lying thick as ever with no sign of thaw.

FRID. 17

Yesterday, about midday the wind went to the South & it at once began to thaw. Last night & today it rained quite a bit.

SAT. 18

Thawed hard all day. Some rain in the afternoon. The Chinook continued to blow hard until about 5 p.m. when a strong North wind came down the Lake.

WED. 22

Since the 18 it has been mild & ,misty with quite a bit of rain & sleet. Today has been better, with a fairly clear sky & a hard frost.

THUR. 23

Hard frost last night, today has been fairly mild & sunny with practically no wind. As the snow has gone I have taken on the sheep-herding again.

Heard two Coyotes howling this evening.

SAT. 25

Since the 23rd it has been more or less damp & rainy.

MON. 27

Frost yesterday & today - 16° at the Point last night. Saw a horned-owl this morning sitting on the dead bough of a fir tree, silhouetted against the dark greenish dawning sky.

TUE. 28

Another hard frost. A bunch of Cayuses were around here today, & among them was Ginger, & I went up with an armful of hay & succeeded in catching him (a thing I have never been able to do before). I led him down & turned him into our enclosure. I think I shall probably use him for the sheepherding, instead of one of the Point horses, if I can fix it up satisfactorily with Mr. Godwin (the Manager at the Point).

WED. 29

I saw Mr. Godwin this evening, & have arranged to use Ginger for the sheep-herding. Mr. Godwin is to provide feed for Ginger, & I shall do the herding for less money Friday.

DECEMBER 1911

FRID. 1

A dull mild day with a strong Chinook wind. In the evening the clouds cleared off & I had a very nice moonlight ride after the sheep. Chickadees & Nuthatches (the Commonest winter birds here) are now showing up in numbers.

Nearly 30 deer have been shot already this season, around here. Last season, & this, the deer have been more plentiful, than for the last six years:

last winter we practically lived on deer meat (Venison is usually known round here by the Chinook name of "Mowitch")

SAT. 2

A calm day, with a chill mist, that extended all along the mountains so low down that it was almost resting on the Lake.

SUN. 3

A day similar to yesterday . A.K. shot a deer.

WED. 6

A light fall of wet snow during the night. A Chinook wind & sunshine quickly melted the snow.

I am using Ginger every day for the sheep-herding, & he appreciates the feeding.

THUR. 7

A wild day, with a frightful Chinook, which swept along with it sleet & rain.

Most of the people who hunt in these mountains are experienced men, but occasionally some green son-of-a-gun goes out, who ought not to be allowed to handle a pop-gun, much less a rifle.

These sort of people have a habit of aiming (if not firing) at any movement in the bush, whether it be a horse, deer, man or anything else – they don't give themselves time to see what it is. For instance a man named Ward, from the other side of the Lake, went hunting above here to day, & he told us, when he returned, that he had seen a buck, & was about to fire at it when it bounded off, & a man appeared, who at once covered Ward with his rifle, & Ward dropped on the ground in terror, fortunately the man saw in time that Ward was <u>not</u> a deer! – & I hope apologised.

Frid. 8

A day much like yesterday, but with less rain.

Coming back from the mail to day, I met a man who is staying with Durant, on the trail, with a fine large buck. He had shot it about 3 miles back in the mountains & had been dragging it for about 4 hours (it weighed I should think 200 lbs.) & he was pretty tired. He had got it down to the trail about half a mile South of Durants, so we slung it across the saddle & Ginger packed it down to Durants in fine style. I reached home shortly after dark.

Sun. 10

A very light sprinkle of snow last night, also a slight frost. At dawn I went out up the hill, & had a long walk around the mountains, & got back at 11 a.m. having been unsuccessful, though I saw hundreds of deer tracks, one of a huge buck, the hoof of which was at least 4 inches long.

The snow up on the mountains, in most places, reached up to my knees.

Tue. 12

A dull mild day. Deana saw a large buck up the hill today, but unfortunately had no rifle.

Wed. 13

Another day like yesterday. Just on the top of the first bench above Shorts" Point, this morning while I was riding out after the sheep, I saw two large does, about 75 yards ahead; Ginger was trotting along & making quite a noise on the crusted snow, & they looked at me for a minute & then ran off, but I whistled & they stopped & looked again. I then slid down behind the horse & waved my hat on the end of a stick, above the saddle, & instead of exciting their curiosity as it is said to do in antelopes, it seemed to scare them & they went off through the trees with their beautiful 15 foot bounds, & I did not see them again.

THUR. 14

Another dull mild day. This afternoon I saw a buck & a doe in almost the same place as where I saw the two does yesterday. I first saw the buck alone - a beautiful beast of fair size, with very upright antlers. He was on top of a ridge, standing perfectly still, looking at me , & about 50 yards away. I rode straight towards him until within about 30 yards, he then moved off over the ridge, & I noticed there was a small doe behind him. As I was riding up the ridge he evidently saw my hat, for he ran forward to within 40 feet of me to see what it was. He then stood & sniffed at me, & then bounded off.

I rode up on top of the ridge & whistled, & again saw the buck & the doe, about 75 yards off, looking at me. As soon as I rode towards them, though, they bounded away out of sight.

WED. 20

Since my last entry the weather has been chiefly dull with a South Wind, & an occasional frost. There have been two falls of wet snow also. Today is dry, clear, & frosty with a North wind, & about 3 inches of snow on the ground.

I saw a large flock of Waxwings (Amphilis cedroram) today

Durant and Nephew, Norcott Christmas 1911

These birds are very common round here in the cold weather, being as a rule in flocks of 50 to 100.

They sit about on low trees & shrubs eating maple "keys" dried Elderberries etc, & are very tame.

THUR. 21

At about 8 a.m. a wild Chinook wind arose, sweeping before it almost a blizzard of fine, whirling snow, which flew along in almost horizontal clouds

Although the snow was somewhat wet (as it always is with a Chinook wind) I found it cold & stinging enough to ride through. (I rode to the Point, but they told me it was too bad to take the sheep out as it certainly was). After midday the violence of the snow decreased but the wind kept up all day.

CHRISTMAS DAY MON. 25

The early morning was cloudy, with fine snow falling. It ceased to snow about the middle of the morning, but came on again in the afternoon.

There was a North wind all day.

We had a very Merry Christmas Durant & Norcott came over for dinner.

Norcott is Durant's nephew, he came out about a fortnight ago, from England. He is a very nice boy of 18, & is going to stay with his uncle for the winter I believe .

TUE. 26

Quite a bit of snow fell today.

Today was remarkably idle – on account of staying up late last night, this morning we got up later than we have done for many months, namely at half past eight.

WED. 27

About 4 inches of snow fell last night, & it also snowed all this morning. There is altogether about 10 inches of snow on the ground now.

Norcott came over & we spent the afternoon tobogganing.

FRID. 29

Yesterday was cold with some snow. Today was very cold (5° above zero) with a North wind, & fine snow continued falling.

SAT. 30

About 3 more inches of snow fell last night Very cold all day.
We had some invigorating tobogganing this afternoon.

SUN. 31

A bright clear day with the usual North wind extremely cold. It must have been below zero last night. Evidently the usual New Year cold snap is beginning.

The snow, which is over a foot deep, is pleasant to walk in, being perfectly dry & powdery with the frost.

Today we had no less than 4 visitors; The two Gammon brothers (who are living at the "Colonel's" shack near Kennard's) John Powell (who lives near Leney's) & Norcott.

In tampering with Ginger's extreme good nature, a little too much, this morning, I received from him a smart kick on the arm, which ached for the rest of the day.

1912

JANUARY 1912
NEW YEAR'S DAY. MON. 1

Another very cold day. The temperature at Shorts Point was 3°
below zero; at Kennard's 1° below, & upon the Bighorn Flats 16°
below.

When I arrived at Kennard's, Kennard, told me that Starky (an
old prospector, who has been staying with Kennard for some
months) went up to a shack in the mountains, where some boys
were having a spree, yesterday, & had not turned up. When the
fellows came down for their mail, they had horrible news. They
said the Starky left their shack in daylight, yesterday afternoon &
they thought sober enough to walk by himself. However on their
way down to Kennard's today they found a mark in the snow
below where he had laid down, & then slid down a hillside into a
gulch. In this gulch they found Starky's body frozen stiff. An awful
way of seeing the New Year in!

When I took off my socks after having ridden back from
Kennard's, this evening I found that I had nearly frozen two toes.

TUE 2

Colder than ever. The sky was clouded over with the steam or frost smoke from the Lake.

WED 3

Several degrees warmer. Big Gammon & Norcott came round for dinner, an hour or so after which, we turned out & spent a glorious afternoon tobogganing.

We have a track about a 100 or more yards long, for the first 50 it is very steep, after that it becomes less so, and at the end is almost on the level; The track is about 6 feet wide, beaten hard, & fairly well banked with snow at each side. One goes down at a frightful speed on a little toboggan or "stomach sleigh" —- I have done it in 8 seconds. Gammon & Norcott were not very good at steering, & were continually capsizing, ploughing into the banks etc. On one occasion today, Norcott & I were at the bottom, & Gammon was coming down, when suddenly the sleigh he was on, swerved rapidly into the bank, gathering snow in front of it; suddenly a mighty cloud of snow & twigs arose, like an explosion of dynamite.

Nothing else was to be seen until a fraction of a second after the "explosion" when the empty sleigh shot out of the cloud, took a jump & skidded down the lower part of the track. When the snow-cloud subsided, there was Big Gammon licking & howling, completely whitened from head to foot.

This _is_ extremely invigorating sport!

FRID. 5

The cold weather seems to show no sign of leaving us yet. Last night about 5 inches of snow fell, which made the early part of the day warmer, but towards evening the clouds dispersed somewhat, & it became as cold as ever.

Yesterday morning Ginger escaped & decamped to a party of his friends, who were grazing about a quarter of a mile up the hill. Seems to prefer "rustling" & half starvation to captivity & being fed. Food! this caused Deana & I to walk to the mail, & it is pretty hard breaking trail this weather though the snow is light & dry, & you can drag your feet through it. The worst walk I ever had through snow was last winter. The distance was about 3 miles, & the snow nearly two feet deep with a crust on top.

Each step you took you would break through the crust, & instead of being able to drag your foot through the snow, as when there is no crust, you had to lift it clean out, & then down again.

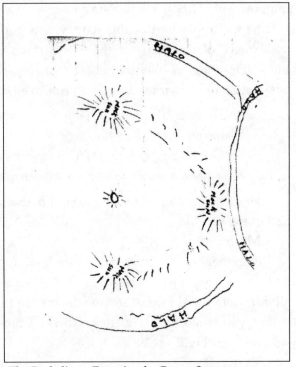

The Parhelion - Drawing by Roger Sugars

Added to this was sunshine which caused the snow to be so dazzling to the eyes that I got a frightful headache.

I heard to-day that up on the Bighorn Flats a night or two ago it was 22° below zero, & at Vernon 20° below.

SUN. 7

A beautiful clear day. Cloudless blue sky, North Wind, & very cold.

There was a parhelion around the sun all the morning (it disappeared at noon). I have never seen one before, & have never heard the cause of them, though I believe they only appear in very cold, & presumably clear weather. There were 3 mock-suns, one at each side & one above the real sun; those were large, bright & shining, with rainbow colours showing in them faintly. Right out round all 4 suns – mock & real – was a mighty halo, like a faint rainbow, only almost a complete circle.

At the upper part of this halo, was a portion of another. the appearance of the shape of the whole thing was somewhat like this:- [Drawing of the parhelion is here] The following is a description of the parhelion from "Primitive Folk" by Elie Rechis:

> *"Now it is the radiant parhelion, in segments or equipolar, oftenest with two or three false suns, sometimes with 4, 8, or even 16 luminous spectra, all becoming centres for as many circumferences."*

The whole thing seemed to extend over most of the Southern half of the sky.

MON. 8

Extremely cold. The temperature last night at Shorts Point , Nahun, & Leney's was 5° below zero. The sky was heavily overcast all day, from the clouds of steam which were rising from the Lake. In fact you could hardly distinguish sky from Lake. as the other side was obscured.

TUE. 9

No change in the weather.

THUR. 11

This is the steadiest cold snap we have ever had. As I have said before the cold snaps are usually short & sharp. This one however, though it has not been very cold, has continued steadily (with a perpetual north wind) for nearly three weeks Every day or night, nearly, during this time it has snowed a little.

All this snow must have been about 4 feet. This of course settles & packs, down to about 2 feet. A short distance up the hill there is about 3 feet or more now. Down here (where the snow has not been trodden) it is about 2 feet. Snow fell most of today.

FRID. 12

About two inches more snow fell last night.

The cold snap came to an abrupt end this afternoon, when a terrific Chinook arose, which swept the clouds along, & more or less cleared the sky.

It sent the snow flying off the trees in great clouds. This Chinook wind had a soft, balmy feel, which reminds one of wild spring days & thaws.

SAT. 13

A slight North wind sprang up this morning, & with it a heavy snowstorm, which lasted all the morning.

It seemed as if we were going to get the cold weather back, but in the course of the afternoon the Chinook returned.

MON. 15

Since Saturday afternoon it has steadily thawed, & about half the snow has gone: what remains is in a dirty slushy condition.

TUE. 16

Bright & cold with a North wind.

Mother & I took the steamer from Shorts' Point to Vernon this morning. (We had an invitation from our friends the Williams, who live in the Coldstream Valley.) We reached Okanagan Landing at about Midday, & hired a sleigh, & were driven into Vernon (about 5 miles North of the Landing)

In Vernon were met by Mr. Williams, who drove out to their place.

FRID. 19

We arrived home today, having spent three days in the Coldstream.

The Coldstream is a wide flat valley, which runs south of Vernon to the head of Long Lake & then east to Lumby (a small town) It is bordered by bare, rolling hills, behind which, are the usual dark wooded mountains. One gets views of miles of open country here. The valley itself is intersected with good wide waggon-roads & is all under cultivation – fruit-trees mostly.

There is a house every half mile or so, & miles of fencing stretch in all directions. The whole Valley has a telephone system. As for the weather, it is more inclined to extremes than on the Lake; the winters being colder: & the summer ! – dust & rattle- snakes!

While we were up there it was very cold (about zero at night). There had been less thaw than on the Lake & there was at least two feet of snow, whereas here (since the thaw) there is only about a foot).

Vernon is becoming quite a city, there being several large & up to date "department stores" etc.

WED. 24

Since we returned from Vernon the weather has been very dull & quite mild.

All day it snowed & rained heavily, & a strong Chinook wind got up in the afternoon.

THUR. 25

A beautiful sunny day with deep blue sky, & a somewhat blustering, & balmy Chinook. Ginger comes in regularly three times a day for his food; between meals he goes out & "rustles". This is very handy.

Today I am 15 years old. (45 Years later: I am 60 years.)

I think the following somewhat strange coincidence is worth putting down:

Over a year ago I had a dream that I was on a steamer, going up a fair sized river bounded by wild wooded hills. For some reason I seemed to know this river as Whiteman's Creek; this of course was absurd for Whiteman's Creek is not deep enough or wide enough to float a canoe. After the steamer had been going up stream for some time she ran on a sand bank & then somehow caught fire in the stern. Crew & passengers then took to the Land, I among them. We wandered about for a time until we came to a high bare ridge, & looking down we saw far below the Sugar-loaf Mnt. & beyond that, Okanagan Lake. After a time we came upon a house, & then a little town called "Twentieth Century" which was supplied with electric light. Somehow the town was connected with gold-mining. Here the dream ended.

At the time I thought that Whiteman's Creek flowed due east into the Lake (so it does according to maps) so I of course thought that it was impossible to be anywhere near Sugarloaf Mnt. (which is a good many miles South of the mouth of Whiteman's Creek.)

Many months after I was told by people who know the Creek

that it <u>does</u> flow North East & <u>directly behind</u> Sugar-loaf. I also heard that a lumber camp had started up behind Sugar-loaf.

At this I said, in fun, that I had better go prospecting up the Creek & find the gold-mine I had been dreaming about. Today, to my astonishment I heard that some gold had been found back near the falls of Whiteman's Creek & that there was a miniature gold-rush (i.e. a few people had staked claims) The falls supplied the power for the electric light which I dreamt about!

TUE. 30

Today was exactly like an early March day. Deep blue sky with bright sunshine, & the usual Chinook.

Beneath all the trees on the sunny slopes, the warm, pine-needle covered earth is exposed. The birch catkins (the earliest) are all out. It seems quite spring like, but it is only one of the midwinter thaws, & next month is sure to bring plenty of snow & frost.

WED. 31

Somewhat cold. The thawed snow was frozen hard enough to bear one walking on it. We saw a portion of a faint parhelion again today.

FEBRUARY 1912

THUR. 1

A thick mist along the hills all the morning. In the afternoon this mist dropped like a blanket right down to Lake-level. Objects a hundred yards away were completely blotted out.

FRID. 2

The mist was almost at Lake level all day. It caused all the trees to be covered in beautiful hoar-frost Hard frost all day. I was told that on the Bighorn Flats, yesterday & today, they have enjoyed a cloudless sky & beautiful sunshine – above the clouds.

THUR. 8

Since the 2nd the mist has remained without a break, low down on the hills. No wind — thawing slightly all the time – Very dismal & depressing weather.

Last night a big Chinook wind arose, & we woke this morning to find the sky cleared.

The brilliant sun & the warm wind thawed the snow rapidly.

Even with all these thaws, in the shady north slopes, there is still 8 or 10 inches.

Last night, in the dusk, I saw a Horned Owl perched on a fencepost near the gate. I went up, to see how close I could get, but he saw me, & flew off without the faintest sound from his great downy wings. We hear the owls hooting every night now (Horned Owls are about most & hoot in the late fall & early spring)

FRID. 9

wind dropped during the night. For some time, early this morning, it snowed heavily, but after a time it stopped, & then for the rest of the day it was thawing hard, & a fine drizzle was falling.

On our way to Kennard's today, Deana & I, twice heard, what we both were sure, were frogs croaking in the <u>trees</u> . Certainly it was a mild day, but could frogs be out & croaking at this time of year? And yet the noise we heard was almost unmistakable.

SAT. 10

A dull, windy day, Rain came on somewhat in the afternoon. I again hear the sound like a frog croaking.

SUN. 11

Windy & warm, with bright sunshine.

TUE. 13

More or less mild & dull. Norcott (a very frequent visitor) came over for dinner.

WED. 14

Weather much as usual. Near FitzGerald's this afternoon I saw a flock of 50 or more beautiful little birds. Around FitzGerald's there are a lot of bushes locally known as spiraea. (I do not know if this name is correct) The blossom hangs in thick clusters of minute cream coloured flowers all over the shrubs. These clusters dry up into brown bunches which remain on all winter, and are greedily eaten by horses.

The birds I saw today were simply covering these bushes &

eating the seeds from the dry clusters. They seemed very tame & I got close enough to tell their markings pretty distinctly. This is a description:

> Nape olive brown, back, brownish with conspicuous white, Wing-bars: tail of brown & white feathers, forked almost like a swallow's: underparts white with a bright salmon breast: sharply defined crimson craw: beak, black & blunt. Length of bird about 4 or 5 inches. they were quite strange to me but I am sure they were some kind of small finch or redpoll.

There seems no end to strange little birds here !

SAT. 17

Very dull & mild – as usual. Every night it rains heavily now. Hope we shall get a change in the weather soon.

Saw a chipmunk the first this spring (can it be really spring so early? & yet it seems like it, though a very dull & wet one: different to last winter & spring very.)

I also saw a great bird which I am almost sure was a golden eagle, soaring over at at considerable height.

The alder catkins are well out. The pussy-willows ought to be showing soon.

SUN. 18

Weather just the same. Saw the chipmunk again. I think it was the one that I saw yesterday. This is an extract from the "Vernon News" of Feb. 8, 1912:

The buxom Lady is none other than Mrs. Kenyon of Ewing's Landing!

Considerable excitement all around this vicinity on account of gold in Whiteman's Creek. There is no doubt that gold does exist and already some ten claims or so have been recorded, among them being an extremely energetic and excitable lady who travelled some twenty odd miles through the deep snow to record her claim. all good wishes and success accompany the buxom owner of Silver Star Ranch. May her star ere long turn to a gold one.

> Considerable excitement all around this vicinity on account of gold being discovered by a Yankee in Whiteman's Creek. There is no doubt that gold does exist and already some ten claims or so have been recorded, among't them being an extremely energetic and excitable lady who travelled some twenty odd miles through the deep snow to record her claim. All good wishes and success accompany the buxom owner of Silver Star Ranch. May her star ere long turn to a golden one.
>
> *Vernon News,*
> *Feb. 8, 1912*

MON. 19

An improvement in the weather. Last night it froze fairly hard, & today was bright, warm & sunny. the pussy-willows are coming out.

TUE. 20

Hard frost last night. A fine, somewhat moist, snow was falling most of the afternoon.

A large number of the little birds mentioned on page 144, came onto the elder tree close to the house & on the ground outside the window, this afternoon.

WED. 21

Dull, & quiet. About 1/4 of an inch of snow on the ground: this melted during the day.

THUR. 22

Another 1/4 of an inch of snow which thawed as soon as the sun rose.

A fairly bright day with a strong wind.

At night very black clouds came up, & Mother saw a single flash of lightning – no thunder followed it. After this heavy rain & hail fell for some hours of the night.

On the trail today I saw a track which I think was that of a skunk. (Skunks do not seem to hibernate properly here)

FRID. 23

More or less dull. During the morning there was a North wind which brought a few flakes of snow, but did not seem to lower the temperature much. In the afternoon this wind veered to the West & blew in terrific gusts like the West wind of summer evenings here.

SAT. 24

Hard frost. Fresh North wind, & a cloudless sky. the frost continued all day in the shade. The most beautiful day we have had for weeks.

SUN. 25

Cold with a north wind: snowed all the morning. In the afternoon a Chinook got up, & it at once began thawing. We were visited, this afternoon by Durant, Norcott & Newbury (a friend staying with Durant)

MON. 26

Cloudy with a Chinook wind. Thawed slightly all day. I thought that I had my list of the conifers of this valley complete but I got a letter from Allan Brooks (a naturalist who lives at Okanagan Ldg.) today, saying that there are two other species: namely: "Foxtail" Pine. Pinus Flexilis or Monticola. This, he says, is a small, stunted, tree (though large to the east of this Lake) & May be found on the summit of Terrace Mnt. and: "Balsam" Fir. Abies sub-alpina.

He says this fir is common half way up Terrace Mnt. & might be found in the shadiest possible North slopes in the gulch of the south fork, Shorts Creek. This is very interesting & I must look out for the Balsam Fir, but I fear I shall not reach the top of Terrace in quest of the Foxtail Pine. Still, it is very interesting to know even the names of two trees previously unknown to me.

THUR. 29

Yesterday & today have been very frosty & bright with a north wind. There was about 20° of frost last night.

MARCH 1912

SUN. 3

Since Thursday, each day has been bright, & sunny, with strong & continual North wind. Every night there has been a hard frost – somewhere about 20°, I should say — & it has continued to freeze throughout the day, in the shade.

FRID.8

There has been no change whatever in the weather, since the 3rd.

Day after day goes by, with an absolutely cloudless blue sky, & the brisk, steady North wind. Towards evening the wind drops & a skim of thin ice covers the Lake in patches.

Among the men who logged on our place three years ago, was a half breed called Albert McDougall,a notorious "bad man" He was only about 24 or 25, but had various knife & bullet wounds on him, which he had got in fights.

He was also somewhat of a thief (as most "breeds" are) Anyhow, I heard today that he has been on a "drunk", & murdered his cousin (or nephew) by pumping three bullets into him! The police have got Albert & he probably will be hanged.

THUR. 14

Since the 8th there has been no change in the weather, till to-day, which has been warmer & dull, with a slight Chinook wind.

FRID. 15

A slight swell on the Lake, from the South. Very dull. A few flakes of snow fell

SAT. 16

Dull & quiet day. Quite mild.

In the dusk, this evening I saw for the first time (The first recognition anyhow) an Oregon Robin. The commoner species here is the Western Robin (Menula migratoria propinqua) It is a large bird - larger than the common English Thrush – it has a slate coloured back & head, & a red breast.

The young have a speckled plumage for the first year. They are most numerous in the spring & fall. The Oregon Robin is much the same but has a more speckled back, a white line through the eye, & a broad black band across the red breast.

The blue birds have returned.

SUN. 17

A dull, showery day with a strong Chinook wind. Deana & I took a walk round the hills this afternoon, to geologise a little.

We saw 8 deer, & a grouse. The result of geological investigations (which have been going on for weeks) will appear later! The depth of snow up the hill is still nearly two feet, in most places; & with constant thawing & freezing very solid & granular, with a hard crust. The snow on all the South-facing slope is gone, & to a considerable height, but on the North slopes even near the Lake the snow remains.

The only signs of spring plant life, are "pussy-willows" & a few other catkins. none of which are very far advanced.

By the way, I heard that the report in the "Vernon News" about the gold in Whiteman's Crk., was a lie – at least, gold has always been known to exist there but not enough to pay – what is one to believe here?

TUE. 19

Slight change in the weather, namely, colder.

FRID. 22

Since the 19th it has been cold & sunny with a north wind , & a hard frost each night.

The first chipmunk was seen on the 17th of Feb., since then they have been very numerous. These creatures are a good deal larger than a mouse, & a good deal smaller than a squirrel (which they resemble in shape but the tail of the chipmunk is not nearly as bushy as a squirrels). They are sandy in colour with dainty, & somewhat faint black & white stripes down the back. They have cheek pouches of which they make great use. They are very venturesome & bold & if you do not keep cats, you can get them to eat out of your hand. The squirrels are almost as "cheeky".

They resemble the English squirrel in shape, but are dark brown instead of red.

Quite a number of migrating birds have returned already namely: Crows, Bluebirds, Robins etc.

This August I saw a Bald-headed Eagle, & during the day I saw another Oregon Robin.

We have heard more startling news – it is the talk of the whole place, i.e.: - Two men – Frank Wilson & Walter James – held up a store South of Penticton, *[I afterwards heard that it was South of Kelowna]* shooting at the storekeeper & missing him. They were arrested & were being brought to jail by a constable on board the steamer, on Tuesday 19th The constable had his own revolver & the revolvers and cartridge belts of the two men. One of them however had concealed, in his sleeve, a tiny revolver with a small bullet & formalite cap. The constable unfortunately fell asleep, & they shot him in the head, seized all the firearms & escaped off the steamer at Peachland. They then travelled North up this side of the Lake. The Police were out everywhere after them. A man called Ramsay, however, met them on the road near Batchels & held them up with a "rifle". They were captured & taken off by Constable Tooth on Wednesday. The constable they shot, has a bullet in his head & will perhaps recover.

SUN. 24

Warm & sunny. Took a walk up the hill alone, saw five deer. In the cañon I saw two groundhogs – the first I have seen this spring.

WED. 27

The last few days have been very warm & sunny At night though there is no perceptible frost on the lower slopes, yet there are patches of thin ice on the Lake. This shows how extremely low the temperature of the Lake must be in the spring.

Celandines are out in sunny spots on Shorts' Point. Butterflies are quite numerous, mostly varieties of fritillary. Each morning, the last few days have been cloudy, but as soon as the sun rose the clouds dispersed, & for the rest of the day the sky has been cloudless & sun very hot.

The prevailing wind on the Lake is from the North but is very slight.

THUR. 28

A Chinook came up today making it very hot, & bringing heavy clouds

FRI. 29

Uncertain wind, blowing in puffs from all directions: light. showery & cold, & hot & sunny alternately.

SAT. 30

Slight frost, Very clear sky. Warm sun during the daytime, & practically no wind – in fact a perfect day for The flower to come out after the Celandines is a pretty little thing like a snowdrop only yellow (we call it "butterdrop") These grow all over the sunny slopes. Mother found the first today. Grass (the "bunch grass" of the sunny open slopes & flats, & the pine grass of the higher & closer pine woods is beginning to sprout a little yet in the shady hollows & "pot-holes" not far up the hill there is still two feet of snow & no snow has fallen since February - it has lain for 2 months.

SUN. 31

A warm sunny, & practically windless day.

A few high clouds.

A flock of five or six wild swans (Olor buccinator?) were about on the Lake all day.

I saw a lizard on the warm rocks on the beach between our place & Durant's.

I also found a very old mountain-sheep (Bighorn: oris montana) at an old Indian camp on the beach. I mention this, as bighorn are very scarce here – a few are occasionally seen (more often their tracks) back of Terrace Mnt.

The Aspen catkins are well out.

John Edward & Lily Sugars Circa 1912

April 1912

Frid. 5

Up to the 4th it has been cloudy off & on with a Chinook wind most of the time.

Today has been clear & very warm & sunny, with little wind. The leaves of various deciduous trees are beginning to sprout.

Mon. 8

Since Friday it has been fine & warm. The constable has died.

Tue. 9

A bright clear day. In the evening it clouded over & there were several flashes of lightning. I saw a flight of martins, the first arrivals that I have seen.

Wed. 10

Some heavy rain fell last night; today was warm & partly cloudy.

Thur. 11

Rained heavily all last night. Dull day, with a Chinook wind.

Frid. 12

A fairly clear day with a variable wind. A few wild sunflowers are out on the hillsides.

MON. 22

Since last entry the weather has been somewhat changeable. Most days have been fairly fine. There have also been several wet days & nights.

Most of the leaves are out - bright green, tender shoots. The Saskatoons are beginning to blossom. The tiny green flowers of the maple are also out. Celandines are nearly over. Butter drops are in their prime, as also are some star-like little white flowers which carpet the hillsides in places.

The sunflowers are coming on well. Except in swamps & all places which are clothed with deciduous trees, the spring does not cause a great change in the appearance of the landscape because of the evergreen conifers which cover practically the whole country.

Up on the high mountains the snow of course still remains but its melting is swelling the creeks considerably.

A few little patches of snow are still on the deep pot holes or dells not far up the hill.

I have seen, lately, two Loons flying Northward looking like small geese. At a height their cry suggests "wild maniac laughter" as it is usually described in books, but heard near to it is more like a loud, hysterical <u>laugh</u> of a girl.

Yet more excitement in the way of "bad men".

Two lumberjacks went to the bank at Lumby, hammered at the door (sometime in the night) & asked to change a cheque. A man came to the door & refused to change a cheque at that time of the night, & slammed the door in their faces, at which one of them promptly pulled his "gun" & fired through the door, & broke the arm of the man inside.

The two then betook themselves to the "bunkshack" at the lumbercamp , & put the revolver under another lumberjack's pillow!

Roger's Drawing

They have been arrested, I believe, & will probably get 7 or 8 years imprisonment. (I found on the "Colonel's" beach, today a nice little stone arrowhead: — actual size.)

MAY 1912

WED. 1

A hot, clear day with cumuli banked on the horizon. A slight North wind all day.

Since the 22nd April the weather has been fairly fine but inclined to showers in the evening.

On all the steep, south-facing hillsides near or not far back from the lake, the pines & first growth in clumps or singly, from 10 to 100 yards apart. In the open spaces between, the tall stately saskatoon bushes grow (which are full out with their beautiful white blossoms, now) between the saskatoons again are the tussocks of yellow sunflowers, (which simply blaze on the hillsides at this time of year) – and the bunchgrass. *[Sagebrush and sometimes prickly-pear cactus in the S.Okanagan.]*

In shady hollows & slopes the ground is much thicker carpeted with grass & low shrubs & many kinds of smaller, though no less beautiful flowers, also the trees grow closer together.

In about two months most of all this spring glory will be withered & parched under the heat & dryness of the summer.

Several flights of geese have gone over to the Northward lately. Blue grouse are very plentiful in the hills, & ruffed grouse are drumming all the time in the swamp & bush along the Lake shore.

We got the awful news of the week of the Titanic about a fortnight ago – the day after its occurrence, I think.

A bunch of 40 or 50 head of cayuses were driven through along the trail a day or two ago, two cowboys with them. They had come from Kruger's (down on the Line) & were taking the horses to Vernon to ship by train from there to Alberta.

FRID. 3

Variable wind, somewhat dull.

In the evening a flight of about 50 or 60 sandhill cranes passed over at a great height.

WED. 22

Since last entry, with the exception of the last 3 days, which have been somewhat wet (we needed rain!), nearly every day has been hot & clearskied. On Monday 13 the temperature rose to 83° in the shade.

The creeks are exceptionally full this year. Shorts Crk., is up several feet, & is simply boiling through the canyon & over the falls.

The lake has nearly reached high water & is full of leaves, branches logs, etc lifted off the beaches with the rise of the water, & also from the creeks. There is still a considerable amount of snow on the tops of Terrace & Little White Mnts.

Many more flowers are out: The sunflowers – which are over – have been, compared with other years, a rather poor show. The saskatoon blossom - also over – has been more than usually beautiful.

It seems quite summer-like In the hot afternoons, the air is heavy with the drone of insects & scent of flowers. The crickets chirrup all the evening.

I bathed on the 14th; the lake is very cold with snowwater, so I only took a plunge.

FRID. 24

A hot day with a Chinook wind in the afternoon. A few cumulus & cirrus clouds about.

I read in the paper (Vernon News) to-day that both Albert McDougall & Walter (or William) James have been sentenced to be hanged on August 9th. The man who wounded the bank-manager at Lumby has got a 12 years sentence.

FRID. 31

Since last Friday the weather has been uncertain Each day has been more or less cloudy & showery, with a Chinook nearly every afternoon. On Monday I rowed home from Kennard's in a tearing Gale from the South.

Wild roses & dog woods (which grow in the heart of the Cedar Swamp) are blossoming.

The Creeks are still considerably swollen & the lake is higher than it has been for 5 0r 6 years, & continues to rise every day.

The following is to give some idea of the force of Shorts' Creek this spring:

Mr. Godwin (the manager at the Shorts" Point ranch has for the past year or so, been employing men on the construction of an electric plant, for the purpose of lighting, irrigation etc.

It is almost completed this spring, & consists of a suspension bridge, about 50 yards long which spans the cañon above the falls. This bridge carries pipes, which tap the creek at the upper end of the bridge, in the bottom of the cañon & at the head of a small fall. At the lower end of the bridge the pipes are brought out over the rim of the cañon, & laid in a ditch which extends about 200 yards down a very steep hillside to one side of the cañon. Here the power is obtained. At the foot of the hill, on the flat the pipes are connected with a dynamo in a power-house The suspension bridge is very imposing & gives access to parts of the cañon which could not be seen or reached before: but I think on the whole it spoils the

Suspension Bridge with flue to carry water from Shorts' Creek to Fintry

grandeur of the cañon.

To return to the subject of Shorts' Creek. At the upper end of the bridge, the water has been coming over the little fall, & tumbling with smashing force into the bridge itself, & has carried away 5 pipes & wrenched or broken two steel cables so that the bridge now sags right over!

JUNE 1912

SAT. 1

A somewhat hot day; cloudy in the morning. Chinook most of the day.

I was coming along a practically disused trail, on the way home from the mail, yesterday, when I encountered a mother grouse (a ruffed grouse).

I came upon her right in the middle of the trail, & almost trod on her. She flapped & scuttled round my legs, with all her feathers & ruff bunched out. I then saw several tiny brown chicks hurrying away up the slope, under the sunflower tussocks. After watching them for a minute (to the rage & distress of the mother) I walked on, but the mother flapped along beside me, hissing & whining, for a short distance, & then stood & watched me out of sight.

SUN. 2

A fairly fine day. Durant took us all out for a trip in his launch (he bought a 25 foot gasoline launch a few weeks ago) this afternoon. He took us as far as Okanagan Centre & back – a run of 12 miles – to his place where we had tea. Wed. 5 – since the 22nd each day has been perfectly cloudless, & very hot. There has been a North wind for the most part.

WED. 12

since the 5th it has been very close & extremely smoky, there is evidently a bushfire somewhere about. The mosquitoes have been terrible, worse than I have ever known them.

Today has been very wet.

THUR. 13

Another wet day. The rain has cleared the atmosphere of smoke, & done the garden stuff a lot of good. I have found a few stone flakes & imperfect arrowheads lately.

With regards to the various means of transport here, I do not fancy I have ever mentioned anything except the C.P.R. steamers, & horses. About 7 years ago nearly everybody owned a flat-bottomed rowing & sailing boat. These boats (except among the Indians) are now going out of fashion, & clinker boats & fast gasoline launches are coming in.

Besides these, there is a considerable traffic of motorcars along the waggon-road of the East side of the Lake. A telephone from end to end of the valley on the east side, & part way up the South end of the West side (but does not pass up here) connects all the "cities" of the valley.

As I have said before fruit-ranches, roads, towns etc., are confined practically to the Lake-shore & lower benches, while the great majority – the mountains & great timbered plateaux – remain wild – & always will as far as I can see. (and hope!)

SUN. 16

The wet weather ceased yesterday. Today has been quite fine & hot.

Newbury & I have proposed to take a three days expedition to climb Terrace Mnt. We start tomorrow – weather permitting.

Newbury is a very nice English man of about 30. He only has one arm – the other he lost when a boy, in a gun accident.

WED. 19

On Monday morning Newbury & I set out on our expedition. We each had a pack – mine consisted of 1 blanket, 1 mosquito net to pull over my head, water flask, 1 loaf bread, 2 tins sardines, 6 hard- boiled eggs, salt, tea, & socks & sweater. All this I roped into a compact roll, which I carried on my back with shoulder bands. It weighed about 9 lbs. In addition I had a camera, rifle, knife, & cartridge belt.

Newbury carried much the same, with the addition of a small axe, compass, & an Aneroid barometer.

We left the level of the Lake (1,130 ft. above sea) at 7 o'clock, & struck across the bench to Attenborough's. Just above Attenboro's

Sheep Mountain Bluffs

we came to the mouth of the South fork up which we went. We travelled along the north side of the creek along a steep hillside openly clothed with Douglas fir & bullpine. We went north like this for several miles until the direction of the creek swung to W.S.W.

Here the open country ceased & we got into "flats" densely wooded with jack-pines, spruces & balsam firs. When we had gone about a mile into this wilderness, we found it was midday, & went to the creek side, lit a fire & had a meal.

Here I found some "devil-club" -a broad leaved plant about 3 feet high, with fierce prickles all up its stems. The altitude was 3,900 above sea. After this we went on for some hours up the creek, until in spite of the heat, I was forced to put on the sweater over my flannel shirt as the mosquitoes were becoming intolerable. We were now in a dense spruce forest. After a time we began to look out for a camp site, but the further we went the wetter the ground became,

& there was hardly room to sit down for dead falls. We saw some bear-droppings at this part. Finally we lit a fire & bolted a miserable supper, with the mosquitoes. We decided to strike uphill & trust to luck for water. The altitude at the point was 4,500 ft. above sea level. So we left the creek & struck off due west, through jack pines (chiefly) On the high plateaux, where the trees grow in very dense stands (except where the country has been fire swept.) the trees – especially jack-pines – are wonderfully tall & straight in comparison to their thickness – from 3 inches to 1 foot – The jack-pines are clear of branches for two thirds of their height, & when they fall the bark comes off.

After we left the creek this was the kind of country we went through. The trees so dense, we could not see 50 feet ahead, & dead falls lying criss cross in all directions, as straight & slippery as fence-rails. The ground was still mossy with damp. Suddenly we saw, towering sheer above us a mighty precipice – the first terrace of Terrace Mnt. The hill became steeper & steeper & the trees scraggy & stunted. Fortunately we had struck the Southern extremity of the terrace & we got up quite easily. We walked about 100 yards North along the terrace, & found an ideal place to stop the night – an open, dry, flat bit of ground, about 50 feet in from the edge of the cliff; a patch of snow handy for water, & lots of little balsams & knarled jack pines. So we pitched camp, that is to say made a mattress of balsam boughs on the ground & lit a fire.

The altitude was 5,600 ft. To the back of our camp was a sort of densely wooded flat extending somewhat downhill to the base of the second terrace or summit.

To the east the view was grand. The terrace we were on was at least 300 feet high. It is about two miles long, & quite impossible to scale except at the extreme ends. It rises sheer out of the forest we had been walking through. I must reserve my wretched description of the view, for that from the summit which (to the east) was almost the same as that from our camp).

We arrived at this point at about 6 p.m. In spite of a cold wind the mosquitoes were simply in thousands, covering our bodies,

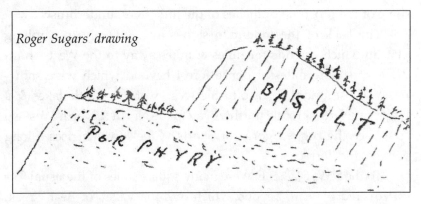

Roger Sugars' drawing

swarming in the air near our heads, dropping into the tea, singeing themselves in the fire, & humming like a swarm of bees.

Newbery killed 20 on my back with a slap of a hand.

We turned in at 9 p.m. got right under the blankets to protect ourselves from the hordes of winged devils. We managed to get a few hours sleep & got up at 4 a.m. In the morning twilight the gloomy forests at the foot of the great precipice seemed to stretch out like the sea, or a great, dark lake. In spite of the chilliness of the morning the mosquitoes were as bad as ever. Shortly the sun rose like a ball of fire through the haze of smoke which lay along the horizon to the east. Everything, the trees & the great rocky terrace, was tinted with red.

We rustled some breakfast, carefully put out the fire with snow, left our stuff in a heap, & set out for the south end of the summit terrace, which we reached in about half an hour. After a short steep climb we gained the summit, still accompanied by thousands of mosquitoes. The top resembles the first terrace, but is a great deal shorter & considerably higher. It is flattish, & fairly thickly covered with little, knarled & sprawling spruce, Jack, & fox tail pines. Also balsam firs. The summit's face is a mighty precipice of irregular frost split basalt. There were several patches of snow, the largest of which was about 20 feet across & 3 feet deep. The barometer gave the altitude as 6,200 ft. above sea level. There were a great variety of beautiful little alpine flowers, saxifrages & beautiful little mosses & ferns. There was no underbrush, unless one would call some of the prostrate branches of the little trees, underbrush.

The back of the mountain slopes away steeply to a rolling plateau which extends for miles & miles away to the West – hundreds of square miles of dense forest beyond which were snow-peaks. Close under Terrace to the west, were two little lakes & a larger one further to the north. Away to the North & North-West we could see the rugged gorge of Shorts" Creek (which rises a long way behind Terrace.)

To the S.W.; S.; & S.E. were many square miles of the usual forest covered plateau, beyond which was the Valley of Bear Creek, beyond that again more plateau & then snow-peaks.

To the east there were several miles of flats & rolling hills sloping downwards mostly to the east, where far below hazy & shimmering in the sunshine, lay Okanagan Lake – the Northern end; the Southern end was cut out of sight by a range of mountains. The eastern horizon was unfortunately veiled with a haze of smoke, but we could just make out a great extent of plateau, beyond which rose vaguely & infinitely distant-looking, a line of snowy peaks – evidently the Selkirks.

After I had taken several photographs, we hurried down to our camp, which we reached at about 7 a.m. We packed up our stuff & set out Northwards along the lower terrace; We walked right along the edge of the precipice for its entire length (about 1 to 2 miles I should say)

We of course, had a splendid view to the east, all the way. I doubt if an experienced mountaineer could scale the face of the terrace anywhere. The terrace dwindles down at the North end, & there is a gulch between it & Goat Mountain. It is a rocky crag about 5000 ft. about sea level. (It lies between Terrace Mountain & Shorts' Creek.) We went down through this gulch, where we were thankful to find some water. We then mounted the slope on the other side & went through fairly open woods until we reached the summit of Mnt. Zion (a green, grassy, treeless little peak just below & in front of the great Goat Peak). The altitude of Mnt. Zion is 4,800 feet above sea level.

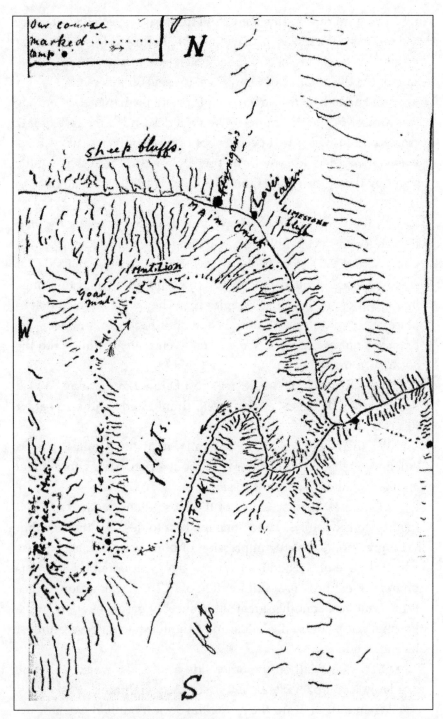

June 1912 - Roger Sugars' map.

There was a very fine view from this peak, especially of Terrace Mountain – which was, by this time, beginning to look somewhat distant - & the bold Sheep Bluffs, which extend along the opposite side of the deep valley of Shorts" Cr. for several miles.

We had a drinkless lunch on this pretty peak (which to our joy was almost free of mosquitoes) We then descended the face of it & crossed a flat which had been swept of most of its trees by fire, & was starting a new growth of tiny jackpines. There was a little swampy flat at the edge of this bench, with a little stagnant lake in it.

At the edge of the bench we found ourselves at the top of a tremendously steep hillsides, with Shorts' Creek roaring in the gulch, about 2,000 feet below us, we descended this hill side for some distance through open firs, & then found we had to plunge into a belt of small young Douglas firs. They were so thick that in places we had to crush through downhill backwards to keep the branches out of our eyes. We got out eventually, & down into the creek bottom, parched with heat & thirst.

We had struck the main creek just below Love's cabin. We sat down under the trees by the creek, drank, had a little to eat, & drank & drank.

We then walked down the trail for about 2 miles, passed Attenborough's & reached home at about 4 p.m. having found that another night out was unnecessary.

In spite of the discomfort of the mosquitoes, we had enjoyed the trip considerably. I have done my best to describe the view but I can give no idea of the impression of immensity & vast expanse which it gave one. The lower terrace is a great dike or sill of por-phyry, & Goat peak is a continuation of it. The upper or top terrace is the remains of another great sill or sheet of basalt, overlay- in the Porphyry; thus lit up the landscape, brighter than day, were almost incandescent.

On top of a hill on the other side of the lake we saw a flame suddenly leap up, evidently a tree struck by lightning.

When a flash lit up the sky & the dark mountain was thrown

into sharp silhouette, we could distinctly see the smoke from the fire against the purple sky. Yesterday morning there was no sign of the fire – it must have been put out by the rain – fortunately.

Last night there was another slight thunderstorm.

Today has been cool & cloudy.

SAT. 29

Yesterday & today have been close & sultry, during the day & almost chilly at night .

A thunderstorm passed to the eastwards last night. Both last night & the night before, we, & most people around, noticed a smell of sulphur in the air. When there is a smell in the air here, it is almost invariably smoke from forest-fires, but this sulphur smell was totally different. though somewhat faint, there was no doubt about it being present. Mnt. Katmi in Alaska is in (or has been in) violent eruption & volcanic ash was seen over Vancouver Island. We thought, possibly the sulphur smell came from this volcano.

In our spare time we are building a new log house, for which is required besides logs, a considerable amount of lumber, which arrived from the mill at Kelowna, today by a gasoline lumber launch.

Shorts' Point 1913

Sugars' first home at Shorts' point

New House Winter 1913

July 1912

Mon. 1 Dominion Day

A cool, dull day, with a strong Chinook wind.

On Dominion Day there are always celebrations in one or more of the towns in the Valley. This year, there is a regatta at Okanagan Centre, with sailing, swimming, launch-racing etc. also horse-racing among which is the usual "cowboy race". However the greatest day ever attempted in the Okanagan, is today at Armstrong. Among other things there are to be two aeroplane flights – the first in the interior of B.C.

I found a very good arrowhead at Kennard's today.

Tue. 23

Since last entry the weather has been very unsettled. According to the "Vernon News" it is about the wettest summer on record.

Some think it is owing to the eruption of Mnt. Katmi in Alaska; possibly it is.

There is a thunderstorm nearly every other day, & considerable rain; only a day now & then that is clear & cloudless.

Usually each day is fine & hot in the morning, & clouding over for a shower in the afternoon: most extraordinary weather for the "dry belt".

On the afternoon of Saturday 20th there was a thunderstorm accompanied with a regular cloudburst of rain & hail. It swept down with a deafening roar on the roof. The trees bent before it, & the landscape was blotted out with mist, & the lake was whipped into foam with the deluge of great raindrops & hailstones.

There are some old logging-trails down several gulches, on our place; down there, during the 15 minutes the storm lasted, regular torrents roared & tumbled, washing out the loose earth, & building little deltas.

Since we have been here, we have never known the the mosquitoes so thick, & the hills so green, all due to the unwanted moisture.

The photographs that I took up Terrace Mt are not very good, but I think I can improve them with a reduction of the density of the negatives. I have written an article on the expedition, & if I should have the luck to get it published, I shall buy a new camera – a $20 Kodak.

AUGUST 1912

SAT. 3

During the past week the weather has been for the most part dry & clear., but today shows signs of unrest in the elements, big thunderclouds & an occasional rumble of distant thunder.

The mosquitoes are getting much fewer.

The deciduous trees are exceptionally green for this time of year. Early peaches are ripe. Blue grouse familys are very plentiful. I hope there will be good shooting when the season opens.

SUN. 4

A hot & somewhat close day. I rode up to Love's today. Had dinner at Attenborough's & then went on up the creek.

Love is an old man with a white beard, he has been an Indian fighter down on the plains, he is a *Civil War Veteran, & a prospector. He lives in a tiny shack, about 5 x 10 feet with a dirt floor. The shack is on the level creek bottom, between the great bare slopes of Mount Zion & the Limestone bluff. These mountains have once been thickly timbered, but some great forest fire has swept

Hercules Love US. Civil War vet. Had a gold mine at Shorts' Creek for several years

them many years ago. Now the slopes are covered with grass, shrubs, a few small firs & pines & here & there a burnt stump, log, or great blackened spike of an ancient tree.

Love's Cabin

The slopes are fearfully steep, & new growth is slow in getting a start.

Love has mined up here for 15 years, & never loses hope & faith. He always talks as if he was going to strike the gold "pretty soon now". He had one tunnel 250 feet into the base of Mnt. Zion (all his own work) which caved in a year or two ago, & he had to abandon it, but he is now 50 feet into the rock.

The old mine is known as "Love's Golden dream" & "Loves labour lost". It is pitiful in a way, & yet the old man, I think is as happy as anyone could be for he has absolute faith.

He told me that this is about the wettest summer since '98.

Mon. 5

There was quite an event today: the mother & sister of Bob & Jack Somerset arrived off the steamer. (Somerset's ranch is on the hillside above Leney's.)

Frid. 9

A hot & fairly fine day. Walter James I believe was hanged at Kamloops today: Albert McDougall however has had a reprieve & has got the life sentence.

Sat 17

The weather remains very unsettled: More wet days than <u>fine ones</u>.

The latest alarm is that there is to be a 5 or 6 years cut of timber, taken out back of here (Attenborough's & Godwin's range) The whole of the logging inhabitants of Naramata will move up her. There will be a big camp, a school, & possibly a sawmill. There will be three or 4 million feet of logs to take out Where they propose to put the great lumber-camp I don't know, not too near here, I hope. The benches between the lake & the first range are clothed openly with firs & mighty red-barked pines; a veritable primeval deer-park.

After this country has been logged over, most of its beauty has gone. There are still many trees, but they are small & crooked or dead.

In place of the great pines are big stumps, wasted "saw-logs", a litter of lopped branches, & tree-tops with the needles turned brown or fallen off. There are roads (torn up, rutted trails through the trees, of about 10 feet wide.) & "skidways" chutes & "dumps" to generally disfigure the landscape. It is a wild & pitiful confusion of destruction.

Fortunately, in the mountains, though the trees are frightfully numerous, they are too small & inaccessible to get out; so the upper forests are likely to remain untouched for many years, if not forever.

However I am glad I reached this country early enough to see the forests of big trees which grow on the lower hills before they were all destroyed.

SEPTEMBER 1912

SAT. 7

I think that I must hurry up & try & finish this diary, as I fancy the "folks at home" are wanting to see it.

The season for grouse & deer opened on the 2nd this year & will be closed, for deer, on Dec. 15th & for grouse on Dec 31st We are busy fruit-picking at the Point, & have not much time for hunting; I have only got one grouse.

The new house is going up by degrees: we hope to get it fin-

Sugars' new log home 1913

ished before snow flies. The log walls are up & half the shingles on the roof.

It is 20 x 20 feet & is to have a "lean-to" kitchen 10 x 10. It is in a more sheltered position than our shack, nearer the lake, & we shall be able to pipe water right in, from our springs.

It is to have a sitting room 10 x 20 & two bedrooms, & a rustic porch.

The weather continues wet off & on. We get a few days of clear, bright weather, promising weeks of fine weather then without any warning the sky will thicken, & we get two or three days of rain. I fancy we shall get another winter of heavy snow. Most years the annual precipitation is about 12 to 15 inches. I should think for 1912 it will come nearer to 25 inches.

I have tried to size up the geology of this district roughly, but it is beyond me.

By the position of the moraines I concluded that the glaciers moved Northwards here, which I verified by a book on the Ice Age.

As old Love says "The country's bin all tore up" The country rock seems to be granite & gneiss, which has been torn by porphyry dykes all about. The plateaux are said to be remains of lava floods. On top of this, the hills have been rounded off by glaciers & round or flat-topped moraines, of granite boulders & gravel have been piled up every here & there, at the bases of the main mountains along the lake-valley.

In a few places there are remains of various strata which once overlaid the land. Up Shorts" Creek there is a mass of limestone which has been metamorphosed to a lime schist.

Then there is a seam of coal overlaid by sandstone. This coal was opened up about 5 years ago & has been prospected ever since, They say it is an excellent quality of coal, & I believe there is plenty of it. Samples have been taken out, & I suppose some day it may be worked.

I have already given some slight description of the general appearance of the mountains, & slopes along the Lake, but none of the shore line. For the most part, except on flats at the mouths of creeks, the hillside slopes almost to the water's edge. The upper part of the narrow beach is usually clothed with Aspens, Cottonwoods willows, maples, Alders etc. In the fall these turn orange & red, & the narrow shore line is ablaze with colour. The fore shore may be of sand, gravel, pebbles, & angular or round boulders. In years of very high water, the Lake may cover the narrow foreshore right up to the bases of the trees. Then again the banks may be so rocky & precipitous, that there is no beach or fringe of deciduous trees, instead there are twisted pines & firs, growing out of the rock almost to the waters edge.

In places there are sheer granite cliffs & bluffs, descending straight into the water. From the foot of the lake, northwards, for about 6 miles on each side the shore is an unbroken line of sheer mud cliffs, from 20 to 100 feet high. In this part of the Valley the lower hills are rolling & barren, & cactus & sagebrush covered; to the back of these rise the high mountains covered in the usual dark forest.

MON. 23

Since about the 8th September the weather has been almost faultless, true British Columbia September weather, day after day without a cloud; cool, almost cold nights & warm brilliant days.

The leaves are not turning much, yet, near the lake, but the autumn is well forward on the uplands.

The timbered mountains are still dark & sombre, but up on the bare slopes of Mnt. Zion & the neighbourhood of the Sheep Bluffs, the saskatoon bushes on the dry sidehills, & the aspens, birches etc. in the steep, little gulches of some side rivulets, are simply ablaze.

The hillsides in this part are mostly of sliding disintegrated rock, covered with bunch grass & saskatoon bushes with here & there a crag.

On Saturday 14th myself & Norcott went hunting up the slopes between the Limestone & Sheep Bluffs. We spent the whole day (a glorious day!), visited Love's, & Pat Kerrigan's shack, (a well built, but deserted cabin, with a deserted mine on the hillside above it) Pat Kerrigan's is about 3 quarters of a mile above Love's.

I shot two big blue grouse. Norcott had a .22 with a fancy wind gauge sight, which of course went wrong & he missed a fine grouse.

On Tuesday evening we had a feast of 6 grouse, with Norcott as guest. Birds are more numerous than they were during the summer, returning from the North I think.

Today, the weather seems a little unsettled, it is windy & dull, & the atmosphere is thick with smoke. The fruit-picking is about over – I have made $30.00 off it. Deana & A.K. are at the Point, Mother has ridden to Leney's on Ginger, so I am alone, except for

Peter, the only remaining rabbit.

OCTOBER 1912

TUE. 8

For the past month the weather has been perfect with hardly a break. One does appreciate this glorious fall weather after the unwanted wetness of last summer (or should I say this summer?) Yesterday & today have been cloudy but I think it will clear again.

There have been several light frosts during the past three weeks or so. The autumn is well advanced. The Tamaracks are lemon- yellow in the mountains.

In spite of the main forest being evergreen it is wonderful how much colour there is – along the lake shore – in the cedar swamps, on the creek flats, little gulches, mountain meadows & sloughs.

Anywhere, there is enough moisture to support deciduous trees or shrubs. All varieties of colour: orange, saffron, lemon russet, scarlet, crimson & delicate pinks.

I saw a queer thing yesterday; A saskatoon bush swept of all its leaves, had on one of its bare branches, three or four blossoms & several just bursting open. The saskatoon is an early spring blossom!

I have shot only a dozen grouse so far (this is with a .22 Winchester & no dog).

The Duke of Connaught went down the Lake on Sat. 5 - or rather he went down on the 4th& returned on the 5th.

All of A.K. & Deana's spare time is taken up on the new house, so the task of sawing & splitting the winters wood has fallen on me. We shall require 5 or 6 cords of wood for the winter, & besides this I have to keep the house in present wood.

MON. 21

Up till Friday the weather was fine.

On Friday afternoon it clouded over, & all Friday night & Saturday morning it rained. When the clouds lifted, the mountains were white with snow within a few hundred feet of the Lake.

I have never seen this earlier than the first week in November before. The snow has melted back 1,000 feet or so, but above that it is staying firm. There was a sharp frost this morning, making the ground as hard as a brick. At present (about midday) a mixture of snow & rain is falling.

NOVEMBER 1912

THUR. 7

I am awfully busy & have little time to write in this diary, so I will now attempt to make a summary of past events since last entry.

Most of the remaining part of October was frosty & clear. So far, November has been wet & dull with little frost. Nearly all the leaves are fallen. There is considerable snow on the mountains.

Newbery is still with Durant. Captain Durant (Durant's son) & a friend Captain Masters are on a two months visit. They planned a hunting expedition, & on the 29th October. got me to pack in their "grubstake" on Ginger, to Pat Kerrigan's deserted cabin (5 miles above Attenborough's)

The pack weighed about 130 lbs. & was pretty full. It took us about 4 hours to get to the shack from Durant's. I rode straight home, with instructions to go up again on Thursday, which I did.

I reached Kerrigan's at midday, & they wanted me to stay over to Friday morning. So I got in the afternoon hunting & climbed the South east end of the Sheep Bluffs – up to the snow.

The Bluffs rise some 2000 feet above the creek bottom.

I saw one wild blue grouse

I returned to

Log boom, Bear Creek mouth

Kettle Valley Railway

the shack before dusk, made a bed of fir boughs on the floor.

It is a fine big shack of cedar logs, with 4 dirty bunks & an old stove, & an earth floor.

We had supper & turned in at 8 p.m. & looked at magazines of 1903-4 that were in the cabin, & then managed to get a limited amount of sleep. The next morning was clear & frosty & the party having had no luck (except Newbery who saw a splendid Big Horn Ram on the Sheep Bluffs), prepared to depart. I packed Ginger, hit the trail, & reached Durant's at midday. Durant paid me five dollars.

Newbery departed for England this morning, & is returning next spring.

WED. 13

Every day it rains, truly strange for this country, but keeping up the good old English story – something – "It raineth every day" which might well be applied to the Coast of B.C. but ought not to be applied to the "dry belt" of the Southern Interior!

The ground is everlastingly mud & the trees are dripping, everything is sodden, even in the intervals the sky is leaden.

So much for the disgraceful weather.

This year in my "spare time" I made a "stake" of about $70. $40 from fruit-picking; the remaining $30. various savings.

About $30 went on clothes etc., leaving me $40.

I had intended to get a $20. Kodak, but I have changed my mind & ordered a $25. Mexican saddle.

The remainder I am going to spend on feed to keep Ginger for the winter.

There is a small camp up the hill on the other side of the creek near Attenborough's preparing for the winter lumber camp, & selecting a mill site. I doubt if the cutting will get fairly started this winter, as the preliminary pitching of the camp, & cutting miles of logging roads, is no small proposition, & they have started so late in the season.

The camp is no matter of tents but good sized, long low buildings of logs. The camp is composed of "bunk-shack", "cook-shack" barn, black smith shop etc. *[This camp has "bust up" & gone, too big proposition.]*

TUE. 26

Since last entry the weather had been dull & mild with not much rain, excepting the last two days which have been dull & frosty: frost continuing throughout the day.

The logging is well under way up the hill: they are not going to put in a mill but are thinking of putting a chute through our place & booming the logs in the lake. Also they are only going to cut Attenborough's timber on this side of the creek, which won't amount to very much.

There are two railroads in construction in the district. One is from the region of Grand Forks, up the Kettle River, over the mountains to Kelowna. There is a great crew working on it, in the mountains about 30 miles South east of Kelowna somewhere up the Mission creek. We can see the smoke out there, where they are clearing & burning the right of way.

The other branch is from Princeton, Similkameen, to Penticton. they are both branches of the main line which passes from the Crows Nest, through Rossland, Grand Forks South of Penticton,

John Brixton, "The Colonel"

westward to Princeton & on to Vancouver.

Both lines are expected to be finished in 1913. Which will cause great changes in the valley, especially in Kelowna, & Penticton.

Later a line is to go Northward, on the east side of the lake, from Kelowna to Vernon & meet the present existing Shushwap & Okanagan branch.

MacNair has returned from the Coast, & is, I believe going to "winter" in the "Colonel's" shack.

The last few seasons deer have been so plentiful that this part is getting quite a name as a hunting ground, & all sorts of people come in from other parts in boats & by steamer to hunt, much to the annoyance of the residents. One never feels safe in the mountains, as in the old days, as half these strangers are "cheechahkos" & may shoot one, in mistake for a deer. This logging camp has added some thirty-five men to the region.

John Brixton, was called The Colonel. No one really knows why, but it is likely because he resembled the picture of the sailor on "Players Tobacco" tins.

Actually, the Colonel's birth name was Mark Joseph Ellis. He was born in Islington, Middlesex, England in 1870, one of eight or nine children born to E.W. Ellis (a professor of music) and his wife Mary Anna Meson Jackson.

Vernon News, 1912

Okanagan district that I have been so far able to identify

Mammals.

x. Blacktailed deer x.	Cariacus virginiansis.
o Bighorn Sheep	Ovis montana.
# Cougar or Puma.	Felis [sic] concolor
# Lynx	Lynx canadensis (?)
# Bobcat	(?)
x Coyote.	Canis latrans.
o Marten.	Mustela Americana
x Weasel	Putorius vulgaris
o Mink	Putorius vison.
x Skunk	Mephitis mephitica.
0 Badger	Taxidea americana.
x Otter	Lutra canadensis.
# Brown Bear.	Ursus americanus
o Grizzly Bear.	Ursus horribilis.
x Bush tailed rat	Nestoma cinerea.
x White footed mouse	Hesperomis leucopus.
x Meadow mouse.	Arvicola ?
x Muskrat.	Fiber zibethicus.
x Northern Hare.	Lepus americanus ?
o Porcupine	Erethizon epixanthus
o Beaver.	Castor fiber.
x Pocket Gopher.	Thermomys talpoides.
Flying Squirrel.	Sciuoplenus volucella.
Red Squirrel.	Sciurus richardsoni.
x Chipmunk.	Tamias asiaticus quadrivittatus.
x Ground hog or marmot	Arctomys caligatus.
x Mole.	Scapanus townsendi ?
x Shrew. Sorex	?
x Red bat.	Atalapha noveboracensis
x Pika.	Lagomys princeps.
? Wolf.	Canis lupus occidentalis.
Within 20 miles,	

There are also probably other species of mouse, deer,
weasel, Hare, Gopher, Squirrel, (& perhaps
Chipmunk) but of these I am not certain.
Those marked "x" are quite common
"#" are rather uncommon.
"o" are very uncommon.

Birds

Turkey Buzzard (Cathartes aura)
Golden Eagle (Aquila chrysaeta)
Hawk (several)
Bald Eagle (Haliactus leucocephalus alascanus)
Osprey (Pandion hatiactus carolinensis)
Big horn Owl (Bubo virg)
Small owl (?)
Wood pecker (several)
Poor-will (phalaenopticus)nutt.)
Night Hawk (????? virg.) (enyi) Ruby
Throat Humming bird(Trochilus colubri)
Rufous Humming bird (Selasphorus rufus)
King bird (?)
Flycatcher(?)
Magpie (pica pica hursonica)
Black-headed Jay(Cyanscitta stellari annectens)
Rocky Mnt. Jay or Whiskey Jack
      (Peri-sorcus canadensis capitalis?)
Northern Raven (Corvus corvax principalis)
Crow (Corvus Americanus))
Clarkes Nutcracker (nucifraga columbiana)Blackird (?)
Western Meadow Lark (Sturnella magna neglecta)
Belted King-fisher (cenyle alcyon).
Cassin's purple finch (Carpolacus cassini)
American Crossbill(loxia curvirostra minor)
Redpoll (Acanthus linaria)
Western Vesper sparrow(Poocaetes graminens confinis?)
Junco (Junco oregonus)

Spurred Towhee(Pipils maculatus megalonyx)

Blackheaded Gross beak (Habin melanocephala)

Lazuli bunting (cyanospiza amoena)

Louisiana Tanager (Pirango ludo-viciana)

Barn Swallow (Hirundo erythrogaster)

Martin (?) Cedar Waxwing(amphilis cedrorum) Virco (?)

Warbler (several) American dipper(linclus mexicanus)

Cat bird (Galeoscoptes carolinensis)

Wren (?)

Rocky Mnt. Creeper (Certhis famileanis montana)

Nut hatch (Sitta-carolinensis aculiata)

Red breasted Nuthatch (Sitta canadensis)

PygmyNuthatch (Sitta pygmaia)

Oregon Chickadee (Parus atricapillio???occidentalis)

Mnt. Chickadee (Parus gambeli)

Chestnut backed Chickadee(Parus Rufescens)

Golden crowned Kinglet (Regular satrapa olivaceus??)

Western Robin (Merula migratonia propinqua)

Western Blue bird(Siala mexicana occidentalis)

Wilson Thrush (Hyloeichla fuscesanssalieicola??)

Grebe (probably several)

Loon

Gull (Larus californicus)

Merganser (Merganser americanus)

Red breasted merganser (M. serrator)

Mallard (Anas boschas)

Cinnamon Teal (Querquedula cyanopera)

Coot or "Mud hen"

Scaup Duck

Canada Goose (Branta anadensis

Trumpeter Swan (Olor buccinator?)

Sandhill Crane (Grus mexicana)

Sandpiper (Arctodromas munitilla)

Richardson or Blue Grouse (Dendrogapus obscurus)

Franklin Grouse: Fool Hen (Canchites franklinii)

Ruffed Grouse (Bonasa umbellus)

Band tailed pigeon (Columba fasciata).

Also quite a number of other birds, species I am uncertain of.

Reptiles

Rattle snake. Poisonous.	average size 2 to 4 ft.	
	confined to certain districts	
Bull snake. Harmless	2 to 5 ft.	Common
Garter snake	6 in. to 2 ft.	Common
Blue racer	1 to 3 ft.	Common
Rubber boa	1 to 2 ft.	Uncommon
Lizard	6 to 8 inches	Common
Turtle	about 6 inches.	Uncommon

Fish

Rainbow trout	Edible.	average length 8 in. to 3 ft.
Speckled trout		8 in. to 3 ft.
Mountain trout		2 in. to 1 ft. in creek
Sucker. poor eating		1 to 3 ft.
Squawfish. poor eating		1 to 3 ft.
Dog fish. poor eating		1 to 3 ft.
Kakkaninny. edible		about 8 inches.

Also several small species.

All of the above except Mountain trout are found in the Lake.

Kikkaninnies runs in shoals of hundredsalong the shore in
  very shallow water, every fall for about a week or more.

Trees

Coniferae.

Pinus contorta.	Lodge pole of "Jack" pine
Pinus ponderosa.	Yellow or Bull pine.
Larix occidentalis.	Western Larch or Tamarack.
Picea Canadensis.	White Spruce.
Pseudtsuga [sic] taxifolia.	Douglas fir.

Thuja plicata	Western Red Cedar ; Cedar
Juniperis communis.	Dwarf Juniper.
x Juniperus occidentalis.	Western Juniper.
Abies sub-alpina.	Balsam fir.

Deciduous trees

Willow	(several varieties)
Populus tremuloides.	Aspen.
Populus trichocarpa.	Black Cottonwood.
Betula fontinalis.	Birch
Alnus oregona	Red Alder
Amelanchier alnifolia.	Saskatoon.
Crataegus douglassii.	Black Haw.
Prunus demissa.	Choke Cherry.
Acer glabrum.	Dwarf maple.
Sambucus glaioa	Blue Elderberry.

Those marked "x" grow hardly bigger than large shrubs.

Temperatures

☐The average temperature at Nahun for June, July and August 1910 was 68.5 F

For December, January & February 1910-11 :
Vernon   1910 Max. 97F   Min - 12   Mean annual 46.0
Ok Mission. 1910 Max 93F Min - 18 below. Mean annual 46.2.

Average annual precipitation, throughout Valley seems to be about 12 inches.

The summer of 1910 was cooler than usual, so I should think the average temperature for other summers would be about 72 or more.

Second house winter 1913

Roger in front of their second house (about 1960) Not much left.

A.K. Menzies (Mingies)

Guy Ford

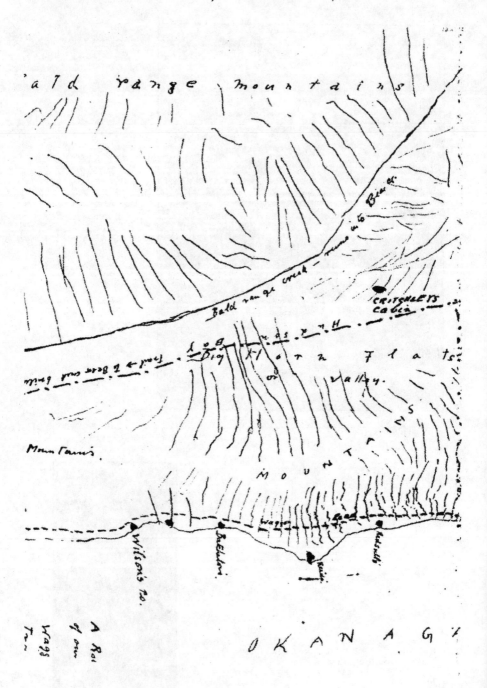

Roger Sugars map

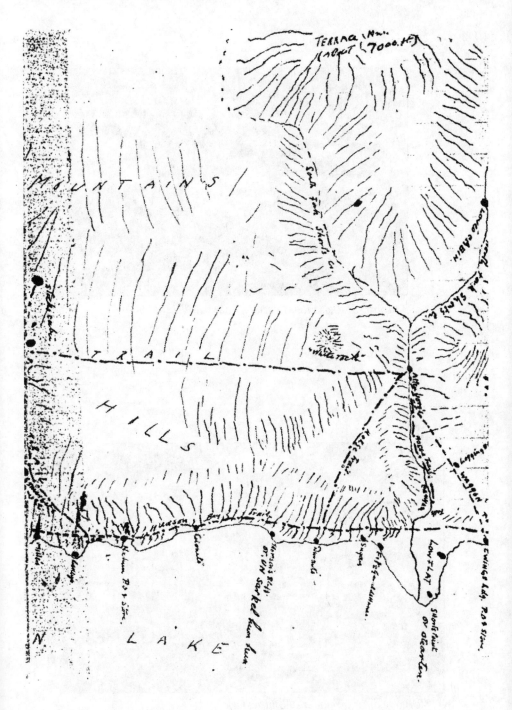

...joined together

Durant, Stocks, Ellis, Loveday, Tozer at Nahun 1909

CPR Barge and Naramata's "Smokestack"

1914

Roger and Lily, 1913
Family photo taken by John Edward

TUESDAY MARCH 31, 1914

On the 2nd June, 1911, I started a diary filling one book which was completed on December 4th, 1912. Since then I have kept no record---to my regret as a diary is most useful to read back for comparison on the weather of various years, etc.

Apart from this though there has been nothing of much account to write about; it would be mostly repetition. We are still here at "Cedar Swamp". Everyday life goes on much the same. However I shall start another diary now, as even everyday life occasionally affords items of interest, especially in this country.

I am paying no attention to the date spaces in this diary as on some days I shall write pages and on others, nothing at all.

In the fall of 1912 I mentioned in the last diary that we were

Lily Sugars (Mother)

building a new house.

This was completed in the spring and we have now been in since May 24th, 1913. It is most satisfactory and comfortable & being built of logs, picturesque and pretty both inside & out. It consists of a sitting room 20 by 10 ft. two bedrooms each 10 by 10 & a kitchen 10 by 10. We have spring water piped into the latter. In front we have banked out a terrace 6 feet wide, and planted white clover & blue grass on it.

The house is very prettily situated and nearer the lake than the old one. The beauty of it is that we did the whole thing ourselves in spare-time.

But what almost transcends the house is the piano. This we installed at the end of June, 1913, and I don't think we ever appreciated so much anything we have had since we came to this country. It is a very nice piano costing 260 dollars (which is but half paid — 10 dollars a month is the system). Better still is the fact that Mother can play splendidly, and we do not have to listen to the usual waltzes, twosteps & ragtime, but enjoy the glories of Chopin, Beethoven and Liszt, and next in order of beauty, Greig, etc.

Last summer I had the great good luck to find a boat, & luckier still, it has never been claimed.

It was washed up high and dry on the shore of our own place; a small

Lily and John Edward Circa 1913

flatbottomed boat without seats, oars or anything else & leaking like a sieve but otherwise sound. I took it home, dried it out, scraped the cracks, then tarred the bottom inside and out, put seats in etc. & have used it ever since. Being of cedar it is very light & is very easy to row & I have weathered some storms in it. This spring I tarred the bottom again and painted the rest green. & I have got a small sail, and it is really quite a good boat.

Our cayuse, poor old Ginger, had to be shot last fall on account

John Edward and Lily playing the piano, June 1913
Finally, some good music!□

of extreme thinness, evidently the result of old age, as it was certainly not through lack of food.

I now have to travel by foot or by boat always.

1913 was the first year that firearm licenses had to be taken out in British Columbia.

APRIL 1914

TUESDAY APRIL 21

Since last entry A.K. has got more photographs – 2 beautiful woodland scenes with deer in the background, also one of a bear! This is the first bear any of us have seen. It was a small brown bear and he had the good luck to photograph it at a distance of about 40 yards. It makes a lovely picture in the trees with a small but conspicuous object that is recognizable as a bear.

I have a No. 2 Brownie enlarging camera to make 5 by 7 from 21/4 by 31/4 negatives. It is most successful and improves pictures wonderfully, especially those of deer, grouse etc.

It cost but $2.00 & seems to me worth more.

Sunday the 19th was a fine windy day & I went out at 6 AM alone and walked solidly for 8 hours. I took my camera and went up Shorts' Creek to my favourite refuge, the Sheep Bluffs.

I have often mentioned the Bluffs before, that great mountain that forms the northern "bank" of Shorts' Creek & which at a distance looks like an unbroken wall of rock, rising some thousands of feet above the creek.

They are faced on the south by the higher but not quite so precipitous Mount Zion and the Goat Peak.

I will attempt to give a slight physical description of the Bluffs. It would be impossible for me to set down on paper any idea of the grandness and awe inspiring splendour of the great cliffs.

They are not beautiful. They are too rugged and gashed and barren to be beautiful. They are more. They are grand.

The Bluffs are some 10 miles long and you come to the first buttress of the bluffs about 6 miles up the creek, in fact at Old

Love's cabin.

From the summit the cliffs drop sheer for 1000 feet or so and then the mountain slopes more gradually to the creek. Here a cottonwoods flat 50 yards wide with the creek winding down it, and then up the other side 3000 feet to the summit of Goat Mountain.

Though the Bluffs look like an unbroken wall, they are in reality gashed by many side canyons. They are escarped into notches and battlements, ledges and buttresses. The summit is flat & the fringe of the forest comes to the very edge.

Shorts' Creek Falls

Then the cliff drops away in the midst of the trees, down, down a thousand feet or so. Then it slopes more gradually another 1000 feet to the creek. These lower slopes, though very steep and broken by many a crag & cliff, once supported a forest growth: 60 or 70 years ago this was burnt off , and all that remains are rotten and blackened stubs and a few prostrate trunks.

The result is a very barren appearance, the remaining growth being bunch grass and Saskatoon bushes & here & there a young pine or fir. There is very little soil and a good deal of the slope is talus slide of pumice rock. There are many canyons cut by the streams which fall over the face of the cliffs above (in spring when the snow is melting). These lower slopes are difficult to climb in many places, & the upper cliffs are impossible.

On Sunday I chose a side canyon and followed it up. There was a small torrent running down it, and I went up from stone to stone, between high rocky walls, for about a half mile. I then could get no further. I found myself in a "cup", a perfect blind alley on all sides except the down side. The rock arched up 100 feet or so and overhanging the basin in a most threatening manner.

The stream no longer came down a gorge, but had divided & was falling in 2 spray-like cascades almost into my face, from a ledge 75 feet above me. The cliffs overhung so much that I was underneath them everywhere except in the middle of the basin, close to the waterfall. Also I could get behind the fall without getting wet, thus:

I did not actually do this, but could have done with a somewhat difficult scramble. I took two photos and hurried away as I heard a rock fall, & the cliffs looked very loose and ready to crash down.

Huge boulders had fallen into the basin, but no doubt the main structure will endure for thousands of years. The Bluffs are full of

John Edward Sugars at Kerrigan's Cabin 1915

places such as this one, & many waterfalls much higher.

After walking over other parts of the Bluffs for some hours I returned home, arriving at 2 o'clock. I developed the films which were all good.

Just above Kerrigan's on the way home I saw a bunch of 6 mountain sheep (Bighorn) at a distance of about 200 yards. I sat & watched them for about a half of an hour & one of the lambs passed quite close to me, & baa-a-ad to its mother up the hill.

JUNE 1914

SAT. 6

Since last entry I have been slack in writing up my diary. Little news however out of the usual run of things. It is a bad and depressing outlook all round this year. During the nine years we have been here work has always been plentiful & well paid, & if you met a man out of work it was because he was a lazy hobo or else a useless cheechahko.

The country has been "running its face" for 10 years: The Okanagan can grow fruit. There it ends. The range is not open enough for stock. The best timber will be exhausted in a few years. There are no mines as yet. There is scenery and there are fruit ranches along the lake; scattered ranches which produce splendid fruit. They have the quality, but greater quantity is the only thing. The population is too large for the industry already.

For 10 or 12 years the whole thing has been a big real estate bluff, keeping the place booming with land at fabulous prices, wages and living away up, the boosters coining money, & then clearing out leaving their victims to glean what they can off the fruit ranches. Expenses being far too great, they find they cannot glean anything, so likewise fool the suckers as they themselves were fooled.

And so the fruit industry "ran its face", but this year the whole works have fallen to the true face value & the fruit industry will go smash, or else go on very soberly on a small scale.

Money is so tight that no one can buy or sell anything, the

stores give no credit. Many ranchers are going bankrupt, hundreds of men out of work.

The meanest thing of all is that the Chinese and Japanese can get work right along with the ranchers who employ them in preference to white men. This yellow peril question is a complicated one.but if they are not stopped soon they will gradually oust the whites of the country.

The moneyed rancher , however, is too mean to look to the good of the country beyond his own generation, much less consider the state of his own countrymen who have to earn their livings. However, if a little wisdom & forethought will only enter the government, and the country run at its true value, things may right themselves yet.

Early in May, what seemed quite an event occurred at Nahun. For the first time in this country, I saw a true golfing "nut". When the steamer came in with the mail, he walked onto the wharf. He was a tall and frightfully emaciated youth with a bored expression. He wore an immense tweed cap, grey flannel trousers & golfing brogues.

He carried a bag of golf clubs & stood on the wharf twisting his little fair mustache, & finally decided he had got off at the wrong place.

There is a golf course at Vernon so I suppose these "things" are beginning to infest the place.

A.K. thought

Roger camping on Long Lake 1905
Photo by A.K. Menzies

that during this hard

season he might make a little by going around Vernon as an itinerant photographer, to see if he could get some orders.

On May 5th he and I set off and rowed to the Landing, (a distance of about 11 miles). Here among the squalid "habitations of men" we camped. The first day proved unsuccessful. Next morning at about 6

John Edward with rattlesnake

A.M. we put our packs on our backs and walked over the hills among orchards and barbed wire fences, to Long Lake, which we reached at about half past 9.

We passed to the south of the rocky crags (the "Old Long Lake Crags" as we called them) and then descended the bare sagebrush hillside below them, striking the lakeshore in a beautiful grove of aspens & good sandy beach. We visited this spot purely out of sentiment, as it was somewhat out of our way.

However we had not set eyes on this pretty spot in 9 years. We threw our

Roger camping on Long Lake (now Kalamalka)
Photo by A.K. Menzies

packs down & rested. This aspen cove is "Rattlesnake Camp". We camped there during the summer of 1905 when we first were in B.C. & before we had seen the lower part of Okanagan Lake. The place was full of associations for us. 9 years ago it was wilder, though within a mile of the saw mill. There were no houses near, no road, and not a motor car in the southern Interior, to my knowledge.

Being near to Vernon, however, it was quite a camping place, even in our day. This visit though, showed signs of many campers since we were there. There were two big ugly houses, directly opposite on the other side of the

Roger hiking to the Sheep Bluffs.
Note backpack he made. Photo by A.K. Menzies

lake, and on the hillside just behind is a good road known as "Kalamalka Drive" with motors running on it about 4 or 5 an hour. After contemplation of about 20 minutes, we "hiked" along, & at the head of the lake, near boat houses and within sight of about a dozen houses, we camped & had lunch. In the afternoon we bought some eggs and things at a house near, pitched our (borrowed) tent on the sand with the lake in front & a large bulrush slough at the back.

During the evening we sat by our fire and quenched our thirst continually with tea. (Long Lake is now unsafe to drink on account of typhoid.)

We were quite comfortably fixed but there was not the pure restfulness that one feels in the wilds.

Motors honked on the road 200 yards away. The sawmill opposite shrieked its song continually. Some mad blackbirds nearly drove me crazy by unceasingly saying "bobdazzee-ee-eedl". This queer liquid note was terribly monotonous, and in the night the frogs in the slough simply roared.

Next day A.K. walked through the Coldstream Valley, while I lay in the tent reading the latest murder case in the "Vernon News" ie, a lumberjack by the name of Berryman, near Lumby. He and 4 or 5 other loggers, all drunk, were drinking in a rig when he was last seen.

He was brutally murdered, for when the body was found it was bruised all over. Five ribs were broken, two puncturing the lung, a ruptured kidney and punctures from caulked boots on his head.

All the men in the rig were arrested, but not enough evidence can be found to convict any of them.

At the end of the day A.K., who had been to many houses, had met with no success. Next morning we broke camp and walked to Vernon (3 miles) and on to Okanagan Landing (another 4 or 5 miles). Here we got into our little boat and rowed out past Rattlesnake Point and across to Whiteman's Creek on the west side. The weather was good and we were glad to be back on the lake. We coasted along slowly past Whiteman's & caught a few fish. Off Ewing's a fish took the bait and broke the trace. We rowed in and got a new bait & trace at Fox's store. Then a south breeze got up & round Shorts' Point and on to home we had a hard pull, shipping a few waves.

We got in from our unsuccessful expedition at about 6 p.m.

The rest of the month elapsed until May 28th when A.K. and I decided on a trip in direct contrast to the one above described. Ie: to climb Terrace Mountain with a view to getting photographs, which would be of great interest & possibly remunerative if we could get them published.

A blanket apiece, a little grub, extra shirt, socks, belt axe, compass etc. constituted our packs . A.K., of course carried his

Summit of Terrace Mountain 1914

camera and films. I did not take my camera as the films did not come in time.

May 28, 5:30 a.m. we started. We were glad to find that Holmes (the fire warden) had re-blazed the old trail to the South Fork cabin. We crossed the first bench one-mile up the creek above Attenborough's. We turned at the mouth of the South Fork, found the blazes, & followed them up the mountain. The trail zigzagged up this hill which was steep and high and clothed openly with bull pine and Douglas fir.

It took us about 2 hours to climb the mountain & the day was getting hot. At the top we crossed an open patch of "bois brule" and got a good view of Terrace which seemed quite near. Then we followed the blazes through the typical upland forest of slender jack pines, spine-like balsams & spruces. At about 9 a.m. we reached the cabin, a picturesque but roughly built little place. The door was fastened by a big forked stick leaning against it.

On entering, we found it had recently been visited, as there was quite a lot of grub, pots and pans, a pack-saddle & blankets hung from the roof, two axes and plenty of chopped fire wood to feed the ancient camp stove.

We walked on and found the blazes continued in the direction of Terrace. We followed them for about 2 miles. When we got to the narrow gulch between Terrace and Goat Mountains (where a small creek rises) we found the blazed trail ran straight on past the gap towards Shorts' Creek.

So we turned through the dense poles of jack pine (more properly called Lodgepole Pine ---pinus contorta) & went up a short but very steep slope which was densely timbered and choked with windfalls. In 10 minutes though, we were up on the first terrace, out on the edge of the great precipice, which drops sheer 200 to 300 feet; a big talus slide at the bottom and then the forest. This was the north end of the terrace, on our right was the dense timber which extends half a mile west to the base of the summit; on our left---nothing, till you struck the tree tops 300 feet below---if you fell!

It was now 10 a.m. & we melted some snow, made tea and had lunch. We then walked on south up the terrace (having hung our packs in a tree). The further we went up, the more snow there was, until on the highest part of the terrace there was more snow than bare ground. It was the remains of the winter's snow, hard-packed and granular and about 2 feet deep, lying in drifts and hummocks.

The terrace is about 1-1/2 miles long. At the south end we struck off through the timber, and it was like walking in the woods in February. I put my extra shirt on, it was so cold & under the dark trees with 2 to 3 feet of snow it was indeed wintry.

We reached the summit at 11:50 a.m. Out on the bare rock the snow had gone but among the beautiful stunted trees it lay in great drifts from 2 to 5 feet in depth.

The trees here must be of great age. They are stunted and contorted with the winds & great depth of snow. They are very beautiful and picturesque. The species I saw on the summit was white-bark pine. P albicanlis. (unknown except on the summits).

Lodgepole Pine. P contorta, balsam fir. Abies sub-alpina?

White spruce. Picea canadensis. Needless to say, the view was grand, quite beyond my powers of description. Far down to the N.N.E. lay the north end of the lake. We could see every detail, even a steamer.

The nearer view consists of miles and miles of rolling plateau, black with densest jack pine forest, absolutely unexplored, with here & there a high point showing snow. On the far horizon in every direction were snow peaks rendered minute by distance. The finest of these lay along the eastern horizon like a row of shark's teeth; evidently the peaks of the Gold Range or of the Selkirks.

Though the photographs A.K. took (numbering 18) do not show these distant peaks, they give more idea of the view than I should ever do with pen and paper, for they are splendid pictures.

We spent an hour on the summit & returned to our packs down on the first terrace, had some more to eat & returned to the cabin which we reached at 4 p.m..

We cut a large quantity of Balsam bows and laid them on the bunk in the cabin, Leisurely cooked supper & ate it & turned in at 9 p.m.

We had a comfortable night & got up at 3 a.m., had breakfast, tidied the shack, & pulled out. A little way out on the trail we saw an enormous buck, the largest deer I have ever seen. A little further we met a Fool Hen (canchitis franklinii) sitting on a log. We walked up to it and A.K. put out his hand within 2 feet of it, when it lazily flew into the tree close at hand.

When we got out on the open hillside, we saw another deer & were attacked by a blue grouse with chicks. We got home at about 8 a.m.

On my former trip up Terrace mountain with Newbery in June, 1912 (before Holmes reblazed the trail), we got wrong in our direction. We followed up the South Fork into a wholly unexplored region of dense, damp, gloomy jack-pine & spruce forest, choked with deadfalls, and finally struck the south end of the terrace at 5 p.m. Also it being well on in June, the mosquitoes were simply frightful, swarming in millions. On this latter trip, there were no mosquitoes at all.

Last fall I made a pack saddle which on these expeditions or any time when I have to carry a load, I find extremely useful. This "human pack- saddle" is made simply of thin flat pieces of wood about three inches wide, forming an oblong frame which fits the shoulder blades. Attached to it are shoulder bands of sacking & rope for fastening the pack. A pack of 40 lbs. is quite comfortable and leaves the arms free (which is essential in woods, walking and for comfort).

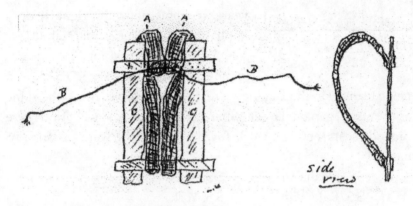

Outside view of pack saddle side view   *Roger's drawing*
A-shoulder straps: B-lashing: C-frame
The whole thing weighs about 1 lb.

As Alfred Stocks remarked on hearing the news: "There are no more heifers on the West Side." The news is the Miss Isabel Somerset is engaged to Mr. Frank Vaughan.

Kennard, who has sold goods over the counter of his 8 by 10 store for about 12 years, and also used this establishment for a Post Office, has had a new building erected on the wharf. It is a pretty place, white with green facings and a red roof. It is built on piles under the trees, on the beach, the front door opening onto the wharf. Inside it is divided into two rooms, each about 12 by 15 feet, the back one being a store room, and the front one shop and Post Office. The walls, shelves and counter in the front room are painted

H.B. Kennard

white, the floor red.

The walls are gay with canned goods and bottled goods, tobacco, soap, medicines, blue & brown overalls etc. Hanging up are saddle thongs, bathing suits etc. In the back room he keeps the heavy goods: flour, sugar, rolled oats, hardware, boots ,rice & so forth.

It is a very compact store, but having known the little old place for 9 years, it seems not quite right. It does not have the atmosphere of "Nahun".

As usual, never a mail day passes without me in attendance. There is a new steamer on the lake now, the S.S. "Sicamous", much the same as the Okanagan but larger. What she was built for I can't say. There did not seem enough work for the boats that were on already, namely:

S.S. Okanagan	S.S. Aberdeen
S.S. Kaleden	S.S. York
Tug Naramata	Tug Castlegar

This last comprises the C.P.R. boats and does not include the various ferries and lumber tugs.

S.S. York

S.S. Sicamous, Courtesy Kelowna Museum

The day that A.K. and I returned from Terrace Mountain, we heard the awful news of the wreck of the "Empress of Ireland". (night of 28th of May)

WEDNESDAY JUNE 24

This month has been fine compared to the last two years, mostly dry and not very hot with occasional wet days.

On Sunday, 21st, there was a big storm on the lake, a fierce Chinook wind which blew the surface of the lake into long rollers tipped with white caps. The breaking seas did quite a lot of damage carrying away a small wharf at Batchelor"s (North place) and somewhat damaging FitzGerald's boat.

Yesterday morning a cold rain fell which was snow in the mountains. The big mountain behind Ewing's (which is as far as I know, nameless) had snow on it. None of us has ever seen snow as low as this in June before.

Bill Norcott, who has had a pretty tough winter & who has

been looking after Durant's place for the past three weeks (while Durant has been away at Fairmont Hot Springs for his Rheumatism) has decided to go out to the prairies and join the Northwest Mounted Police.

THURSDAY JUNE 25TH

I rowed to Kennard's this morning & bade farewell to Bill who took the morning steamer to Vernon. He is going to see a dentist in Vernon, & then going straight through to Regina, Sask.

Bill is an exceedingly nice boy & we shall miss him very much.

While I was at Kennard's, I was shocked with the news that H.L. Fox had died at Ewing's yesterday. I saw him when I went to his store about two weeks ago, & he was as well as possible. He wore an eye glass & talked & dressed as though he were taking the "nuts" part in a play. He was somewhere about 45 and was a most entertaining man to talk to. But he was, unfortunately, somewhat given to drink, & no doubt this brought on his sudden death as it has done with many other men.

JULY 1914

WEDNESDAY JULY 8

Since last entry the weather has been perfect, perhaps a trifle too hot. Unlike the past two or three seasons, this year we are having a fine "Dry Belt" summer, such as those we had in the years 1906-7 & 8. In those days forest fires were frequent in the valley & the smoke was intolerable. This year, however, there are fire wardens and forest rangers throughout the district, and so far there have been no fires, though several on the point of starting have been extinguished.

Last summer was about the wettest on record.

As I have already remarked, since last entry there has been perfect weather. Day after day goes by with a blazing sun in a cloudless sky, and not a drop of rain has fallen.

Once or twice in the evenings it has looked like a change, but in the morning the clouds have dispersed, & the sun rises with increasing heat into the cloudless sky. Beautiful weather indeed, but far too hot for working.

Still, I think it is better than the unsettled rainy weather of last summer

A.O. Holmes, the Nahun fire-worker returned from an expedition into the hills on Friday. He, with one extra man, went to the head of Shorts' Creek (25 miles back) & then turned south & followed the divide 15 or 20 miles to the head of Bear Creek. He came down Bear Creek and reached Nahun on the 8th day from the start.

He told me that there had been 3 to 6 feet of snow in places, & that the mosquitoes were in the tens of millions.

The Okanagan -Nicola divide in this part lies about 15 miles west of Terrace Mountain & about 25 west of the lake. It is mostly dense forest and probably no white man has ever been along it before.

I had a letter from Geoffrey Haddon a week or so ago, saying he had been in B.C. about 7 weeks. He has joined Colin at his place at Gray Creek, Kootenay Lake.

Astonishing things do happen in this country sometimes. Fox's store at Ewing's has been taken over, Wallace Colquoun, who had been engaged for two years, has married Patty Kenyon, (who is only in her 16th year) & they are running the store together. As Colquoun is getting on for 30, few people thought that it would really end up in a wedding.

I am now somewhat busy sawing cordwood for next winter- very hot work in this weather.

TUESDAY JULY 14TH

The fine weather broke on Saturday evening when a thunderstorm passed eastward, with a deluge of rain which lasted about 10 minutes. Sunday was unsettled and rain fell continuously throughout Monday afternoon. Today dawned clear and bright, but soon clouded over. No rain has fallen however, & this evening is clear & promising over to the west.

Mail day at Kennard's is often amusing. Most of the

Nahun wharf circa 1910. Ms. Okanagan coming in

community gather there , mostly the men but frequently Mrs. Leney, Mrs. Powell and Miss Somerset.

The congregation always arrives hours before the steamer, some in boats, some on horses, and some walking. In winter amounting to a dozen or fifteen, in summer less. They buy their stuff, haggle with Kennard over his prices, etc. (his prices are always the standard prices). They then sit about or eat Kennard's cherries, & curse the boat for being late.

Vaughan & Cheeseman & a few others discuss tennis or dancing at Okanagan Centre, whilst the broader minded engage in violent arguments on politics & commercial questions.

A very hard-working Canadian named Denby, who settled on a piece of land near Wilson's Ldg. about a year ago, is remarkable on arguing. He is a man of wide knowledge and interests. He is altogether eloquent & never gets stuck for words or breath.

"Now then, Denby," Kennard said on Monday, "are you on the

voters' list?" "No, sir!" "Well, will you be put on it?" "No, Sir," said Denby, "I wouldn't walk across the street to vote for anyone in this place."

Kennard & another man at once took up this point & a stormy argument ensued. Faster and faster they shouted and all the time at once.

Nahun 1909 Getting the latest news

"Don't you know, bellowed Kennard "that to be without a vote is to be nobody, you----" "That's all very well, Now looky here----"

"Darn it, I tell you, you aren't anybody, you're not known if you haven't a vote!" "Lovely gentle ----now looky here now," shouted Denby, thumping his middle finger on the palm of his left hand (the first finger was missing), looky here, the only thing to do is darn ignore this gol darn government. There's no one to vote for.

One's as bad as the other. Now, take Old Dunsmuir," he cried, shaking his long middle finger in Kennard's face. "That old devil down on the Island made millions shipping in Japanese - er-er- Chinese, no Japanese smuggling 'em in without paying their head money."

"The way things was run down on Vancouver Island!

Waiting for mail at Nahun

Mail day at Nahun Circa 1911

Why, I couldn't a'thought it possible for things to be like that in the whole Dominion of Canada! God darn it, think I'd vote when there's men like that in the government? They're not fit to touch! Oh, Lordy, give us a drink a'water, Charlie. This is dry work." And on he went and Kennard at the same time.

Later on the same day Durant took up an argument with Kennard. What about I cannot say, nor could they, I expect. However, it was heated and wordy. Durant gesticulated & shouted about "carloids of coil oil" in his confusion. When it became deafening, he walked out & left his followers to finish it.

He said to me, "You know Kennard can't argue a bit, he gets so excited. The great thing in arguing is to be calm & quiet, and not lose your head."

I thought, "You might well apply that sentence to yourself!"

The shouting continued in the store. Miss Somerset escaped and ran up the road.

Then it was interrupted by the arrival of the steamer. It was the "Sicamous" & her first call at Nahun. A few comments were made on the ungainliness of her lines, then everyone went into the store and waited in a hush of expectancy, while Kennard sorted the mail, with his usual slowness, absentmindedly reading aloud the names on the letters, & occasionally remarking that he was the fastest sorter in the province.

After a great lapse of time, Kennard called out (as is his wont) "Does anybody want any mail?" He then hands out the mail to the eager bidders. This is usually followed by grunts of disgust, "Is that all there is for me?" "Humph! Not a blessed letter." "Good Lord", said Durant, "The post offices in this country are a disgrace."

SATURDAY JULY 18TH

The weather has once more settled, clear and hot, but with a refreshing light breeze continuing most of the day. On Thursday we were somewhat surprised by a visit from Mr. McGeorge, the piano tuner.

Having tuned our piano (which was badly needed), he went along to the point to tune the Godwin's & the Dun-Waters' pianos. After he had left we found that one note was altogether wrong. (We found next morning that it was caused by a small fruit knife which had got lodged in the back of the piano, producing a ringing sound on this particular note.) so I at once went off and found him tuning

Circa 1908 Roger with crowd waiting for mail boat

the Dun-Waters' piano.

The Dun-Waters were all away, so he asked me in to look at the piano.

When he had finished the tuning, I helped him to replace the player attachment. He then put on a short record to see that the mechanism was in order. On looking through the player records I found Liszt's "Rhapsodie Hongroise" (no. 2) and expressed my desire to hear it on a player. He very kindly put the record on and played it for me. It is a long composition & magnificent to listen to. When it was finished I thanked that piano tuner emphatically. This with Beethoven's "Moonlight Sonata" and some of Chopin's Polonaises, is the finest piece of music I have ever heard.

Mother has been practicing the "Rhapsodie" for some time & I feel convinced that if she stays at it, she will play it splendidly.

AUGUST 1914

AUGUST 4TH

Weeks have gone by without a drop of rain. Since about July 15 there has only been one thundershower which lasted but a few minutes. The days go by one after the other with scarcely a cloud. Usually in the morning there is a light cool breeze from the north and sometimes from the south, which dies down towards noon, leaving the lake like a sheet of glass in the shimmering heat. The temperature at this time is up to 90 in the shade or more. Perhaps during the afternoon a hot wind comes in puffs from the hills, laden with the smell of distant forest fires.

The last week the atmosphere has been thick with a haze of smoke. As the sun swings westward, its light grows feeble, of an orange-red colour. Clouds, there are none, but the smoke hangs thick in the still air.

The heat grows more oppressive, but after the sun has sunk behind the western mountains, the evening quickly becomes cool..

Rain is badly needed, but the sky tonight is perfectly cloudless.......

Europe is indeed in trouble now. First we heard that Austria had declared war on Servia.

Monday brought news of a war likely to implicate the whole of Europe & today we heard that England had declared war on Germany last night and that warfare was being waged almost throughout Europe. It is said that there has been a naval battle off Flamborough Head.

It is also stated that in a battle in the Mediterranean two German warships were sunk. A third class German cruiser is steaming for Vancouver, but a Japanese warship is waiting for it. A terrible thing, this continental war & I hope to God it will come to an end soon.

SATURDAY AUGUST 15

The weather continues dry and cloudless. There has been only one shower of rain, since my last entry, which lasted about 10 minutes.

Thursday was as cloudless as usual, but in the afternoon a dry scorching wind arose & the sky rapidly became veiled with a haze of smoke.

Later in the evening the smoke thickened & rolled in a great brown cloud across the lake from West to East.

Little puffs of hot air came at intervals bringing tiny specks of white ash.

Thursday was Regatta day at Kelowna, the chief attraction of which was an hydro-biplane flight which I was told was very successful.

This is the first aeroplane flight ever made on the Okanagan Lake.

Friday was almost cloudless but calm, with the hills dim in the haze of smoke.

Though the sun shone with a pale light & the temperature was not so very high, yet the heat was fearfully oppressive.

Today has been much the same but somewhat less smoky.

Have been busy fencing lately. I have cut cedar posts, packed them out of the swamp on my back, have charred the ends of them which go in the ground to preserve them from rotting too soon; have dug the post-holes and tamped most of them in, & it will be ready for the barbed wire. The fence is about 300 yards long and enclosed the house from the open range, the lakeshore forming the eastern side of the enclosure.

Fencing has, however, been suspended for a short time on account of fruit

Roger and John Edward picking fruit

picking at the Point. Was picking crabapples on Wednesday, Thursday & today---. Fruit picking will now continue at the Point more or less steadily until sometime in November.

Fruit-picking is a deplorably monotonous occupation, & my only compensations are the mail days, Sundays and evenings.

A.O. Holmes, the fire warden, has gone off to the 30th B.C. Horse (who are mobilizing). I have written to the district forester to see if I could get his (Holmes') position until his return. If I could only get it I would see the fruit picking to hell!

The war continues as bloodily as ever.

We get all the latest news, but it is most unsatisfactory. So much of it seems to be untrue or confused. However, the poor foolish Germans seem to be having a fearful time.

Most of their calculations seem to have gone wrong. They got such a terrible stand-off from great little Belgium. It is said that all the other countries are holding their own against the Germans. Dreadful seems to be the slaughter amongst them. Poor devils!

It is damnable that the German authorities should have brought about such a fearful war, forcing their own, probably unwilling, countrymen to fight & be butchered in thousands. I feel bitter resentment toward the German government, but I think the German people deserve the greatest pity.

Old Love, up Shorts' Creek, who has fought in the north and south war, & with Indians on the plains, truly says, "War is hell."

At Love's were camped two fire fighters;* they were just breaking camp & were leaving that afternoon. There is a big fire up at the headwaters of Shorts' Creek, that was probably started by lightning. It was first seen from Okanagan Centre. The news was telephoned to Vernon & three men were at Attenborough's (the end of the road) in a motor car 2 1/2 hours after receiving it. The next morning they toted their packs up the creek on foot.

On arriving at Love's, they found another fire. Old man Love was in a desperate state. He had fought the fire all night alone. He "saw he was beat" so he had moved his stuff out of his little shack, across the creek.

Some men had already gone up the creek to the upper fire. One of the three went on to them while the other two stayed at Love's to fight the fire there. It had started from a campfire that some careless person had left.

It spread through the bush near the creek a little & then ran through the bunch grass up the limestone bluff just behind Love's cabin. Fortunately it was checked before it reached the timber. The two men had been there a week & the fire was just about out. If they had not arrived when they did, no doubt Love's cabin would have been burnt, & the fire would have reached the dense timber on top of the Sheep Bluffs, which would have caused a very serious forest fire.

The big fire up the creek is said to be under control but by no means out. Four men are up there.

I visited Mr. Love. He seldom has visitors & he seemed pleased to have someone to talk to, to judge by the extent of his conversation. He talked about the present war and the Civil War in the U.S.A. (in which he fought) chiefly, & never paused a moment. However, his conversation was never uninteresting.

His knowledge is very extensive & he can talk on any subject, from experience in the old days on the plains, to politics in Germany. I should like to write down all he told me, but it seems to me it would fill a book.

I noticed that the beavers have been at work among the aspen trees in the creek bottom near Love's. They had built a small dam across the creek at one point. Between Love's and Kerrigan's (about 1/2 a mile), the creek being so low, the water disappears in the ground, leaving the rocky watercourse dry. The water reappears about 400 yards lower down.

On reaching home, late in the afternoon, I saw a large covey of ruffed grouse within 50 yards of the house. I secured three. Only the other day I said that the way to get game was to stay around the back door!

WEDNESDAY AUGUST 19

Rain fell all Sunday night, but by 10 O'clock on Monday morning all the clouds had disappeared.

There is very little fresh war news.

The following items from the Vernon News are, I think, worth writing: Aug 13 "Two motor loads of men came over from Vernon to the fire at Irish Creek, which spread up the mountain, but is being extinguished."

"A fire had been raging all the week from Grande Prairie toward Fish Lake.

Two bands of workers, one under the control of V. Whiting, forest ranger of the Monte Hills Timber reserve, the other under W.F. Smith of the Fly Hills timber reserve, have been busily engaged warring with the devouring element.

Long trenches were dug to keep the fire from spreading & every precaution taken, but it was not until Friday that the fire was put out." This explains the smokiness of the atmosphere lately. And again "An Indian was killed by a grizzly bear near Pinous Lake (up Whiteman's Creek) one day last week. It is supposed he had gone to hunt for huckleberries. His horse was half eaten when it was found.

SEPTEMBER 1914

SUNDAY SEPT 6

Not a drop of rain has fallen since August 16th. The fine days go by without a break. When there are clouds, they are white and fleecy, and floating at an immense altitude. Everything is parched. Running water with the exception of springs and the larger creeks, is all dry.

Forest fires are raging in all parts of the country. The air is thick with a blue haze of smoke which occasionally thickens to brown clouds from which fall little flakes of white ash. The days are no longer so very hot, & the nights are quite chilly.

Fruit picking continues steadily, Fifty tons of crabapples have gone, also a great quantity of different kinds of plums and prunes. We are now picking "Wealthy" apples.

A.K. got Thursday off from work & went hunting, & succeeded in getting a buck. It was a good size and the meat is beautiful.

On Friday I walked over the hills from 7 a.m. until 1 p.m.. Today I left home at about 6 a.m. & went with my 22 up the creek to that bare region near Kerrigan's where blue grouse were so plentiful last year. On the first level I saw a coyote at a long distance. I saw no grouse at all!

TUESDAY SEPTEMBER 8

Monday 7th dawned gray and quiet. Later a strong Chinook arose, bringing some heavy rain. Today has been very windy and dull & it rained a good deal during the afternoon.

WEDNESDAY SEPTEMBER 30

The wet weather let up on Monday the 21st; since then there have been a few wet days, but for the most part it has been bright and sunny, fresh and autumnal. As I write, it is raining heavily, but I think that it is only a shower. Yes, as I finished the sentence, it stopped & the sun is coming out.

On Friday 25th we were laid off from apple picking for a week or ten days in order that the late apples should ripen up; so we are having a "holiday", that is to say we have plenty of work to keep us fit, but we are our own bosses. I have been hunting several times, but have seen no deer as yet. I have lately taken to carrying, in addition to my Winchester 38-55, the 22 slung on my back & have been glad of it as I have shot several blue grouse. With the beautiful lights and gorgeous colours, walking in the mountains at this time of year is simply delightful.

A.K. had the luck to get a deer this afternoon.

OCTOBER 1914

SUNDAY OCTOBER 11

We have returned to apple picking & expect to finish at the end of the month. The weather has been beautiful; many days are absolutely cloudless, though it is sharp in the mornings, there has been no frost here yet. At the Point and not far up the hill there has been an occasional slight frost. Last Sunday, the 4th, Deana and I spent the day up the creek. We went as far as Jack Pine Point, where we had lunch with a gorgeous view all round.

Jack Pine Point is a spar at the foot of the bare Sheep Mountain. It is flat and covered with a growth of young jack pines. The creek flowing from the North-West, with the tawny cliffs of Sheep Mountain on the right, & steep, sombre, heavily timbered mountains on the left, rising about 3000 feet to the plateau, swings around Jack-Pine Point to the East. I wish I could describe the scene that lay or rose about us. We sat on the bare ground on the edge of Jack-Pine Point. A cliff dropped away beneath us, some 50 ft. to the creek bottom.

Opposite a small creek came down & a high and narrow gulch, dense with dark timber, from behind Goat Mountain, which showed its great sheer face in profile a little further to the left.

Behind us rose the cliffs of Sheep Mountain terminating at the painted bluff at the summit. All the low shrubs and aspen that grow in the lesser canyons of the Sheep Bluffs, were ablaze with scarlet and orange, which could be seen for miles and miles. Up and down the valley, the wide creek bottom, being filled with a thick growth of cottonwoods, birches, aspen, maples, willows & other deciduous trees, was a mass of the most dazzling colour.

The day was perfect: a deep blue sky & wonderful cleanness of atmosphere. In the canyon the light was a sharp contrast between brilliant sunshine and deep shadow.

The sombre mountains on the left & the deep shadows they cast set off beautifully the bright sunshine on the cliffs to the right , and the gorgeous autumn colours. There had been frost & the air was deliciously fresh.

On our way down from Jack Pine Point, we decided to ascend one of the little creeks (now dry). After going up its steep, rocky bed for about half of a mile, the cliffs closed in round us & we could go no further. Above this point, when the creek runs in the spring, it descends from the top of the Bluffs in a series of sheer cascades for

Roger and "Deana" 1914
Taken by Roger pulling string joined to camera shutter

about 1000 feet. On the way up I found on the boulders, a dried branch of a strange tree.

I kept a twig and decided it must have been washed down the creek from the heights. However, I kept my eyes open & on the way down, close to the place where I found the branch, but about 20 feet up th cliff, I saw the strange tree. It was a low shrub and much like the dwarf juniper in general appearance. I climbed up to it, secured a twig & looked for berries or cones, but could find none. It was an extraordinary piece of luck that we should have chosen to ascend that particular creek and that we found the dried branch.

The tree was absolutely strange to me & I could make nothing of it. When we got home, we consulted Sudworth's "Trees of the Pacific Slope", & decided it was Western Yew (taxus brevifolia). In giving the range of this tree, he says it occurs west of the Coast Range & again farther east in the Selkirks and gives no mention of it in the central interior.

I have never heard of this tree. Allan Brooks, the Naturalist at Okanagan Landing, does not know of its occurence here, for he gave me a list of the conifers in this region, and this was not among them.

From this I am inclined to think it is unknown in this part of the country. I have sent a specimen to Mr. George B. Sudworth (author of "Forest Trees of America" & dendrologist of the Forest Service, Washington, D.C.).

While we were up this canyon with the rock walls all about us, it became very cool and the shadow was so deep that we were led to believe that the day was closing in to the evening. On looking at my watch I was very surprised to find it was only about half past two. We descended from the late, chilly evening of the canyon & 20 minutes later emerged into the bright sunshine of early afternoon. Later on when the sun was nearing the Western mountains, the Bluffs looked magnificent, wonderful contrasts of light and shadow, every cleft and canyon was filled with dark mysterious shadows, throwing into sharp relief the projecting sunlit cliffs and buttresses. In the bottom of the valley where it runs east and west, the sun still shone brilliantly, but when we turned the corner at Kerrigan's & walked southward with the eastern slope of Goat Mountain (its eastern side is known as Mt. Zion) on our right, we were again plunged into the dusky evening of middle afternoon. Between Love's and Attenborough's the trail goes along the creek bottom on the level and is walled in on either side with dense woods of maple, birch, willow, cottonwood, young firs, cedars and spruce.

In these deep woods, the "afternoon-evening" developed into dark mysterious dusk. Scampering rabbits would now & then dash across the trail and disappear like phantoms into the dense brush. And still the time was but half past three. When we left the woods of the creek and were approaching the lake to the bull pine bench, the day seemed to become earlier.

Between Kerrigan's & Jack Pine Point where the valley runs east & west, & the precipitous slopes of Goat Mountain rise 3000 feet on the south side, the sun never shines on the lower parts of the canyon for the whole winter I got only three grouse on this expedition.

SUNDAY OCTOBER 25

Since my last entry there have been several very wet days, but the majority of days have been fine. On one or two nights lately, there have been slight frosts. The leaves are falling rapidly, & the rabbits are turning white on their ears & feet. We gathered the last of the apples yesterday & expect to be laid off work at the point on Monday or Tuesday.

There are two men camped on our place cutting telephone poles for the government.

Each pole is 30 feet long and averages 10 inches at the butt, & has to be of fir & peeled. They are paying us 25 cents a pole & expect to get a hundred or more off this place. Civilization is indeed coming upon us! This telephone extends along the road survey from Westbank to Whiteman's Creek, connecting with already existing telephones. It will probably be in working order by next spring, though it was promised this fall.

The war continues as fiercely as ever, but in spite of all reverses the allies seem to be gaining step by step. Some weeks ago Durant's son, Captain Hugh Durant of the R.J. Rifles, was wounded & returned to England & is now in hospital. The wounds were fairly serious, a bullet in the groin which went in with a tobacco pouch, & shrapnel in the leg. However he is doing very well and we all hope he will make a quick recovery. Durant is of course somewhat worried, but at the same time greatly relieved, for he thinks his son will probably be unable to return to the war.

As is the case in most new countries, the waste of material resources is a disgrace. Here it is most noticeable with timber. About 50 years ago in Michigan, they thought that the forests were almost inexhaustable. Ask a Michigan lumberman now why he left that state, & he will say, "Oh they're about picked up there now", the forests have almost gone. I have read that Indiana was once a forest state, but is now open prairie country. Here in the Okanagan the waste of timber is wicked.

About three years ago there was a tract of country behind Ewing's landing that was logged. The camps were working off & on for two years, & they boomed about 5 million feet. This spring I was up in the hills there & passed about 8 skidways of logs which had been left in the woods. Each skidway had perhaps 60 logs in it which had once been magnificent forest trees which took hundreds of years to grow. These logs were already useless for lumber, but would have made second rate cord wood. But they will never be used, they will be left to moulder until there is nothing left but a decayed heap of punk.

Two winters ago a big camp started work about two miles up the creek. They cut several hundred thousand feet of saw logs, found they were going in the hole and quit, leaving three large unfinished log buildings and hundreds of logs lying in the woods. The poles that are being cut for the telephone along here have to be 30 feet long & not less than 10 inches at the butt. In getting such a pole, very frequently there is from 2 to 15 feet of butt cut off the tree. These butts which would make excellent cordwood are left to rot.

These same poles are being set 5 feet in the ground & the butts are being preserved either by creosote or charring. The result will be that in 15 years or so all the poles will have to be renewed. Then of course, in B.C. millions of feet of timber is destroyed by fire.

These are only a few instances. The same sort of thing is going on all over the country. The B.C. Forest Service is of course doing a lot to prevent this sort of thing, but as it was only established in 1912, it is not yet very effectual.

NOVEMBER 1914

WEDNESDAY NOVEMBER 18

After a day or two of frost & north wind, the first snow fell on Monday 16th. Fine dry snow fell all that day & by evening there was about 2 inches on the ground. Up the hill the snow is five or six inches deep.

Yesterday a Chinook arose, & today it has been thawing, so there is not much snow left near the lake. I have been out hunting several times lately, but have seen no deer except on Tuesday last, when I saw a small doe (shooting of does is prohibited this year). However there are lots of tracks, so the deer must be coming down.

I have never seen Terrace Mountain look so beautiful as it did on Tuesday morning. At about half past seven I was a short distance across the first bench. Snow lay on the ground & rested on the boughs of the red-trunked bull pine & sombre firs. The dark mountains rose beyond, the forests dusted with white.

The sky was grey & overcast, & to the east there was no sign of the sunrise. Suddenly, ahead of me, I saw a glow like fire through the trees. Coming to an opening I saw a break in the clouds just over Terrace. The rising sun was shining on the summit, turning the pure white of the snow to deep rose- gold, which slowly changed to lemon-gold.

Behind the mountains was a small space of clear sky of the most delicate blue. Wisps of grey mist floated across the summit. It was wonderful, this glimpse of the glories of the day above the clouds. In 10 minutes it was over; the cleft closed, the summit was hidden by leaden snow clouds. The curtain had dropped and the tableau was over. Terrace Mountain might never have existed.

DECEMBER 1914

TUESDAY DECEMBER 15

During the past fortnight or so there has been a steady north wind with continuous but not severe frost. There have been two falls of snow, each about two inches. It is as dry & powdery as dust. A.K. & I have been hunting more or less steadily during the past few weeks. I saw about two weeks ago a very fine buck, but was unable to get a shot. A.K. succeeded in getting a deer last week. Today we both went on the last hunt of the season. I had been out about two hours & was walking along the rim of a steep gulch which was choked with underbrush all laden with snow, when I heard tramping at the bottom of the gulch. I crept up to the rim & waited. In a minute or so I could make out through the thick brush two deer walking along the bottom of the gulch.

I could not see them properly & still waited, then they turned off & made up the hill on the other side. Still I could see glimpses of them through the trees. There was a bare space above them directly opposite me about 100 yards away, across which I guessed they would go.

I leveled my rifle on that bare patch and waited. The leading buck appeared strolling up the hill with his back to me. I fired & he went on as though not hit, then he staggered, turned around & tottered down the hill again into the brush. I could only get glimpses of him as he moved about in the trees & I wasted several shots trying to finish him off. Shortly he appeared in an open place to one side, when with another shot I completed the work. I then went across and found him lying in the snow. He was a nice buck with perfect antlers, 3 points each side.

I cut his throat & removed the entrails. It was my first deer and I felt decidedly elated, but I could not get over a feeling of remorse.

A.K. on a hunting trip circa 1914

He was such a beautiful beast, and it was pitiful to see him lying in his blood on the snow. I have worked hard to get this deer. I must have hunted 31 times this season, but the triumph was mixed with sorrow. There are many of the most hardened hunters who cannot get over this feeling.

I decided that I could not haul him out of the gulch alone, so I set off home. When I arrived, I found A.K. butchering a deer that he had just shot, a fine two point buck it was. In the afternoon we all three went up the mountain and hauled out my deer –it was about 2 miles away—

We now have nearly a deer & a half hanging in joints in the meet safe & a whole deer hanging in a tree outside. We are going to give joints to the FitzGeralds, Durant & Parson Smith at the Centre. (Okanagan Centre)

This last was the fourth deer A.K. has had this season.

DEC. 16

We cut the antlers from the skulls of the deer this morning. We boiled them to remove the meat, scraped & washed the bone until it was as white as chalk & polished the horns with oil. They are now ornamenting the sitting room along with another good head of A.K.'s, shot in 1909. As to the hides, I think I shall remove the hair and cut them up for thongs. According to the law, we are to dispose of this vast quantity of meat before the first of January, 1915. The law evidently overestimates the capacity of our stomachs. If we eat to repletion at every meal & between meals, we could not get rid of our Mowitch in that time.

We therefore feel that the only remedy is to cache the mowitch for we do not feel at all inclined to throw it away. It is an immense help in these hard times. It will keep indefinitely in this weather, for it freezes as hard as wood. A joint has to be cut with an axe & saw.

Shorts' Point 1914

Fintry 1914

*Too many stones
for farming 1914*

Nahun as it is today (1997)
John Sugars' photo

Nahun as it is today (1997)
John Sugars' photo

1915

Photo by A.K. Menzies

JANUARY 11: MONDAY

Eleven days of the New Year already gone! All the old sayings about a "Happy and prosperous New Year" and so forth, are likely to remain sayings, it seems, this year at any rate.

The war rages on in its mad game of murder. The outlook for B.C. and Canada, generally, is about as bad as it ever was; railways suspended. Trusts going smash. The fruit growers are now being paid for last years' crops and instead of getting the face price, (which is always low), they are receiving about 20% of it! The telephone along here is nearly completed. Great numbers of trees have been cut down along the trail to make way for the wire, causing an unsightly and dangerous confusion on the ground. It is dangerous for the reason that nothing is so likely to start a fire as felled trees and branches, especially in the vicinity of a trail or road. It seems strange to see a telephone wire intruding into these hitherto undisturbed woods.

Since about the 20th of Dec. there have been several falls of snow now amounting to a foot, but the weather has been remarkably mild. There is a slight thaw nearly every day. A thin drizzling rain has fallen nearly all of today. Miserable weather!

Christmas was anything but cheerful. Doffles, who has been with us for over 10 years and was far more to us than any mere dog, died in the small hours on the 27th of December after a week's illness. The main trouble at first was that she could keep no food down, we did all we could and sat up with her on the last three nights. It was evidently the breaking up of old age, for she became weaker and weaker and went out perfectly quietly in her sleep.

There seemed to be a strange emptiness about the house afterwards, and we all felt exceedingly miserable. It is a terrible thing, this capacity for loving animals like humans. When our poor old cayuse had to be put away I could have cried. There are some callous people who are saved much pain in this way.

I have read three books lately, on Socialism, two by Blatchford ("Merrie England" and "Britain for the British") and one, "New Worlds for Old" by H.G. Wells; this last is particularly good. Until I have further knowledge I say, without hesitation, that I am a Socialist.

After two weeks soaking in the lake the hair came away with the greatest ease, from my deerskin. I have succeeded in tanning it quite well, after the Indian fashion. I proceeded as follows: I stretched the skin on the wall, scraped off all meat and left it until it was nearly dry. I then selected two small trees about 8 feet apart and nailed two poles between them, one almost level with the ground, the other about 6 feet up. I then cut holes every 10 inches around the edge of the deerskin and laced it onto the frame thus formed, stretching it tight. I then lit a small fire to one side of the skin. While it was drying I worked and scraped it with a trowel,

Roger tanning a deer skin. Photo by A.K. Menzies

with the point slightly flattened and sharpened. Putting all my weight on the trowel I pushed and scraped it all over both sides of the hide. I did this for two days, working about 6 or 7 hours a day. I then made a slight hollow in the ground and bent three little withes over it, bow-wise. I lit a tiny, clear fire in the hollow and then smothered it with green cedar tips, which created a dense smoke; I put the skin over the withes like a round-topped tent, closing all gaps as much as possible to keep the smoke in. I sat by it for about 5 hours smothering the fire from time to time with fresh cedar tips. When one side of the skin was smoked to the tawny colour of Indian buckskin, I turned it and treated the other side in the same way, each side taking about two and a half hours. When it was sufficiently smoked I restretched it and worked it again with the trowel for a couple of hours when I considered it finished. The result was a thin, tough, soft leather, in appearance like chamois leather, with a delicious aromatic smell of cedar smoke. It was not, however, as soft as the buckskin tanned by the "Klootchs" (*Chinook for squaw*).

I have made a tolerably good pair of moccasins out of this hide also 5 pairs of bootlaces and an 18-foot rawhide cord. I have various scraps of buckskin left over.

JANUARY 31: SUNDAY: 1915

During the past two or three weeks the weather has changed but little; continuous but not severe frost and the snow powdery and dry. The winds seem quite local, no real North winds and no Chinooks. What wind there is blows alternately from the North and South-East, both are cold but seem to cause no rise and fall in the temperature to speak of. A few evenings have been wonderfully clear and brilliant, but for the most part the sky is dull and gray.... I have been working since the 19th of January on the "slashing" of the right of way for the road to come between Nahun and Ewing's. There are five of us, Clarence (the "Boss"), Critchley, MacAlister, the "Colonel", and myself. We are following the survey stakes and removing all "brush" roughly to the width of 33 feet. Standing trees, "deadfalls", and other brush have to be removed and piled into heaps and "wind-rows" ready for burning. A good deal of the work is on the sidehill at an angle of 30 to 45 degrees with much rock and little precipices. It is mostly axe work and sawing, with the addition of a little cant hook work in rolling logs out of the way. I am the "Colonel's" partner on a crosscut saw and he and I are chiefly engaged in felling the larger trees. We started at the "Golden Gate" above Kennard's and have now come about two miles; well no, perhaps a mile and a half. I take my dinner along with me in the morning and walk home at night. The others are "batching" in the "Colonel's" shack. We work about 8 hours a day, and the pay is $2.50. The weather is perfect for this kind of work. I have grave fears, however, that the weather is about to change. There has been a fall of wet snow today and the temperature has risen 4 or 5 degrees above freezing.

I got a letter from Newbery a week or so ago, thanking me for the Terrace Mountain photos which I sent him. He is now married and settled down at "York House".

MARCH 5: FRIDAY: 1915

Since the above entry the weather has been very mild, next to no frost and no snow. There has been a little rain and nearly all the snow has gone from the lower hills. Altogether, the weather has been peculiarly unseasonable; I do not think we have ever had such a mild and open winter before. The dirty and objectionable stages of early spring are now well advanced. Everything is "soggy" and damp. The roads and trails near the lake are very muddy. The early spring flowers such as "butterdrops" are sprouting: the cock willow grouse are drumming, and some of the Robins have returned. This is a grubby, depressing time of year., but it will improve greatly towards April, when the thaw is over and the flowers and young leaves are out. We finished slashing the right of way on February 17th, our wages amounting to $62.50 a piece. I have missed this work.

Clarence and the "Colonel" are very nice men both around 40 and old-timers in this country. Both interesting and amusing. Critchley, who is 26, is remarkable for good nature. MacAlister is notorious for pomposity and a knowledge of everything. He always contradicts, argues and asserts his own opinion and delights in finding fault. However, if you humour him, he is very amusing in the capacity, for he is really quite harmless. The order of the day was yamming, next to this, work was considered. My saw-partner, the Colonel, was in the habit of indulging in sudden attacks of an "awful weary feelin". I was told emphatically that it was not laziness, it was pure incapability. "I'm not a lazy man," he said. "I don't like work, hard graft, but you can't call a man who hunts in these hills day after day as I do, lazy". Of course I like huntin'", he added, "but it's damned hard work just the same."

MARCH 9: TUESDAY: 1915

The Colonel has since enlisted in the B.C. Horse (3rd contingent). There is some doubt entertained as to whether the 2nd contingent will be sent out of the country. There seems little likelihood of the 3rd ever being used. The British Columbia section of the 2nd contingent is encamped at Victoria, On Friday the 26th of February I went up to Critchley's where I stayed till Monday the 1st. He holds, in my opinion and of course his, the best of the pre-emptions on the Bighorn Flats at present - Horner and MacAlister's; Stock Bros., Mark Ellis's and Critchley's. Each have their clearing, the whole amounting to some 40 acres. Critchley's lies farthest from the lake. MacAlister's at 3000 feet elevation is on the edge of the hill overlooking the lake about 1600 feet below. Critchley's is about 2 1/2 mi. down the valley southwest. Stocks is halfway between. His pre-emption is in the valley of the Bald Range Creek; a high ridge of hills divides him from the lake slope on the East and steep mountains rise on the West in the direction of the Bald Range. The flat between the slopes is from 100 to 200 yards wide; a small stream, called Bald Range Creek, flows through the flats and on down the valley to Bear Creek, about 6 miles south.

Unlike the other pre-emptions, which are covered thickly with jack pine and spruce, these flats of Critchley's are covered with alder, a few spruce, jack pine and cottonwood. This alder land is said to be perfectly fertile. Critchley should be able to grow fine hay here but of course there is no way of conveying it out to the lake. However, they hope for a road up from Bear Creek sometime in the future.

There is a trail up from Kennard's and on down the valley to Bear Creek. Critchley's shack is somewhat of a dog kennel, being about 10x12 feet and rather low; the mud roof leaks slightly, and the bark has not been taken off the logs on the walls. Critchley is, however, a clean individual and that is the main thing.

After a vast supper of "mulligan" I was initiated into the elements of cribbage on the first evening. At about 11 p.m. we retired into the two bunks, head to head: my bunk was 6 or 8 inches too short for me. Critchley insisted on lying awake and telling me the history of his life; how he had risen from pageboy to butler, chemist's assistant, butcher, farm boy, etc. That he was one of a family of 16, the last being only three months old; that he had been engaged and jilted but had not broken his heart over it. But after all this excitement he found the life too dull and humdrum and craved for the free life of the woods. So he came west where he has now been for five years and is never happier than when going over his trap line on "webs" [*snow shoes*]. The second and third day passed more or less uneventfully. The coyotes were howling their spring fever round the hills each night. The horned owls were hooting much more than they do near the lake. I saw several whiskey jacks and also heard a raven. The former never seemed to come down near the lake, and the latter is a somewhat rare bird. The snow up here was lying to the depth of a foot, though it had all gone near the lake. One Monday morning, after a somewhat late breakfast and a smoke, I returned home leaving Critchley's in blazing sunshine, with cloudless blue overhead.

I reached the top of the mountain at MacAlister's. I looked down and behold, no lake to be seen, but billowing white cloud filled the valley below. There was not a break in the dazzling white, it was almost like looking down on the sea, or a much larger lake than the Okanagan. In the gorgeous sunshine with the blue sky above, it was indeed a lovely sight. But after descending the mountainside about a thousand feet, I suddenly left the sunshine and plunged into the mist. In a few minutes the sun was blotted out and objects 50 yards away were almost invisible on reaching Kennards. I found the mist was resting right on the lake.

MARCH 25: THURSDAY: 1915

For the past few weeks there has been the most perfect weather, almost every day being bright and cloudless. There is a slight frost almost every night but the days are very warm, almost like summer days. Winter left us very early this year; the snow has all been gone for nearly a month and it is only to be seen now on the tops of the mountains gleaming in the spring sunshine.

The dull, dead and dirty appearance of early spring has vanished. The landscape is taking on a delicate green tint. The range grass is coming up and most of the leaf buds are opening; "butterdrops" are out all over the open hillsides.

The day before yesterday we planted our potatoes, a sack and one half, and reserved a piece of ground for carrots and tomatoes etc. About two weeks ago I put a fresh coat of green paint on my boat and refinished the bottom and am now using her again regularly. Since having the boat out we have been doing some fishing but without much success until today, when A.K. caught an 8 pounder. It is said that the road from Nahun to Ewing's, which has been expected for so many years, is actually going to be constructed this season and is to be begun on the 15th of April. The work is to be for the benefit of Westsiders. So we, no doubt, will be taken on. The work will probably last all summer. Some weeks ago we went up to see the Somersets, Mrs. and Miss only being at home, Jack having enlisted and Bob working at Armstrong. We borrowed a book from Mrs. Somerset (as somewhat of a favour I fancy, for the book had been presented to her late husband when at school in the year '67 or thereabouts). The book was entitled "British Columbia 1862" by Commander Mayne, being a description of four years explorations on the Coast and in the interior of this Province. This book, of course, was of particular interest to me, but I might have been more so had he treated more fully of details. At that time British Columbia must have been a fine country holding far more interest than it does now. There was, of course, no railroad across the Rockies. Vancouver was not in existence, Victoria with Esquimalt as its harbour, was only a Naval Station, Hudson Bay post, and jumping off place for the Cariboo miners. Gold had just been discovered in B.C. and there was a rush to various points on the Fraser River, the "Cariboo goldfields" in particular. The famous Cariboo Road was under construction at that time.

The Siwashes of the Coast had already become degraded from their contact with the whites but those of the interior appear to have been a somewhat superior race, and uncontaminated; most of the tribes were mounted. The present district and Lake called Nicola was named after an old chief of that country by the name of Nicola or Nicholas. Mayne, on one of his expeditions into the interior, visited the Nicola Valley (which is but fifty miles west of here, over the mountains) and the valley of the Thompson River on which is now situated the town of Kamloops. It was then Fort Kamloops, a Hudson Bay trading post, which was still visited by the great pack trains of three northern fur brigades. Mayne did not reach the Okanagan but mentioned it occasionally. It seems to have been less known than Cariboo country (which today is still a thinly populated and wild country). The Okanagan appears to have been known only by a few prospectors and Jesuit missionaries. The valley of the Okanagan River and Lake seems to have been a route from Washington territory to the Cariboo goldfields. I wish those days were here now!

April 12: Monday: 1915

Spring has advanced rapidly in the last few weeks. Everything is extraordinarily early. The deciduous trees are quite thickly clothed in tender green leaves. The Lower hills are beautifully green with the new grass. Many wild flowers are out, most conspicuous of all, the tussocks of yellow sunflowers growing on the steep sunny slopes among the pines and Saskatoon or "olally" bushes, though not yet in full leaf, are already bursting out into their white blossom.

The creeks are rising and the lake (which dropped lower this winter than I have ever seen it before) has come up about 3 inches; the Lake will probably not rise to its usual level this year on account of the somewhat light snow fall in the mountains. The "willow" grouse are drumming in the swamps and thickets and the blues are booming on the hills. The weather is, for the most part, warm and sunny; and as is usual in April somewhat inclined to be showery.

On Sunday the 4th Deana and I were caught in a heavy shower of sleet driven by a bitter wind. When we were up near the summit of Mt. Zion, where spring had advanced but little, the snow still lying about in deep patches. The morning had all the promise of a bright fine day so we set out with the intention of climbing Mt. Zion. After 4 hours steady walking we stopped for lunch on a "bench" near the top of Zion. In front of us the long, bare 2000 foot slope up which we had just climbed, fell away to the creek, to rise again 1500 feet or so on the opposite side of the gorge. This formed the "Lake Ridge" running north and south and then at the "Kerrigan bend" of the creek joining the bald Sheep Bluffs, which sweep round to the Northwest. Behind our ledge was dense wood of small jack-pine, sloping back a quarter of a mile or so to the foot of the bald summit of Zion, which was not in view on account of an intervening ridge. Looking Northward we saw a dark rainstorm swooping over the battlements of the Sheep Bluffs; in ten minutes it had crossed the canyon and was on us. We sheltered in the jack-pine, but were soon very wet and cold; it was over in 5 minutes but a bitter wind was sweeping over the mountain. We decided not to go on to the top that day and shortly descended. In a short time the sun burst forth and we sat down and had a smoke and basked for half an hour in the warmth, the great bare steeps stretched above and below us. Love's cabin, straight below looked like a matchbox beside the ribbon of the creek. On the way down, Tom and Mrs. Attenborough shared their usual boundless hospitality, had us in to some tea and loaded us with parsnips and eggs to take home. Tom, who is one of the old timers and has lived on his ranch up the creek for 18 years. is in my mind the finest and most good-hearted man in the country (with the exception, perhaps of Durant). He used to have a weakness for Hudson Bay Rum and four years ago, when Billy Rilands and 'Red' Marshall were up there, it was pretty tough. In the last few years, however, he appears to have given it up. Old Love, once said that "Tom may get full, but he's never mean with it..."

I am sorry to say that Bachelor, one of the Westsiders, has been killed at the front.

APRIL 21: WEDNESDAY: 1915

After all the talk and "hot air" about the road coming for a certainty it has, as usual, been "postponed". And as usual, they are kicking and bucking about the money that shall be put out on it, and various other things. Rumors run that the South member wants half the money for his section, the North member wants it all for this section, and so and so says if so and so is having his right of way fenced at government expense, why shouldn't he have it.

Somebody wants the road to start at Nahun and somebody else wants it to start at Ewing's. We all have to vote Conservative for fear of getting out of favour with the Conservative member (a rank grafter!) and thereby losing the road altogether. In other words we are being bribed for our votes. The Conservative member dangles a road before us and says, "Vote for me or I'll take it away again". In all probability he will keep up the road bluff until he secures his votes and then will "postpone" it again for a few years.

The "Colonel" was talking to Mabee, some months ago, about what a farce the B.C. government was, there being absolutely no opposition to the Conservatives. He said if a goodly number were to vote Liberal, it would rouse them and do some good: "I've a good mind to go myself for Ch-'s sake, don't do that or you'll lose your vote," said Mabee. Such is the government of B.C.!

APRIL 29: THURSDAY: 1915

Three weeks or more have gone by without rain, each day being clear and sunny and almost hot enough to be late in May. Yesterday was a cloudless, hot day with no wind; towards evening the sky thickened gradually until it was heavily overcast and in the night the rain started. All day it has been dull and wet with a chilly south wind in the afternoon. The rain will do the garden no end of good. Potatoes, carrots, maize, and radishes are all up. The artichokes and white carrots have not yet had time to come up. The "lawn" (the blue grass and Dutch clover terrace along the front of the house) is growing splendidly this year and will soon have to be "mowed". This I do with a well-sharpened butcher knife! Along the front of the house against the wall we have Japanese cucumber, which are already beginning to climb. In the shady corner where the kitchen meets the log house we have a couple of "bearrines" or clematis: a true blue flowered clematis which is abundant in the swamps. These were planted last year and are doing well. Next year they should be halfway up the wall and flowering. This little corner is bordered off from the clover-turf with a few stones among which we planted some wild ferns, Along the foot of our grass terrace Deana has planted various little wild plants. Saxifrage (golden moss) box, ferns, and others I know not the names of. Some weeks ago, when in an energetic mood, I made a "drive" of clean beach gravel, about 15 feet long by four wide past the front door, bordered on each side by green turf. It took an immense quantity of gravel to cover even a little space like this. I carried on my back, from the beach, about 30 coal-oil cans full of gravel each weighing about 60 pounds. I also had to bring the gravel in the boat from a beach about 300 yards away. Having made my gravel "sweep", I then made some steps down in front of the house to meet the zigzag road from the beach. But better than all our improvements are the wildflowers, which are particularly profuse this year. Up the steep slope, behind the house the sunflowers and Saskatoon have been a gorgeous sight. The air is full of the sweet scent of the Saskatoon blossom. Sunflowers and Saskatoon are now nearly over and the later and less conspicuous flowers are taking their place. Masses of the pale purple "snap dragons" (called this for want of their proper name), squaws paint brush, deep blue lark spur, a delicate, dark red brown flower with a yellow green pistil, of the lily family, I think, and somewhat like a small dropping tulip in shape. It is hopeless to go through them all, there are dozens of others, and many more to come and yet, by July there will be hardly a flower left in all the hills. The two rarest and perhaps most beautiful flowers that grow here are the Tiger Lily and the Wild Columbine. The former grows in the thick brush and grass on the fringes of swamps and gullies. The columbine I have only seen once, growing in fairly thick undergrowth among the thick timber in the creek bottom just above Attenborough's. The plant was 18 inches high and the flowers pink and yellow, and in size and shape exactly like the cultivated Columbine.

MAY 30: SUNDAY: 1915

This has been an exceptionally wet month. Since the long period of fine weather mentioned in my last entry there has been scarcely a single fine day. Rain, indeed, was wanted, but in moderation; there has been so much that the garden stuff is somewhat at a standstill for want of sun and warmth. On Friday last a stranger entered our family circle; we find him a very amusing guest. He is at this moment in my shirt pocket. A baby squirrel he is, and I found him alone on the ground under a birch tree but 10 yards from the house; he was crawling about with his eyes only just open and came to me, apparently for help. I called the others out and we debated over the best thing to do about it. We thought that the mother must have been killed, or that the little thing had fallen from the nest (which is a hole in the birch; under which I found him). We finally decided to do our best for him. He is thriving and takes warm canned milk and water out of a spoon about every two hours. He is a beautiful little creature, and very entertaining. Every now and then he becomes restless and climbs out of his basket and explores the broad desert of the floor and finally climbs a chair or somebody's leg.

Having scaled your leg he proceeds up your shirt and tickles round your neck attempting to get inside your shirt. On one occasion he took me unaware and succeeded in doing so the tickling of his sharp little nails as he crawled down the bare skin on my back was almost unbearable. Today he discovered that the most delightful thing on earth next to eating is to get into your shirt pocket and sleep there for hours, enjoying the warmth of your body.

Just as I entered the bay on my way back from Kennard's today I saw an animal swimming rapidly close to the boat. I thought at once it was an otter and gave chase, and rowed up within 20 feet of it. We both, (Mother was with me), were able to see it to good advantage as it slid though the water making a wash like a little steamboat. It looked not altogether like an otter and when it dived I saw there was no doubt about it. As he dived the great flat tail struck the water with a loud splash. I knew at once it was a beaver. Twice again he came up and dived each time striking the water with his heavy tail. We then rowed ashore, and he swam about in the bay and after some time went in shore near the old otter's den, among some big boulders which are half in the water and over hung by tall slanting cedars. I very much hope he will take up his abode there. It is the first live beaver I have ever seen. I once saw a dead beaver and have often seen trees that have been cut down by them. I saw a small new beaver dam up Shorts' Creek last fall and have seen several ancient dams, large affairs now on dry land; these last are the Bighorn Flats near Critchley's pre-emption.

Beavers are, undoubtedly, increasing every year. Eight or ten years ago they were only known in remote sloughs back in the hills. Now their workings can be seen all down Shorts' Creek right to the very month, also in places along the lakeshore.

JUNE 8: TUESDAY: 1915

About ten days ago three half-breeds rode past with several packhorses late in the afternoon. They stopped and camped for the night close to our old house. In the evening one of them came down to see (or ask) if he could buy some bread; from his appearance one would have expected him to pull a couple of guns and hold up the establishment! As is the way with Indians and "breeds", especially the young bucks, he was very elaborately dressed. On his head he wore a soft, fawn coloured Stetson with a wide trim and a very high crown 'round it was a narrow leather band studded with silver. He wore an unbuttoned waistcoat made of the skin of a pinto horse, a green handkerchief round his neck and buckskin gauntlets. A pair of high-heeled tall riding boots with the trousers tucked into them completed his costume. We gave him a loaf of bread and he politely withdrew; and we thought no more about it, it was nothing unusual. Siwashes and 'breeds' are frequently passing to and fro on the trail. However, on the next inspection of the old house (the day before yesterday) we discovered that the front door had been forced open, and my saddle and bridle were missing! These three breeds may or may not have taken them, but we naturally suspect them as they passed the night within 50 yards of the old house. We have written to the chief of police at Vernon, but I think there is not the slightest chance of recovering the saddle. It is an ordinary Mexican saddle of smaller size and almost new. I should know it anywhere but I could not prove that it was my own.

JUNE 16: WEDNESDAY: 1915

A couple of days after we discovered the loss of the saddle, I was walking round investigating when I found, near the ashes of the campfire where the breeds had spent the night, some advertising leaves out of Harper's Magazine. It seemed to me unlikely that these breeds should just happen to have a Harper's Magazine with them and I knew there were several Harper's in our old house. This struck me as being fairly good evidence, but I have since seen Dundas (the Game Warden) and he thinks it most unlikely that any of the McDougall (these three were of that "Clan") would have done such a thing. He said they might steal horses and so forth but he had never heard of them going in for petty "swiping". I know most of the McDougalls and thought they may be "toughs" who get to "taking down their old Winchesters when they're "full" (as Art Johnson put it). We have hitherto found them honest and decidedly interesting. Several of them were logging on our place under Johnson all the summer of 1909 and though they had many opportunities they touched nothing and only had one "drunk" during the summer, quite an inoffensive affair. Johnson came up from the camp in the morning with a cheerful expression, a jug of whiskey, asking us to "drink merry" and then politely retired. There was a little whooping and yelling and the next day they were at work. The best of all the McDougalls is old Henry the guide. The McDougalls who camped here, however, were strangers to us and I am very much afraid it was they who took the saddle, the evidence is pretty strong....

The roadwork has been under way for about three weeks, under George Smith a very nice Canadian road foreman who lives at 6-mile creek (North of Whiteman's). It is very complicated and hard to understand but it appears that Smith had instructions to do some preparatory work such as blowing stumps, etc., until he had orders to proceed or not to proceed. The latter has happened, or rather, it is said there is no money to finish the road. I am told, however, that Smith hopes to complete the grade between Ewing's and Shorts' Creek before what little money there is gives out. He is

Working on Westside Road with pick and shovel

maintaining about ten men and changes them from time to time so that everybody may get a chance of some work. Deana and A.K. have had two weeks and were laid off last Monday.

JUNE 26: SATURDAY: 1915

Monday's mail brought us very bad news. My cousin, Jack Semple has died of wounds at the front. We heard no details except that he had been doing well in hospital for three weeks and was expected home at anytime, then something went wrong and he died. He was only twenty-one. Another old friend, George Concannon has also been killed in action. He spent about a year with his cousin Kennard at Nahun six years ago. We got to know him well and found him one of the most entertaining and brilliant men the Westside had ever seen. He was a poet and had also written a play, a fantastic and somewhat blasphemous play in which the Australian squatter sells his soul to Satan. He was given to periods of insanity and as Kennard said that perhaps it was just as well, he had died fighting.

JULY 13: TUESDAY: 1915

I have worked for two weeks on the road (pick and shovel) and took this morning off on account of bad weather. Yesterday afternoon while at work we were caught in a fierce rain and hailstorm. We (Joe Wood, Mark Ellis and myself) sheltered under some birches, lit up our pipes and waited. In ten minutes we were drenched to the skin and in twenty the creek had risen six inches nearer to our feet and was frothing over the boulders as thick as pea soup. We waited and shivered for nearly an hour when the storm began to let up. Soaked to the skin, we put in an hour's work shoveling sticky mud and glistening wet stones, and then quit, the hail still lay about in patches, and on my way home across the bench I noticed the patches grew larger as I went south. On reaching the brow of the hill above our place, the country presented an almost wintry appearance. The sky was grey and overcast, a thin rain was falling and the ground and nearby hills were covered with large patches of hail lying to a depth of 2 or 3 inches. If it were not for the leaves on the deciduous trees one would not have believed it was anything but a wet day in early spring with the snow still lying here and there. Following the old logging road down the hill I found that a torrent had been boiling down it, washing out the soil to a depth of a foot in places. The very center of the storm seemed to have swept over our house. Here, hailstones as large as small cherries lay in drifts 3 or 4 inches deep, the roof appeared to have 2 inches of "snow" on it. The ground was covered with ice and riddled leaves and twigs from the trees. The big leaves of the salmon berries were torn and ripped and smashed off.

At first sight out the garden appeared to be wrecked; potatoes and carrots were smashed flat, the ground was guttered out and grooved and potatoes lay exposed in places. These we covered over again. Our garden consists mainly of potatoes and these will probably recover, the other stuff - tomatoes, beans, marrows, and carrots - no doubt will be ruined. It is the fiercest hailstorm we have ever seen. Patches of hail are still lying unmelted this morning. It has rained all the morning and it is threatening to do so all the afternoon. Five minutes before the storm, yesterday Mr. Clarence rowed into our place. On his way back to work on the road (He rows home - 12 miles - on Saturday nights). He slept here last night and walked up to the road camp at Shorts' Creek this morning. He told us he had never seen such a hailstorm before and he has been in Canada 18 years.

All the fruit in the region of the storm is badly damaged. The entire crop at Shorts" has suffered heavily; a large quantity ruined and the rest will have to be shipped as "thirds" or "hail marked".

SEPTEMBER 13: MONDAY: 1915

Two months since I made an entry! A somewhat uneventful two months perhaps, but very busy. On the 9th of this month the roadwork shut down on account of lack of money, the road being built from Ewing's to a point within three-quarters of a mile of the end of the road at Nahun. This part is still traversed by the old trail. I have had about 10 weeks work on the road; Deana and A.K. a week or so less. It was good congenial work and I felt in good shape after it.

The work was varied to some extent, rock-picking (boulders and half-blasted bed rock), pick and shovel, rock-cribbing, with a certain amount of sawing and axe-work, also some brush burning followed by a little fire-fighting. The pick and shovel gang consisted latterly of Clarence, MacAlister, Lawrence, Landale, Mark Ellis and ourselves with old Muirhead as "straw boss". The "skilled" gang was Tommy Struthers - teamster and grader man, Bob - teamster, Thompson - teamster Lou Everett - powder man and the brothers, Adam and Nin. All these are decent men; especially Thompson and old Adam; he and his brother Nin (Niniam) are regular old Canadian "Mossbacks" from old Ontario. Their western cousin Lou is a squawman and a bit "tough", peculiarly unkempt in appearance. Tommy is also a squawman. Bob is a breed. Thompson comes from Nova Scotia and his wife and daughter cooked for the road camp (a more excellent cookery could not be found in any camp in this country). It would be interesting to describe all the various tricks and traits of these men, but I am not equal to it. Muirhead is a particularly interesting man.

He is a tough old Scotchman of 64 with a keen hawk like face and a grey mustache. He has been 42 years in America and in that time has been practically all over the continent. In his youth he spent a year and a half on the survey of the Topeka and Santa Fe - from Couejos, Colorado to Graymas, Mexico, passing through the desert regions of New Mexico and Sonora. This was in the days when the Apaches were hostile. In the Mexican towns also, he said the "Greasers" had a way of shooting one on sight. Consequently the survey party traveled armed with Winchesters and Colts.

As is the way of the old timers he tells his stories with great precision, mentioned all such details as so and so's Christian name and the fact that the Engineer was having his breakfast when he applied for the job of front chainman...

August was a clear, dry month on the whole and not too hot. September has been slightly unsettled so far and today has been grey and cold. Our squirrel, after spending about 6 weeks of her youth with us, took to the woods for the first few weeks, she came regularly once or twice a day to the house for peanuts and having submitted to a little petting would scamper off into the brush. For the past month or so, however, she has not put in an appearance, but we hope to see her again when the cold weather comes. A prettier and more interesting little creature I seldom saw. She is the second wild creature we have reared from infancy. The other was a snowshoe rabbit, which also took to the woods when about half grown.

One would never have credited a squirrel with so much intelligence and vivacity: for playfulness a kitten did not approach her. In her milk - food days, the voracious scenes over the teaspoons and saucer were truly disgraceful. The first peanut was also a great joy but nibbled very slowly with the baby teeth. It was not long, however, before she could devour half a dozen peanuts in a very few minutes.

The deer season this year is as usual, from September 1st to December 15th, It is also lawful to shoot does. The season for grouse does not open till September 15th and closes Nov. 30th.

On Sunday the 12th A.K. shot a doe - a fine fat beast with haunches weighing 21 lbs apiece. I was also hunting on Sunday and saw two deer vanishing in the thick woods and 7 grouse.

I also walked right into a bear - a medium sized brown bear. I was topping a little rise and Bruin was coming up the other side; we both stopped on top facing each other, with 20 feet between us. I sank down and cocked my rifle

A.K. with a deer - Note: No belt loops on pants

(forgetting that I required a $5 license to shoot bear) but the bear decided not to wait any longer and made off into the woods at top speed, crashing through the deadfalls. It seems that bear are somewhat more plentiful than usual, this year, as four were seen near Nahun a few days ago.

OCTOBER 15: FRIDAY: 1915

There seems very little material for a diary these days; for the most part the weather has been fine during the past month. Of course the fall is now well advanced, the season of bright fresh days and frosty nights, superbly tinted woods, mellow golden sunshine and blue shadows. The time of year when the crisp air is scented with the decaying carpet of damp, yellow leaves and when everything is pervaded with a sort of delicious melancholy.

On the 23rd of September I shot a two-point buck and, as A.K. had shot a big doe a week or two before, I decided to ship it to the butcher for sale, so next day I sent it to Casorso Bros. Kelowna. In payment I received $6.50! Their excuse was that the CPR only advised them of its arrival the following morning and the meat was tainted in consequence. I wrote and said that I failed to see that that was my fault, as I had advised them over the telephone that the deer was to be shipped that afternoon and that if they had not time to do so that evening they should have said so over the phone and I would have not shipped the buck. As a matter of fact their reply on the phone was simply that they would allow me ten cents a pound on my buck (it weighed 126 lbs. gutted). The last deer I ship to the meat market!....

On Wednesday night I finished up 15 days of work at Somerset's. Mrs. Somerset gave me $1.50 a day and my board and lodging. The main part of the work consisted of painting the roof red, the window casements green, and the window sashes white outside, doors, windows, and two walls oil stained inside. In addition to this I mudded up the stables and did many other odd jobs. Jim Gleed, a contractor from the Centre was also there and had been for some weeks shingling the roof, building two chimneys, and generally refitting the house. It is a large house of logs with three rooms downstairs and three upstairs (one of which Gleed and I slept in) also a "lean to" kitchen at the back. I found Gleed a very nice little man and also succeeded in getting on admirable with the notoriously fussy and cranky Mrs. Somerset. Being about sixty-five she is too settled in her English ideas to adapt herself in the least to the ways of this country. However I found that by humouring her and by conducting myself in a seemly manner I could get at the best side of her. I only made a few mistakes such as attempting to smoke when she was in the same room and also attempting to pour out a cup of tea for her. This latter was a rather amusing incident. While at dinner Mrs. Somerset handed her cup to be refilled and (as I do at home) impulsively seized the teapot to do so. Miss Somerset at the other end of the table was the authorized tea vendor and as most of her time was taken up in pouring our tea, I thought there would be no harm in relieving her for once. But Mrs. Somerset reproved me by saying precisely: "Miss Somerset will pour out the tea".

I smiled inwardly and handed the cup on. I was also careful not to tell Mrs. Somerset that I was a socialist, or that I had never been to church since I was christened. I thought she would think no better of me if I did. In spite of her somewhat prim ideas in some things, she is capable of telling quite frivolous and even vulgar stories. The following, though very mild, is surprising from such a person.

A Sunday school teacher asked his pupils "who was the Son of God? No answer. The question was repeated, still no answer. "Come, come" said the teacher. Surely you know who was the Son of God". A short pause and then a little boy suddenly jumped up exclaiming "Oh Christ!" "Of course, that's the right answer," said the teacher. "You'd have said 'Oh Christ' too if you'd had a pin stuck into you!"

NOVEMBER 14: SUNDAY: 1915

The first stages of winter have come. The leaves have fallen, the snow is down within a few hundred feet of the Lake, and a week of stiff frost has just passed. Today is milder with a heavy Chinook. There was a beautiful display of the Northern Lights about a week ago; I think the best I have seen. It was a dark night and it began like a moonrise and spread until half the sky, from the mountains on the northern horizon to the Zenith, was illuminated. All the Northern sky was bright and here and there shot through with still brighter shafts of whitish yellow light radiating from the North and turning a pale red near the Zenith. These beams of light quivered and changed their position continually. I have just finished three weeks work for Thompson (who was one of the teamsters on the road).

I got to know him and to like him on the road this summer, and he told me he would give me a job this winter, and he kept his word. We were clearing 5 or 6 acres of land for Colquhoun up at

Ewing's - pulling stumps, slashing and mowing small brush, blasting stumps and polishing. We "batched" together down at the Lake in a well-fitted little log shack of Bob Ewing's. I cooked the meals while Thompson attended to his team. In the evenings we would stay and read or talk or, more often, took the lantern and went visiting. The settlers all live close together at Ewing's and we had not far to go to make an evening call with a choice of 4 or 5 houses. There is a gramophone or piano in nearly every house so we had plenty of entertaining and everybody was most hospitable. The excellent and colossal Mrs. Thompson and Marie came down in their rig from Whiteman once a week with supplies of bread, cakes and jam.

Thompson, who is a lumberman by trade, I found very interesting. He spun many yarns of his wild youth in the lumber camps of "Nova Scotia" and "New Brunswick" and his four summers on an ice wagon in Boston. He had various affairs with young women which ended finally some 15 or 16 years ago in the present Mrs. Thompson. He came West 8 years ago - put in two years on the Prairie, 3 years on the Crows Nest running camps and 3 years in this Valley also logging. Colquhoun has offered me a month's work at $1.00 a day and board, (the same as Thompson was paying me - wages are going down while cost of living is as high as ever)...... A.K. shot a two-point buck a few days ago.

NOVEMBER 15: MONDAY: 1915

About 4 inches of snow fell this morning and was followed by a slight thaw but tonight it is freezing again. I came home from Ewing's on Friday and was to have gone to work for Colquhoun today but I am suffering from a very sore left hand and shall be unable to use it for a few days. It started nearly a week ago from a thorn or something and continued to swell; by the time I got home on Friday the back of my hand was a huge size and on Saturday was worse. A.K. lanced it with a razor for me, and we have been treating it with poultices all the time. It is much better now and I am once more able to find the knuckles in my left hand.

NOVEMBER 29: MONDAY: 1915

The past week or so has been fairly mild, with an occasional frost and several light falls of snow. I have done quite a bit of hunting lately and yesterday I succeeded in getting a big buck with five points on one side. I already have two deer skins tanned and this third one will enable me to get the buckskin shirt which I intend to have made out of them.

My job with Colquhoun is "all off" on account of a little disagreement with that gentleman.

DECEMBER 15: WEDNESDAY: 1915

The last day of hunting season! And though A.K. and I have been hunting steadily day after day we have not succeeded in getting our third deer (the law allows three deer to every one holding a license.) We have had two deer each, so have not done so very badly. The greater part of my last buck is still hanging up in the meat safes, enough to last us well past the New Year, but after that? We really cannot buy meat this winter and if you don't eat meat you have to eat something else in its place.

We laid in a supply of flour, sugar, rolled oats, canned milk, tea, etc., some time ago - sufficient for the winter. Without potatoes and Mowitch we are spending next to nothing, but when the Mowitch gives out we shall have to eat about twice as many spuds. This would not do at all so all I can say for it is to do as we did (and everybody did) in the days of old when there were no game wardens, no gun licenses, and only nominal closed seasons, namely poach! We shall have to kill a deer and cache it and then bring it down from the hills at dusk in sacks.

MacAlister has just been unfortunate enough to be fined $25 for shooting a bighorn ram; the head, which was a particularly fine one, was also confiscated. He shot it just up on the hill between his own place and Somerset's. This is the first instance of a Bighorn being seen anywhere in this district for many years except on the Sheep bluffs (where I myself once saw a Bighorn).

There have been several light falls of snow lately (it is up to your knees on the mountains) and it has been freezing for the last few days. R.N. Dundas, the game warden, has retired and joined the army. It seems that he was getting rather tired of the job, as it meant being in the saddle all day and every day. The game protection in the interior is somewhat of a farce. In this section there are only three game wardens to patrol a district nearly 200 miles long by about 40 wide (from Sicamous on the CPR south to the America line and from divide to divide east and west).

Eight or nine years ago Dundas and his family were our neighbours at Shorts' Point. He has been in the country many years and was considered one of the best hunters in the district. He was a broncobuster at one time and was also notorious as a poacher! He was certainly the right man for the Game Wardenship!

DECEMBER 29: TUESDAY 1915

Another Christmas gone! Quietly but cheerfully. I succeeded (for the first time in my life) in making two excellent plum puddings! One of these, with a piece of pork, which the Attenborough's gave us, made a very good dinner. Since the 15th there have been several feet of snow, and it is now about 6 inches deep and some two feet on the hills. There has been almost a continuous south wind but yesterday morning the North wind came galloping down the lake; last night there were 15 degrees of frost; tonight it promises to be colder. The day has been cloudless and sparkling - white and blue, the most perfect winter day possible, the dry, powdery snow has a crisp "squeak" under foot.

There were 24 degrees of frost last night - 8 degrees above zero.

1916

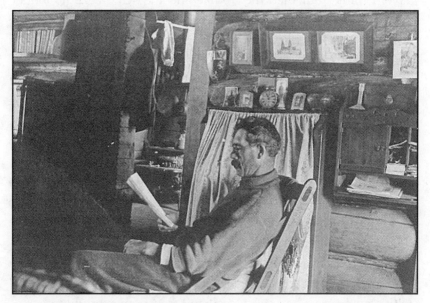

John Edward Sugars, Roger's father

WEDNESDAY JANUARY 19, 1916

The New Year brought in a severe cold snap, the longest we have had for years. From the date of my last entry to the 10th of this month the weather was cold and sharp with a north wind. Then on the morning of the 11th the temperature suddenly dropped to 11 degrees below zero; since then it has gone several degrees below zero every night and only a few degrees above in the daytime.

This particular spot seems more sheltered than nay in the district; the coldest we had was -11 degrees, whereas at Durants' it was -12 1/2 degrees, at Shorts -16 degrees, Ewings -20 degrees, Stocks' -33 degrees. and at the old tie-camp at Whiteman Creek, 39 degrees below. At Kamloops it was no less than -41 degrees. The snow is now about eighteen inches deep and probably six feet in the mountains.

Very pleasant weather except that it has frozen our water pipes up, about every other day. With great patience and perseverence we have, I think, remedied the trouble and they can feeze no longer. A.K. and I, though not plumbers, did some noble work during the last few days; in this country it is a case of "every man his own everything."

The cold snap has come to an abrupt end this afternoon and now (8 p.m.) there is a heavy Chinook rolling up Lake and the temperature has risen to 14 degrees above zero.

This morning it looked as though the cold weather might go on for eternity. The other side of the Lake was shut out with great clouds of grey frost smoke rising from the surface of the water, the sky was overcast with it, and the sun was not visible. The Lake was dead calm, and through the rising mist could be seen a long white floe of thin broken ice stretching for miles, North and South.

The hills were white - whiter than usual for the tress were white, all except the trunks, eery twig and needle was white as if with age; the mist had condensed and frozen on everything.

I am going across the Lake on Monday (D.V.) to work for Thompson. He is going to do some logging and he offered me a job (swamping) at $30a month and board. It will probably last two or three months.

Jan. 21. I have heard that towards the end of the cold snap, the Lake was frozen for two or threes miles northwards from Penticton (at the food of the Lake) and the steamer could not get beyond Summerland. The Siwash Arm at the head of the Lake was also frozen up, but the steamers never go up there.

The weather is warmer but there has been no thaw as yet. Today has been calm, with a fine snow falling almost continuously.

MONDAY FEBRUARY 14

Roger being away, I feel it is up to me, J.E.S., [father] to write up this. The zero snap ended on the 5th, but temperatures remained fairly low, about 15 degrees above, with an unusual fall of snow. There is about 2 feet on the level, pretty well packed. As the temperature rose, the lake began to freeze over more & more, until there seemed to be only a channel, well towards the other side, where the steamer went. We were now fairly cut off. The trail is in an awful state, & we have given up going regularly for our mail. A.K. went to Nahun on Saturday, & returned pretty well 'all in'. Kent came from the point the same night in much the same condition. Also on the same day, Durant tried the ice at his place, and fell through. So on Sunday afternoon, with

John Edward Sugars, Roger's father

a distinct thaw going on, we were setting in some depression, when we heard a hail from the Lake. We hurried out & saw Durant seated on a sleigh & propelling himself with two sticks with great rapidity over our bay. He was followed by Macalishen [sic] on foot. We all went down & 'sported' in various fashions on the ice, which was 2 to 3 inches thick. We were very excited, & two pairs of skates were dug up, one of which Durant took home to fix up for Lily [Mother]. Of course it thawed all last night, & has been thawing ever since, but this morning we locked up the house and all walked over the ice to Durant's.

To be more exact, I walked & A.K. drove Lily in the wood-sleigh on skates. It was one of the most enjoyable walks I have ever taken. To be walking over a flat even surface after plunging & ploughing through snow, was a positive luxury, though after a bit my ankles got quite tired. I came on a deer track running out into the lake, but did not venture on following it. The ice stalagmites from the rocks were very beautiful. As Durant's ice did not "Seam over" safe, we came back, and A.K.'s last film was blown in honour of the event. Lily & A.K. skated most of this afternoon, & I played about with much satisfaction. then a curious thing happened. There was a solitary coot on the ice about half-a-mile off. (The Coots have had a frightful time this year. They live regularly in the shallows of the lake at Penticton, & on the Siwash Arm, but were frozen out of there quite early on. There was a large flock in our bay. In the zero snap, many of them were frozen, & coyotes & bald eagles were very busy after them). Well, we saw another dark object moving near this coot, which we took at first to be a bird, but which turned out to be a coyote, after the coot, which was now rapidly nearing us. The coyote saw us, & struck right out across the lake, and passed us nearly a mile away, going towards Durant's, & stopping every now & then to have a look at us. Soon after he had got out of sight, we heard repeated rifle-shots from Durant's way, but of course do not know what happened. The Lake has not been frozen to bear at this point for 30 years. **[This is the end of J.E. Sugars' writing.]**

[Roger John Sugars takes up the narrative again.]

MONDAY MARCH. 13, 1916

I am storm-bound on the west side of the Lake, so am taking the opportunity to write up my diary. I am still working for Thompson. I usually come home on Saturday night, & return to the camp on Sunday night. I could not get over last night though, & the Lake is still rough this morning, so I fear I shall have to take the steamer from Nahun to Okanagan Centre. Two Sundays in January

Winter 1916 Okanagan Lake

& February I had to stay at the camp on account of the ice on the Lake. I went over on the 24th of January.

It was about 10 below zero that night & the steamer did not reach Nahun till long after dark. Thompson was on board with two men & all his outfit. We got off at the Centre, & by the light of a lantern we had the big bobsleigh loaded up with the stove, a few boxes of grub & our "turkeys". (Just what was required for the first day) & in about 20 minutes the team was hooked up to the bobsleigh & the mare to the cutter; Thompson & I drove ahead in the cutter with the lantern, Joe Goodreau & Billy Wilson followed with the bobsleigh. It seemed very wintry that night, with the jingling of the sleigh bells, the squeak of snow under the runners, & the icy North wind. The steaming horses were covered with frost, & their nostrils were full of ice. We reached the camp in about half an hour, (it is about 3 miles North of the Centre, on the Lake shore) A desolate place it was, a little white board shack, with half the windows broken.

We first fixed up the great sheet iron cook stove (which only just went through the door), we then shovelled out all the old beds, boots, bottles, tins, newspapers & trousers that littered the floor. Later we had a supper of fried fish, bread & butter & water (hot).

Thompson had left the box which contained the tea at the wharf! We made our beds on the floor, removed our boots & retired for the night. The next day Joe, hauled the rest of the stuff from the Centre, & Thompson & Billy & I cleaned out & generally fixed up the shack, barn & bunk shack. The latter was a miserable little hovel, leaky roof, rotten log walls, & dirt floor Thompson suggested that I should fix up my bed in the loft of the cook shack, which I gladly did, as I did not fancy the look of the bunk shack. I was cook for that day, Mrs. Thompson & Marie arrived by the afternoon boat, & by the next day, things were pretty well straightened up & we were able to get to work. For the first two weeks we worked in the woods with the temperature varying from 15 or 20 below zero to a few degrees above.

My work as swamper was varied; limbing the logs, cutting out sloop-roads, helping to load the sloop. Billy Wilson & Charlie Parker (who arrived a few days, & later than the rest of us) were sawing, Joe driving the sloop, & Thompson skidding. Towards the middle of February the snow reached a depth of some 27 inches.

On the 10th of February. the cold snap showed some signs of breaking, having continued with hardly any 'let up' since the 4th of January. The temperature rose slightly & a faint breeze from the South began to sweep the hill tops, & shake the snow from the trees.The next day the thaw was well under way. But the frost had continued long enough to freeze the Lake from end to end – two feet in thickness at Penticton, 14 inches at Summerland & 2 to 3 inches here. From Shorts' Point north & south, for a mile or two, however there was open water right through the winter., which enabled me to cross the lake in a row boat, but I was always encumbered with loose floe-ice & slush, & considerable caution was necessary to avoid being hemmed in by the ice.

The thaw made little impression on the ice for some time, & there is still some loose ice drifting about the lake. Penticton has been cut off from the steamer service for about two months.After about a   month Charlie Parker was "fired", & Joe was put in his place to saw with Billy, & Thompson & I continued with the skidding & swamping. By this time there was not enough snow for slooping, & the logs had to be skidded out of the woods, singly with Tongs or chain, & dumped in various places over the hill, to be taken to the lake later   I preferred teaming to axe work, so Thompson let me do the skidding while he swamped.

MAY 6

Nearly two months since I made an entry!

I may as well take up the story at the point where I left off: Towards the end of March the sawing was finished, the cut amounting to 200,000 feet. Joe departed & Billy was kept on as "skinner".

The next move was to make a couple of roads through the woods up to the two main dumps: (each nearly half a mile from the Lake) The "dollies" were then overhauled & greased, & Thompson & Billy began hauling averaging six loads apiece per day

The "dolly" is a two wheeled truck, with a long Tongue & a heavy "bunk" between the two wheels.

The logs are loaded on to this bunk by means of a skid on the wheel, & some hard lifting with canthooks; They are allowed to project forward over the bunk (to which they are chained) nearly to the horses tails, the backs ends drag on the ground. The dolly is designed expressly for logging on steep hills, the dragging ends of the logs acting as a brake. On level ground a four wheeled truck is used. Of course it is always prepared to haul when the snow is on the ground, with sloops or sleighs.

One to eight or more logs can be loaded on a dolly, according to their size: a good load contains 700 to 900 feet: The largest load we brought down was one I hauled myself, two logs, each scaling 457 feet. While Thompson & Billy were dollying I was kept on to help load, & roll the logs at the skidways on the beach, & had not a great deal to do. When there were still about 80 000 feet up at the dump, Billy Wilson announced that he was going to quit, on account of his wife being sick he said (I guess he was tired). Billy is a quarterbreed & his wife a Siwash. This left me the sole survivor. Thompson & I had to do what was practically three men's work; it kept us clipping from half past six in the morning till eight at night, to get down enough logs to make the thing pay.

We each drove a dolly, & got down about 4 or 5 loads a day apiece. After supper we rolled the days haul out on the skidways (which by this time were from 10 to 20 feet high & stretching from the waters edge, some 50 yards up the beach – We made 3 skidways altogether). When the logs were scaled & rolled, there was always something that needed doing; The dolly-axles to be greased cant hooks to be filed, a chain to mend, or harness to be repaired. The last chore was the barn, the horses to be fed & cleaned, & the manure thrown out. Thence wearily to bed. Of course I was working over time, but I did not mind, because Thompson was doing it himself, & he had been very decent to me. He was only getting $5. a thousand for the logs & at the end of it he cleared $7!

As he said it was better than doing nothing, for he had paid the winters expenses for himself family & horses. A finer logging team than Thompson's it would be hard to find – George & Dan, two splendid horses that know their work by heart. I got very fond of the pair when I was dollying. To stand atop a load of logs & drive that team down the winding, humpy road to the landing at the lake, was the most enjoyable work I have ever experienced.

A somewhat amusing incident occurred one day in February. It was a Sunday, & as the Lake was frozen over, it was impossible for me to go home, so Charlie Parker & I decided to walk down to the Centre on the ice. Charlie, like all half breeds gloried in his Sunday clothes, so after dinner he put on his best brown suit, his high-heeled riding boots & big Cowboy hat, & we set off over the ice & made the Centre in an hour. The ice bore with perfect safety. We bought some tobacco & a few things at the one-horse little store, called for the mail, & started back for the camp. It had thawed a little, & the ice was a trifle soft in places, but still seemed safe enough, When within half a mile of the camp, the ice suddenly gave, without the least warning, we were about 20 yards from shore, and both went in to together, side by side! I don't know how deep it was, probably 20 or 30 feet. I do know, it was the coldest water I ever went into in my life!

If the ice had continued to break when we tried to climb out, I should not care to say what would have happened to us, but as it was the ice around the hole was strong enough to bear us, & we got out without much difficulty, wet only to the waist ; I was wearing a pair of heavy shoe-packs, & short mackinaw trousers, & my legs weighed about 50 lbs. each. Charlie's long boots contained several quarts of the icy water. We ran to the camp, had supper, & then changed our sodden clothes; Charlie hung up his boots behind the heater in the bunk shack to dry. Charlie was highly amused at the affair. "Gee, dat was kinder funny eh: I thought I'd die laughin'; say pal, you give a awful whoop when you fell t'rough!" But Joe Goodreau, the little French Canadian, met us with a serious face "So you was fall t'rough eh: Goddam, she was foolish ting to walk on dem ice, Jes' Chris'! you fellers is lucky you aint was drown, yes sir, dem ice she aint was to be trus' (Joe Goodreau, "she was raise tirty mile from Montreal, & she was lumberjack more dan it ees 40 year," "Yes sir, I was drive de river twenty- t'ree spreeng, in Meechigan. Meechigan, she's fine contree; 'O by God! she's fine contree all t'rough dat contree!) The next evening Charlie found the leg of one

Sugars' house and A.K. 1917

of his $8. riding boots all shriveled up with the heat from the box stove! Strange to say, neither Joe nor Charlie could read or write, Charlie is but 19 but Joe is a man of over 50.

I wrote one or two letters for Charlie, & he marveled at my skill! [*This bright youth has since got two years for desertion from the army.*] Billy Wilson was more intellectual, he could both read & write & "figure" a little. He was born at Whiteman's Creek, & has been in this region all his life: by all appearance he is a white man, but has some of the unmistakable traits of the breed.

He was interesting to talk to, he could tell you many things about the country: old Indian names of places mountains, & creeks; Indian methods of 'jerking' venison, tanning buckskin, & preserving huckleberries & olallies. He told me that the original name of Terrace Mountain did not arise from the terrace like formation of the summit, but from the name of a squaw – Thérèse, who happened to go up the mountain with some hunters. This squaw died but a year or two ago. Terrace Mountain is still known among the Indians by its original name of Sheep Mountain. What we call Sheep Mnt., or the Sheep Bluffs, no doubt had another name with the Indians. The old Indian names were always the most suitable & it is ridiculous the way Englishmen come & rename places to their own fancy. Whiteman's Creek was Birch Creek; Siwash Cr. was Cedar Creek; Coyote or Irish Creek was Kettle Creek, on account of a kettle-like basin of rock through which it flows at one point Otcarten or Shorts" Point has been renamed "Fintry", by Dun-Waters, after some place in Scotland, doubtless a good enough name in its place, but quite meaningless here. Captain Shorts' was the first man to "squat" on the Point. Many years ago at this spot the Sushwap braves came down, & seized some escaped Okanagan Squaws, whom they had captured in a previous battle on the Point. Hence the name "Otcarten", which means "the place where they caught them."

A.K. came over for the last week to help Thompson & I to clean up the logs. We finished up on Saturday the 29th of April – three months & five days since we started in. I drew a cheque for $84.40

& came home. Thompson is hoping to put in about two million feet at Bear Creek next winter, so I may get work with him again. Jones, the Kelowna millman has limits at Bear Creek, with timber on them, estimated at 20 million feet.

Wednesday: May 10

Last week we thought summer had come, the days were hot & sunny: the trees were in full leaf, saskatoon blossom & sunflowers nearly over. This week there has been a setback, cold nights, & cool days; twice, lately the thermometer has dropped within three degrees of the freezing point. This morning a North wind came down the Lake & it started to snow; wet snow, of course, that melted as soon as it touched the ground, but nevertheless snow! & on the 18th of May! when the clouds lifted about ten o'clock the mountains were white within a few hundred feet of the lake. It melted off within half an hour though.

Three more are now in the list of killed, from this district, Bob Somerset, & Frank Vaughan. The last was awarded the V.C. after his death. How many more is this war going to take!

Saturday June 10

Another month gone, & now we are well into summer; a cool, late, spring it has been, & very dry. I took a plunge in the Lake last Sunday, but as the snow-water is still coming down the creeks, it was very cold.

Having had six weeks 'loafing', I am now at work again; in fact all three of us. Godwin has unexpectedly taken us on again, for the summers ranch work – thinning apples, haying & picking, three or four months work. "It never rains but it pours"; no sooner had we promised to work at the Point, than I heard that Thompson wanted me to go logging for him again – 100,000 up on the Commonage, across the Lake; however I had to stick to Shorts", as it was the longer job.

It is hard to describe the degrading influence, which thinning & picking fruit has on one. The first two hours this morning I was in a desperate & rebellious condition, instead of delicately snipping with precision & care, I felt more inclined to tear off the measly little apples, or to take an axe and cut the trees to bits. This passed off, & I fell into a black depression, myriads on myriads of superfluous little apples awaited my snippers on all sides, everything seemed hopeless, evil thoughts filled my mind, & I muttered profanity against all manner of fruit & fruit-growers. Could any wages be adequate compensation for such misery? After some weeks, dinner time arrived, & my stomach was like a vacuum. The afternoon was better. This dislike of orchard work is not laziness, in me, it is the awful monotony. I longed to get hold of a shovel, axe, saw, canthook or something & <u>work</u>.

TUESDAY AUGUST 8

Another two months gone: the thinning is finished, the second crop of hay is in the barns; this with the first crop amounts to something over a hundred tons. We have now begun picking the earlier fruits, cherries, plums etc. Ranch work is uninteresting & monotonous, but not too bad once you get settled down to it. For the first three weeks in June there was no rain at all, & some very hot days, the temperature rising to 90° or over, & as high as 104° in Vernon. Most of July was cool & inclined to be wet.

So far this month we are having two or three clear, hot days, followed by a storm. There have been several heavy thunderstorms this summer. One day in July a tall pine-tree was struck, not far from us, at Shorts' (we were sheltering in the root cellar) & it continued to burn for some hours.

THURSDAY AUGUST 17

Among several books (apart from novels) I have read in the last year or so, three have impressed themselves on me particularly. The first is Henry George's "Progress & Poverty" a very logical reconstruction of Political Economy, showing that, unless some step towards Socialism is taken, a decline in progress & civilisation is likely, if not certain to follow the present conditions. The other two are Sir Oliver Lodge's "Man & the Universe" & "Life & Matter". The first is a defence of Christianity on a scientific basis & the second is an attack on Haeckel's [Hegel's?] hard, materialistic views. The result is that I am an Optimist & a Socialist (of course one could not be a Socialist without being something of an Optimist) By Optimist, I do not mean that if anything goes wrong, or I hurt myself.

I at once say it was the best thing that could have happened! Yet I cannot help feeling that, though life is a pretty "tough proposition" it is not without purpose.

I believe that everything is moving on some definite system & is rising towards perfection. Nor do I think this Earthly life is the end of things for us; I believe that we shall move on with the universe to all eternity. But at the same time I do not think that this earthly existence is stagnant, I think that there is earthly, everyday progress as much as any other. I believe that Socialism is a step towards perfection, & I believe that Socialism will come, in spite of everything the pessimists have to say!

It seems very strange to me, that the average, respectable person is often a frightful pessimist (though he would be deeply offended if you told him so) Orthodox Christians, who think that a Church is the most essential thing to a community (though they seem to spend most of their time quarreling with the clergy) will tell you that God is merciful & all-powerful, & at the same time will banish all hope from earthly existence, by assuring you that human nature will never improve, that there will always be misery & sin, that wars, such as the present one will undoubtedly occur from time to time forever more. They laugh to scorn the very idea of Socialism, "Ridiculous idealism" they call it, but if you were to call the Gospel "ridiculous - idealism" they would be intensely shocked, & yet it is said the Gospel is the purest Socialism!

Some of our neighbours belong to this type. Durant & his wife (she is now in England after a two months visit) Mrs & Miss Somerset, old FitzGerald & his wife, at the Point. All these people had received what is called a good education, but they seem to be under the impression that everything they learned at school is all there is to be learned. They all have many good points. They have quite a lot of everyday knowledge, but beyond this they wilfully blind themselves. The result is, ordinary, pleasant people, whom you may mistake for good friends, until you discover this shallowness & their narrow mindedness with regard to philosophy, & all religious & social questions.

Snobbery seems to nearly always accompany these narrow ideas.

J.D. Godwin, our boss at Shorts", is a man who has been in many parts of the world, & has read considerably, the result is a man, with a broad mind, interested in many subjects, & always eager after new ideas.

Most of the people at Ewings are broad minded & willing to learn, & the result again is that you have beings who are unaffected, genuine, & free from snobbery.

The most broad-minded man I have ever known is my own father free from all prejudice & snobbery, he recognises the fact that there are two sides to every argument.

I don't quite understand why I have written all this, excepting that the thing worried me; I have reached the age when the peculiarities of human nature are beginning to dawn on me.

FRIDAY SEPTEMBER 15

The summer has gone: for the past month fine clear days have been in the majority. At present we are having the best weather that September can offer, cool nights, crisp fresh mornings with a stiff north breeze & warm cloudless days.

There is a certain sharpness in the air which one cannot mistake, it means that the summer has gone.

Something like half the fruit is off amounting to about 10 carloads (a carload is the amount a railway car will hold – 500 to 600 boxes of apples)

On the 27th of August I borrowed a couple of saddle horses from Godwin & took Mother for a ride up the creek as far as Jackpine Point. It was a beautiful day & we enjoyed ourselves immensely. It was the first ride we have had together for many years.

Early in July, George Smith got together a gang & came down to work on the road at the point where it was left off last year. It is now finished & open right through, but owing to shortage of funds is a very rough job for the last mile to Nahun.

Smith asked us to go & work for him, but we were already working at Shorts" so we declined the offer.

On the 26th August at about half past eight in the evening there was a beautiful display of Aurora Borealis.

SUNDAY OCTOBER 8

Every day becomes sharper & cooler, the leaves are rapidly becoming richer & more varied in their colours, every night for the last ten, there has been a touch of frost, the near mountain tops were dusted with snow a few mornings ago; that season which is the most sublime of all seasons is now advancing – the bright, mellow, fresh melancholy fall.

A.K. & I have hunted nearly every Sunday since the season opened but we have seen no deer. There is plenty of bear sign in the hills & there are said to be cougar about. This morning I shot a Coyote, about 4 miles away to the north-west, I skinned him on the spot & carried the hide home, tied up in a bundle: I intend to dress it, to make a rug: Speaking of dressing skins – the three deerskins which I tanned last fall I made up into a shirt this spring. I am rather proud of this garment: it is cut on the line of an old flannel shirt, & sewn with a buckskin needle & linen thread, it is laced up at the neck & cuffs & is made short to be worn outside the trousers like a sweater. I think it should prove useful in zero weather.

A couple of weeks ago I gave up picking fruit, & took a step up to box making.

This is piece-work; for apple boxes I get one cent; & for "Economy" apple-crates 1-1/4 cents

I can now make $3.00 to $3.35 a day with boxes & a little less with crates.

An apple-box is about 10 x 12 x 18 inches in size & consists of 5 pieces & 24 nails. It is the simplest possible thing to make, but in order to turn out 33 an hour one has to 'go some', skilled boxmakers can make over 400 a day. It is rather pleasant work, & the time simply flies. The faster you work the faster the time goes.

SUNDAY NOVEMBER 19

We finished work at Shorts" on Sat-11-Nov. having put in exactly 5 months work.

On Sat. 4. the last of the apples were shipped the entire crop amounting to 34 cars – something over 400 tons. Up to the day of the last shipment, I was packing & boxmaking. Towards the end of the job I was able to turn out 45 boxes per hour but I never made more than $4.00 in a day owing to the failing daylight.

I was quite green at packing, & I couldn't make more than $1.75 a day, while the regular packers were making 3 dollars & over. Great care has to be taken in packing a box of apples; in putting up a No. 1 packing, your apples have to be well-coloured a quite free of blemishes. Each apple has to be wrapped in paper (there is considerable skill in wrapping an apple properly - & quickly) & packed " 2-3 width: 7-8 length; 2-3: 5-5 2-2: 4-4 etc., according to size; the top layer of apples must project above the top of the box about an inch to 2-1/2 inches. The box contains from 72 to 225 apples. For packing a box, you are paid 5 cents The boss packer hails up the boxes & stamps on the outside of them, the name of the apple, the grade, number of apples contained, & place where packed.

The boss packer for this season at Shorts" was Jim Muirhead, a smart young Canadian who has had two seasons experience in the Vernon Fruit Union packing houses. He was drawing a salary of $100 a month; & extra pay for overtime. Packing is paid as skilled labour & it is becoming quite a profession in this country.

There are undoubtedly good openings in it, & it is a thing which any quick fingered person can learn. I intend to take it up each season, & learn all I can It is not a thing I should care to go in for entirely but it is well worth knowing, for, other things failing, one can always go out in the fruit season & earn good wages at packing . . . . . .

Last week was very cold, there being 10 or 12 degrees of frost each night – 18 degrees one night -. It is warmer & suggests snow, but it has been dry all the fall & the snow seems reluctant in coming. There is very little snow in the hills & the deer are not down yet; seldom has it been so hard to find deer as this year; A.K. shot a stray one some days ago, but I have been unable to see one much less shoot one.

Thompson's logging contract at Bear Creek has fallen through, but he is going to log the Jones limit over here, this winter.

He came over with his wife, daughter, horses outfit & one man, on Friday & is camped at Batchelor's. I am going to work for him about the 1st of December.

The limit he is going to cut, is to the west, adjoining our place & Batchelor's. It is 640 acres & stretches a mile west of our back line (& Batchelor's) that is a mile & a half from the lake. The timber on it is estimated at three million feet. It takes in the greater part of that beautiful deer park, which we call the "firstbench". When this section had been logged there will, practically, be no saw timber left in this region, except a few millions on the Shorts" Point range & back of it. In most places around here the good saw timber is limited to the first benches within a few miles of the lake, back of that it merges into the dense upland forest of smaller growth, usually termed "brush" or scrub.

TUESDAY DECEMBER 26

Since the 4th of this month, Deana & I have been cutting saw-logs for Thompson. He is cutting everything that is left on Bachelor's before he touches the Jones limit, so we are working within a quarter to half a mile of home.

He is giving us a dollar a thousand, & we are cutting from three & a half to 5 & a half thousand feet a day, which is not so bad considering that we only work about seven hours - owing to lack of daylight. We take a lunch & boil tea at noon. The saw usually needs filing every day; this I do at midday – after dinner. After the first few days (which are very hard on the back) sawing is very pleasant work especially when you are on comparatively level ground, among long, clean pine timber, running four or five logs & scaling a thousand feet or so, to the tree. Fir is usually hard sawing & inclined to be limby.

The dollar per thousand pays for, felling & cutting into 12, 14, 16, & 18 foot logs, only.

We have to do no limbing beyond what is necessary to make the cuts on the tree trunk. A sawyer's outfit is not merely a saw; he has to pack around a paraphernalia consisting of, cross cut saw, axe, sledge-hammer, saw-cut wedge, a measuring rod, & a bottle of coal-oil! In addition to these he has to have a filing stand, & filing & setting tools (which are, fortunately, not bulky) in some place, convenient for use every day . . . .

There have been several falls of snow this month, amounting to about 8 inches. The prevailing wind is from the north, & there have been no thaws. The last day or two it has become colder, the north wind has increased in strength, & is coming down the valley with a sort of quiet roar.

In the evenings the sky is pink fading into cold steel blue, to the east & north; the snow facing the west is rose tinted, that in shadow facing east is bluish: it has a crisp "squeak" & is as dry as dust. It feels as if a cold snap was approaching; in fact, at this moment the temperature is only 6 or 7 degrees above zero, I think the thermometer will touch zero degrees before the night is out.

We are going to work again tomorrow, having been off since Saturday for Christmas. We gave each other useful presents, & "did" ourselves pretty well on the whole; we had an excellent dinner-turkey, plum pudding etc. also the usual Hudson Bay Rum, "Native" Port & various sweetmeats. All over for another year! What will it be like next year?

Where will we all be? Here, I guess, if we're not killed at the war first. Will the war be over this time next year? Oh hell, what's the use of asking fool questions? 'Sufficient unto the day' –

Mother & Deana presented me with a briar pipe & a beautiful pair of seven dollar stream-drivers shoe-packs (a pack with a heavy sole & high tops, specially made for log- driving on the rivers, but equally good for any kind of hard wear. I have rather a passion for footwear, particularly shoe packs; I have closely studied the question of suitable footwear for this country. I have worn (& worn out!) many kinds of shoes, high boots & low boots cheap boots & dear boots, rubbers, shoe packs & moccasins, & have come to the conclusion that for summer, the most comfortable footwear (but perhaps not the most economical) is a high laced boot, not too heavy, with the soles well studded with nails or caulks; for such boots you pay from 5 to 10 dollars a pair! They will not, usually, last more than 6 or 8 months. For winter & spring I think there is nothing better than a good quality of oil- tanned shoepack; they are from ankle-high to knee high, & can be had with just the plain moccasin sole, or with another light flexible sole, nailed or sewn on; or with a full heavy sole & heel like a boot.

They are light & comfortable, wear like iron, & are wonderfully waterproof if they are well greased. They are, evidently, an evolution of the moccasins of the woods Indians, but almost exactly like the Scandinavian winter boot. For zero-weather there is nothing to beat a pair of buckskin moccasins. I wore them all through the very cold weather last winter, & never suffered from cold feet.

1917

Picnicking with friends 1917
Roger and J.E. Sugars next to wagon

SUNDAY JANUARY 14, 1917

The Christmas cold snap only lasted a few days & was followed by about ten days of Chinook & thaw, wet snow & a little rain & sunshine. The last few days have been cold, & at night the mercury is only a few degrees above zero.

On the 5th, Thompson took us off the sawing for a while, & since then I have been working by the day (Deana has been at home with a cold), swamping, road making & sloop loading. Nearly all the logs are slooped to the Lake bank now, & we shall resume cutting tomorrow. The cut amounts to about 200,000 so far, half of which, Deana & I reckon to have cut (the scale is not complete yet.) Not a bad cut for us, I think; 100,000 in about 20 days. Thompson's crew is now reduced (2 men quit at different times in the last month) to 4 men; Laurie Morrison, "Skinner" Walter Rogers, hookman & swamper, & Deana & myself; Thompson himself drives the second team. He is expecting another pair of sawyers shortly . . . Wages are away up this year, of course – three to four dollars a day in the lumber camps, living is more or less in proportion; flour has risen from $1.75 or less to $2.75 & $3.00, the price of sugar is almost doubled, wool & leather goods have risen considerably, in fact almost everything has gone up from 5¢ to 50¢ on the dollar. However, there seems to be no shortage of food whatever, & we are evidently much better off than they are in England.

SUNDAY FEBRUARY 4

We are having a winter of constant change in the weather; I mentioned in my last entry that the temperature was down near zero; that did not last long, & was followed by a mild spell, then last Monday night there was a heavy sudden fall of dry snow followed by a three days cold snap when the temperature seldom rose above a few degrees from zero, & dropped to 10 & 15 below at nights, (it reached 20° in Vernon) There were four miles of ice at Penticton, & the lake started to freeze up here. It snowed gently but continuously on Thursday & Friday , & on Saturday the Chinook came. The wind dropped today, but it is still quite mild - thawing slightly - the Chinook comes like a warm breath from the south, & sometimes turns the snow soft & wet, within 5 minutes of its arrival.

Our entire household have been hit with influenza; Deana & I had to to quit work for nearly two weeks. We are all better now & I have been back at work for the last ten days (swamping & loading – by the day -)

Thompson has got another man now – Bill McQueen, who is sawing with Walter Rogers. Deana & I will return to our sawing as soon as another swamper can be secured.

SUNDAY MARCH 4

We have just had two weeks of steady cold weather. The first few days of the cold snap were accompanied by a fall of dry snow amounting to about 6 inches, & a bitter north wind. The second week was bright & sunny & the wind was not quite so strong; the lake started to freeze & there was much loose ice floating down on the North wind. Each night there was from 12 to 32 degrees of frost, & in the morning the lake would be skimmed right over with thin ice, which started to crack & tinkle as soon as the sun rose & the wind stirred.

Deana & I have been sawing again for some weeks we are clearing up the trees along the bank at the North end of Bachelor's. The trees are small (8 or 10 logs to the thousand) & the ground is a fright; side hill, rock & brush, so we are cutting far less than we did among the bigger timber up on the bench.

The Chinook came up the valley yesterday & spring seems to have begun.

TUESDAY MARCH 28

It is a very stormy & backward spring. Nearly the whole of the month it has been windy, with snow storms, & sleet, frosts nearly every night, & sunshine between the storms. A good deal of the original snow of winter is still lying in the unexposed places, & a short distance up the hill it reaches a depth of two feet. The ground is still full of frost, & becomes very muddy in the daytime. Of course there is no sign of young green grass or any other early plants. Even the celandines have not appeared. A few chipmunks are out, & the robins are back.

Deana & I finished cutting on Saturday week (17th Mar.) having cut about 85,000 (in addition to the 100,000 we cut in the winter) Deana is at home now, & I am working by the day swamping, twitching out logs with tongs & single horse (little Matilda) decking etc.

The cut on Bachelor's is now finished (nearly six hundred thousand). There are a few more logs to be dumped over & decked on the beach; & a short chute to be built up to the main log piles. After that, Jones will bring up his boom sticks, & the big skidways will be broken out & the logs put down the chute into the water.

SUNDAY APRIL: 15

The spring is slowly advancing; the weather for the most part is quiet & fine, grass & early plants are beginning to grow. The snow is gradually retreating farther back into the hills. Crows, robins, chipmunks, ground hogs butterflies etc. are plentiful: the fish hawks are back, geese are coming north, & the mosquitoes are out. Though there was a fall of wet snow a day or two ago, I think that winter is nearly about over.

The chute was finished about a week ago & the first boom is now filled with logs (200000 feet), the tug-boat is coming for it on Monday. The chute is about 200 yards long & very steep. It is practically dead straight, & narrow, the two parallel sides logs being about a foot thick, with an eight or ten inch space between them, this space is filled with a slim fir pole; on each side, on top of the side-logs a "sheer"-pole is bolted to keep the logs from jumping the chute. Joints occur every 30 feet the logs being notched flush, & spiked with 18 inch drift bolts. The sills or ties are every 15 feet, It is braced & reinforced at each tie. During the first few days, logs frequently jumped the chute, doing considerable damage to the lower length's of the chute. Thompson did much swearing, but patiently mended the break each time with additional precautions to keep the logs in the chute. A big log well under way in a chute is a fearsome thing, it travels with the speed of an express train, & when it strikes the water it sends up a shower of spray 25 feet high, if it happens to leave the chute it leaps end over end, tearing the ground at each stride. Anything in its way is smashed or displaced. Latterly the chute has been working well, & we have been putting down forty thousand a day without a hitch.

The head of the chute has to be greased for a length or two & each log is started with a horse. Thompson starts the logs with George, while Lorie with Dan, snugs them in beside the chute. Walter & myself roll the logs & break out the skidways "Taking a tumble" out of a big skidway is good fun. The skidways all stand side by side with a narrow passage-way between each, some of them are perhaps 30 yards long & 16 or 17 feet high Two men tackle the face of the pile each with a canthook or peavey – one man on each side – They select what they think is the key log - sometimes it is not the key & it is only followed by one or two logs while the rest of the skidway remains solid - & pry & jerk at it, till it trembles, then "look out for yourself she's goin" & a final pry with the hook, followed by a jump to one side, the whole face of the pile totters, a cascade of logs & perhaps half the skidway rumbles down

Walter is a sawyer & hook-man, he is one of those tireless, rapid sawyers, with a featherweight touch which is never hard on the man at the other end of the saw: with a cant hook he is skillful & quick. Walter with his caulk-boots stagged trousers, & little round black hat, is only a "rough" lumberjack, but a more decent fellow it would be hard to find; a man of few words, full of quiet humour & good nature

FRIDAY MAY 11

Spring has at last got well under way. All the leaves are out, sunflowers & saskatoon are flowering; all life is busy & moving.

The warm bright days of late spring are here though the nights are unusually cool; on May 5th when the sun rose in a cloudless sky its light glittered on a lake that was covered with a film of ice. Spring has hardly started on the big mountains, for the creeks, as yet, are but half full.

The last of the logs were put on the beach on the 28th April, but Jones did not come to collect the last boom till Monday (7th My). The main bulk of the logs went down the chute, but 60,000 or so were scattered along the beach in small skidways. This last bunch we put in on Monday:- Thompson & I (Lorrie was away) & two of Jones' men – Norman Day & Charles Somebody: old Dave Jones stood on the deck of his tug calling directions. To roll the logs until they were afloat it was a case of wading in the icy water to the knees Nobody grumbled at that, though, & I think we quite enjoyed ourselves that day. Charlie is a "jack boot" man, & can walk the bobbing rolling logs as if he were on solid land, he spent most of his time with a pike-pole out on the following timbers, packing the logs into the bight of the boom, as they were rolled in, & poling the boom sticks ahead, along the shore as each skidway was rolled in.

He poled along the end of the boom next to the shore, while the tug towed the outer end, the logs floating in the semicircle of boom sticks thus formed. On Tuesday when all the logs were collected the boom was closed, & lines fastened across it & tightened, to draw it into an oblong shape for towing.

By noon the last of the winters cut was moving slowly down the Lake in the wake of the tug boat, the distant figure of Charlie still on the boom with his pike-pole, inspecting the boom- chains to see that they were all plugged tight.

That day I drew a cheque for $271, the great part of Deana's & my own wages for the winter's work. The job is over.

Thompson will now start logging the Jones limit with a small crew, - namely, himself, Lorrie Morrison, Deana & myself (Poor old Bill McQueen went to town, got drunk & joined the Foresters over a month ago, & Walter Rogers left about 3 weeks ago but will probably come back to work for Thompson in the fall).

The old Jones limit which was cruised at three million has run out, but they have now secured a new strip of timberland, estimated at six hundred thousand; it is a mile long, north & south & a quarter of a mile wide, east & west, & adjoins Bachelor's on the west, so the timber will come out by the same roads as the last.

The country is almost drained of able-bodied men. I am very fond of Thompson & I hate to have to leave him in the lurch. I hate having to leave my beloved woods & the prospect of military discipline and all that sort of thing, but I am looking forward to seeing a bit of the world, & my friends & relations in England.

_1919_

SALMON ARM. BRITISH COLUMBIA.
SUNDAY AUGUST 31, 1919

Going on the third year since I wrote anything in this diary! I returned to Canada in good shape over four months ago. I might as well continue the story from where I left off on May 26, 1917 & write down the history of my army life (this to be done in my spare time, which isn't much these days.)

Well on June 4th '17, I proceeded to Kelowna in all my old lumberjack clothes, expecting to get fitted out with a uniform at the

Headquarters of the "Kelowna Forestry draft". On arrival Capt. Rose introduced me to the "barracks" – a small house rented for the purpose - & the "draft" which consisted of three men, all in their civilian clothes! After 3 or 4 days 100 uniforms & kits arrived from Vancouver Great excitement "dressing up" though we all felt like damned fools the first time we walked out in our uniforms.

My calves ached with the tightly wound puttees which I didn't know how to put on & my neck was choked & chafed with the high stand up collar of the Canadian tunic. Much time was spent in dressing each other, for several days until we got better knowledge of the strange garments.

We did practically nothing in Kelowna. A few more men were recruited, & at the time we left I believe the draft numbered ten! – About 1600 men had already been picked up around Kelowna – At first we had our meals down at the Hotel; then a cook - Jack Stewart, enlisted, & then believe me, didn't we feed, the best in all my army experience.

The movies were our chief amusement (I never having seen them before!)

After a week we all got recruiting leave - I went home for a week, & never bothered my head about the recruits. That week was the last time I was down on the West side.

Easy days! Capt. Rose was a genial, sleepy sort of bone head, & didn't give us much trouble.

3 or 4 days later the remainder of the uniforms (about 90) were repacked & sent back to Vancouver. The draft followed them. The trip to Vancouver. This was really the start of my visit to the outside world. We left Vernon by the 4 p.m. train & reached Vancouver about noon the next day. A fine journey for scenery, particularly down the splendid canyon of the Fraser. We had dinner at a "White Lunch" cafeteria, & then went up to Hastings Park in a Street car. Hastings Park is about 3 miles out of the city. All the big exposition buildings had been converted into barracks, & several hundred men were quartered in them, including, 11th Irish, 72nd Highlanders, Forestry, & Railway Construction. Things were a

little more military now, fatigues, guards, bugles, passes drill, & physical jerks & other atrocities. Our little bunch was put into No. 3 Coy Forestry draft which included Major Haddock's draft from Merrit B.C. & men from all parts of the Pacific Coast, from San Diego, Cal, to Alaska.

We were quarantined for the first 10 days on account of a suspected case of scarlet fever, somewhere. After that we could leave camp every day after 4 p.m. & after 1 p.m. on Saturdays & about 10 a.m. on Sundays. As in all military camps we were supposed to be in by 9.30 unless we had a midnight pass. Along the Street in front of the camp was a long high fence of white palings. It was an amusing sight during the quarantine to see the solid row of Khaki on top of the fence, & almost as solid a row of frocks outside: right up till lights out. I was 3 weeks in Vancouver altogether, one week of which I spent in hospital with bronchitis. Mother & Deana came down & spent the last week with me, & we certainly had a very pleasant time, theatre or movies nearly every night, much eating in "White Lunches" & Ice Cream parlours, many street car & jitney rides (anywhere in the city limits for a nickel) afternoons at Stanley Park or English Bay.

Vancouver has the reputation of eternal wet weather, but while I was there the sun shone every day but one.

It is a fine, clean, up to date Western town; beautifully situated on Burrard Inlet, with the big snow topped mountains on either side. Stanley Park is a large section of the primeval forest which has been reserved Here you can see some fine specimens of the Giant Douglas firs & cedars of the Coast. There is a fine asphalt auto drive clear round the fringe of the Park & many walks & roads through the heart of it. At the near side of the Park is a sort of zoo of various B.C. animals, including some wood buffalo. Here also, are the tea rooms ice cream parlours, bandstands & lawns of the conventional park.

The whole of Vancouver seems to flock out to the Park on Sundays.

So much for Vancouver, where I had a good time.

Mother & Deana left the night before we did & waited for the troop train at Sicamous We entrained at Hastings siding, amid much fervent cheering & good bying. The troop train pulled out for the east at 11 a.m. July 29. We got into Sicamous about 12 that night, the train stopped about 3 minutes Mother & Deana met me on the platform, & said goodbye. That was the last time I saw them until my return on April 11th of this year.

Five days later we detrained at Ottawa. The train journey across the continent was most enjoyable to me. I slept well & ate well & only for the cinders in my hair, I was happy! All the western towns turned out to see the troop train, & wish us luck.

As we got towards French Canada, this feeling was not so strong.

The C.P.R. mainline passes, I think, through the most barren parts of Canada.

Three days of bald headed prairie after we had passed out of the grand old Rockies. A thousand miles of plains dotted with dreary, boring homesteads & a little prairie town every 70 or 80 miles. There are about five cities on the mainline in the prairies, Calgary, Medicine Hat, Moosejaw, Regina, Winnipeg. The rest with names like Indian Head, Pilot Butte, Grand Coulée, are just "one-horse" burgs.

After the bald prairie comes the desolation of N.W. Ontario. From Fort William to Sudbury (The North shore of Superior, country) A howling wilderness of scrub pine & spruce & rocks, picturesque; but hard & cruel.

At Mattawa you strike the valley of the Ottawa & begin to see some sign of civilisation in the shape of logging operations along the banks of the river. The log drive on the Ottawa is almost world famous I suppose.

Old Bob Carswell (the mill owner from Vernon who joined the Kelowna draft) told me many of his reminiscences while we were passing down the Ottawa, & later when we passed through his home town – Renfrew, Ont.

We detrained at Ottawa, the Capital of Canada in the evening,

July 16 & were at once taken out to Rockliffe camp, in motor lorries.

We stayed at Rockliffe under canvas for 3 weeks, having the usual squad & company drill, physical jerks, rifle drill & much route marching. The regulations of the camp were practically the same as at Vancouver except that we now had to wear belts! The food was still good, & sufficient. Rockliffe was about 3 miles out of Ottawa but there was a street car service right to the camp.

The town of Ottawa is picturesque & finely situated on the banks of the River. It is probably of more interest than Vancouver on account of its age, but it is dirtier, slower & altogether behind Vancouver – more like an old world town. Ottawa was "dry" while Hull – directly opposite, across the River, was "wet" hence, much lawlessness.

The population of both towns is mainly French Canadian, who were sometimes openly hostile to anyone in khaki. I used to go to town nearly every evening, get a good supper go to the movies or theatre, or merely walk around. On Saturday afternoons or Sundays I usually took a tram out to Brittania Bay - a sort of pleasure ground, with 2 long piers running out into the River. Boating swimming & Ice Cream Sundaes were the chief attractions at Brittania. The swimming was poor but better than none – you could hire a wet bathing suit for 10 cents. The Sundaes – well, they were the best I ever tasted!

The girls of Ottawa did not run nearly such a high percentage of good looks as those of Vancouver.

Rockliffe Camp was in two parts, one side being the Forestry Depot, the other, Signal Corps. - only a few hundred men in each.

Capt. Laidlaw's Company which left Vancouver a week before us, was the entire strength of the Forestry Depot when we got there.

There were now two companies, ours, under Major Haddock being No 1 Coy, & Laidlaws No 2 Company; with Major Tidy as Camp O.C.

By the time we left Ottawa both companies were considerably augmented by recruits from the Ottawa district. I was now beginning to feel quite an old soldier, & was eager to get to England

& go on shore leave, which they told us we would get as soon as we landed.

None of us expected to be foresters very long; in fact we were told that we should be turned into infantry as soon as we got overseas. By this time I had fallen in, (as men in camps always do) with a set or clique of my own. We always got the same tent hut or stateroom up until the time we were split up into companies for France. We consisted of: Bob Carswell, of Vernon, Deana Chastelain of San Diego, Dick Best of Enderby, Ed, Hewlett of Westbank, "Mac" MacLachlan of Okanagan Centre & Marsack of Salmon Arm, & Little Willy *[Roger Sugars]* himself.

About ten days or more of the time we were in Ottawa we suffered the worst heat I ever struck. 100 degrees in the shade & no coolness anywhere: lying flat on your back in the shade, doing absolutely nothing, you would be drenched with sweat. Hot, humid nights too: oh it was a corker! The heat of the Western country is nearly always dry & light, with cool nights, but this Ottawa heat, it was just like a hot, wet blanket.

On the 7th of August 1917 we marched down to Ottawa with our full equipment, & entrained for Halifax.

The train travelled steadily & took the northern route, instead of going through the state of Maine. We were now on the Canadian Govt. Railway instead of the C.P.R. We kept to the Province of Quebec, on the South bank of the St. Lawrence, clear up to the Gaspé Peninsula & at Metapedia we turned southwards into New Brunswick.

Early on the evening of the 9th we pulled up in the freight yards on the water front of Halifax N.S. There, the train, & ourselves lay inert all night & next morning.

My first glimpse of Halifax was very depressing. It was a murky, foggy, morning & nothing was to be seen except the filthy, smoky freight yards, & the masts & funnels of ships, showing dimly through the fog. The yards were full of filth & garbage from waiting trooptrains, & I will never forget the stink therefrom. I was very sick that night on the boat, before she ever lifted anchor, in consequence of that awful stink.

We embarked on the H.M.T.S. "Grampian" in the afternoon of the 10th. They towed us out into the harbour & there we dropped anchor till the evening of the 13th!

Halifax is a splendid harbour, but even then, before the great explosion, which took place 3 or 4 months later, the outlook was dreary in the extreme; a good deal owing to the dull weather.

To be on board a moving transport is bad enough, but to lie at anchor for 3 days, was like imprisonment. No chance to go to harbour, of course.

The bumboats were alongside nearly all the time, doing a great trade in oranges, apples & chocolate.

The "Grampian" was a solid looking old barge – a small Allan liner, converted into a transport. I do not know how many troops were on board, possibly a thousand; anyhow quite enough!

There were, perhaps, 3 companies of C.F.C. 1 Company of Newfoundland Forestry , some Newfoundland Infantry, & some C.A.M.C. & C.A.S.C. I, & my little bunch got a cabin (6 bunks) somewhere below the water line & away up forward. Late in the evening of the 13th August our convoy steamed out of Halifax, & said goodbye to the shores of Canada.

I then resigned myself by looking forward to the good time I would have on leave, in England.

The convoy was made up of six ships - "Missanabie", "Calgarian" (a converted cruiser which was torpedoed a year or so later) "Cedric" & Grampian; the other two ships I cannot remember the names of. We travelled two abreast across the Atlantic, & always quite close together. We didn't do very much on the voyage: physical drill now & then, a few fatigues & guard. There was an armed guard posted all the time – 2 hours on & 4 hours off, & a new guard every day.

The Newfoundlanders who were supposed to be keen eyed mariners, were detailed entirely for the submarine lookout. The deck was usually crowded with gamblers playing: "House" & "Crown & Anchor"

For ten days the "Grampian" was our home – a miserable ten days for most of us. I was not actually sick – that is to say I did not vomit – but I felt on the verge of it most of the time! The quality of the food went down considerably at this stage. - margarine had taken the place of butter. This was the first time I had ever tasted the stuff, but I certainly became very familiar with it, in all its phases during the following two years. The taps in the wash houses were usually dry: usually, the best time to get a wash was in the middle of the night.

We had a salt water bath <u>once,</u> several <u>hundred</u> men lined up to <u>two</u> baths; just a dip & out again, to make way for the next man. The water in the bath was changed after every <u>third</u> man. Of course one could only expect a shortage of salt water in the centre of the Atlantic!

The atmosphere between decks was always odoriferous, & foetid – the natural musty stench of the ship's interior, mingled with smells from galleys & latrines. The officers, of course, enjoyed the comforts of the saloon deck.

We had one or two lectures, on what to do if we were torpedoed, but thank God we were not torpedoed, for if we had been, I think half the troops would have been trampled to death under the other half.

Quite a number were sea sick, of course – I remember one man in the C.A.M.C. (a Jew named Rosenthal) who sat at our table; ("mess 22, 1st sitting") he never missed a meal, & he never missed being sick after it!

We had one storm 5 or 6 days out. I happened to be on guard duty that night & had a post on deck – right over the propellors. If I had not felt so rotten, I might have enjoyed it, for it certainly was a grand night. The sea was intensely phosphorescent, & the crest of each great wave, was a mass of white fire, & the wake of the ship was fairly ablaze.

A wave would break over the ship, & as the water streamed down the decks, you could see the phosphorescence , like hundreds of little electric sparks.

CPR Bridge at Montreal, 1917

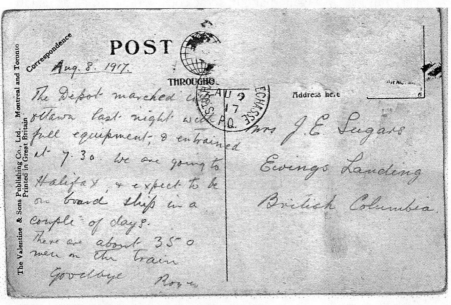

Correspondence

Aug. 8. 1917.

The Depot marched into Ottawa last night with full equipment, & entrained at 7.30. We are going to Halifax, & expect to be on board ship in a couple of days. There are about 35 0 men on the train

Goodbye   Roger

Mrs J. E. Sugars

Ewings Landing

British Columbia

The Valentine & Sons Publishing Co., Ltd., Montreal and Toronto
Printed in Great Britain

Roger Sugars' to Mother before embarkation

Two days out from Liverpool we were met by 6 destroyers, - one for each ship of the convoy Much cheering & waving!

On the evening of the 23rd of August 1917, we steamed into the Mersey, & were towed to dock. "It won't be long before I'm having a good time now" I thought to myself.

Liverpool was most depressing that night, scarcely a living soul to be seen, & all the lights dimmed. Just about dark we disembarked, & gradually worked our way into the Riverside Station & into a passenger train (troop special) The Canadians were much amused by the little English coaches with their small compartments.

What a glorious relief – to get off that damned boat & onto dry land once more!

Our train rolled out sometime that night "we didn't know where we were going, but we were on our way", & that was the main thing. Somewhere about ten, the next morning we pulled into a pretty little country station, called Sunningdale, in Berkshire. We were ordered to detrain, so we tumbled out with our packs, stiff, & very hungry. We waited about, some considerable time (as usual) formed fours half a dozen times or so & finally marched off in "column of route" five miles they said we had to walk; it was five miles, believe me! A beautiful walk it was, through country lanes & oak woods. Finally we came to a very big, high opening in the woods; Smiths Lawn they said it was, & the Base Depot of the Canadian Forestry Corps.

The camp consisted of a lot of draughty huts on one side & a lot of leaky tents on the other, with a large parade ground between. We were marched onto the parade ground & after an hour of dilly dallying, were dispatched to a row of the leaky tents. We afterwards learned that this was called the Segregation Camp. Fresh troops arriving, were put into this camp & imprisoned there for a week or ten days, & practically starved, in order to hurry any disease which they might have in a dormant condition! After that they were made up into drafts & moved over to the hutment camp to await departure.

Well by this time we were getting pretty hungry as it was now 20 hours since we had had a bite! We proceeded to make ourselves "comfortable" in the tents, & about 1 p.m. the "cookhouse" blew. A wild scuffle ensued; the ravenous wolves were anticipating a hearty meal. But – Oh, never shall I forget the disappointment, & the altogether unsatisfied feeling about the middle, after that travesty of a meal. I would have been ashamed to have set such a meal before a Kitten! And so it was for ten days 3 snacks a day & no chance to get out & buy a meal.

The segregation camp was perhaps 10 acres in extent, & there we were stuck for 10 days with nothing but a beer canteen

Of course, we were dirty after our travelling, but there were nothing but open air wash tables. One day we were paraded down to a little lake in the woods (at the bottom of the Cumber- land Obelisk) the water was ice cold & did not clean much. Of course we had much rain & the streets between the tents were usually a quagmire. Most of the tents leaked, but fortunately they had board floors.

They kept us fairly busy in the segregation, Drill & physical jerks & plenty of fatigues & guards. After 10 days the C.B. was lifted & we were free to wander anywhere, in the usual off duty hours. Smiths Lawn is in Windsor Great Park, & there is some beautiful country all around. Egham, a town of about 13000 inhabitants, is 3 miles away. Nearly every evening I walked to Egham & bought a good supper. When I say a good Supper, I mean as good a supper as you could get in a country town like Egham in War time.

Egham boasted a picture house, the "Gem", & some delightful pubs., with names such as: "The Coach & Horses" The "Red Lion" "King's Arms" or the "Castle Inn" The Speech of the people was practically Cockney, & horrible to listen to. On Saturday afternoons there was usually a baseball game in camp, with large crowds of spectators. The King & Queen attended one of the matches. The Initials "G.R." were frequently to be seen on notice boards throughout the park, These were said by the troops to stand for "Gut Robber" There was a Y.M.C.A. in the camp, the "Princess

Victoria Hut" Outside the "Y" you could buy a messtin-ful of milk from the milkman for 10d; inside the "Y" it cost you a shilling!

After being in Smiths Lawn a week or so, I began to think it was time, we were getting that landing leave that was supposed to be coming to us. In the end, of course we were fooled out of it. Four men out of each company were granted four days leave. I am bound to admit, I was intensely disappointed.

The D'Oyleys came down to Egham one afternoon from London. I got the afternoon off, & spent it with them. They had not seen me since I was 7 years old, but after the first five minutes we got along quite free-&-easily.

On arrival in Smiths Lawn we became known as the No. 3 Ottawa draft & ours was No 2 Coy. Gradually we were all split up into different companies, under new officers. On the 7th of September my turn came: I, & perhaps 50% of No 2 Coy. were transferred into 76 Coy. There were a lot of strangers in the this newly made Company, but the bulk of it was from the Ottawa draft. We moved into the huts which was a pleasant change; & the food in the hutment camp was a trifle better than in the segregation. It was exceeding cold & damp; there were little stoves in the huts but no fuel, so we used to go out at night & rustle sticks in the woods, & steal coal from the camp coal yard.

About this time we turned in all our Canadian Oliver equipment, & were issued with the Imperial web equipment. The Medical board passed almost every man as "A 11" which means physically fit but untrained.

We did absolutely no drill while in the hut camp, but they kept us on fatigues pretty well every day.

I saw old Bill McQueen in Smiths Lawn; he went away with some company before us.

We were now under a Capt. Verge, & the N.C.O.s were mostly new to us.

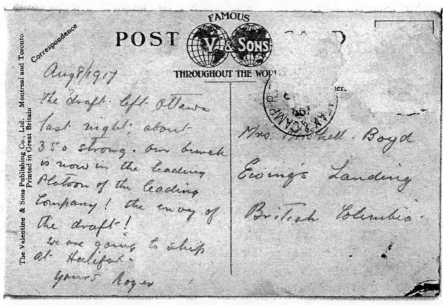

Roger's postcard to family friend, August 1917

Postcard photo of Mantello Tower, Halifax, 1917

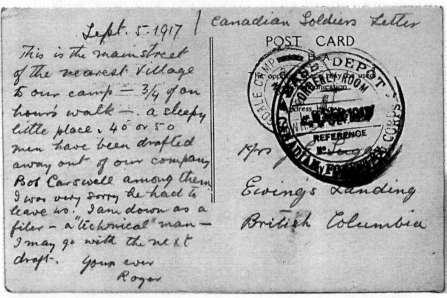

Sept. 5 1917 / Canadian Soldiers Letter

POST CARD

This is the main street
of the nearest village
to our camp — 3/4 of an
hour's walk —. a sleepy
little place. 40 or 50
men have been drafted
away out of our company
Bob Carswell among them
I was very sorry he had to
leave us. I am down as a
filer – a "technical" man —
I may go with the next
draft. Yours ever
    Roger

Mrs J
Ewing's Landing
British Columbia

Postcard to Mother, Sept. 1917

High Street, Egham.   W.H.A. 2528.

Postcard photo of Egham, England, 1917

Our Sergeant-Major was a clear headed German (?) named Schmell, who had excellent organising ability & a good command. Just before we left for France, Lieut. General Turner looked us over; & came to the conclusion that Canadian uniforms were much too light (a conclusion I had come to, about 3 months previously) The only one of my original tents mates now in 76 Coy. was Ed. Hewlett. At the last minute, almost, our O.C. – Capt. Verge, was changed for a Capt. McKeigan, who was with us until we were demobilised, & a bigger blockhead it would be hard to find. A "herring choker" he was, a boob from Nova Scotia.

At midnight on the 21st of September, we marched out of Smiths Lawn camp, with full equipment. It was a bitterly cold, foggy night, & we shivered around Egham Station for an hour or so before entraining. We got into Southampton early the next morning. We lay about the platform of the dockside station until about 4 in the afternoon when we boarded the "Archimedes" Besides ourselves & 75 Coy, there were a battery or so of Imperial Artillery, & some South African Heavy Artillery, on board. We had a quiet crossing, & anchored in Havre Roads on the morning of September 23rd.

"Where do we go from here, boys?" was the general silent question of all. "France at last, wonder when I'll leave France, if ever?"

We disembarked about 2 p.m. & marched up to No 2 Rest Camp, about 2 miles from the docks This camp is generally known as the "Cinder City", its foundation being mainly cinders & clinkers There were no cookhouses, so troops had to subsist on their own travelling rations – bully beef & hard tack, with a little jam & cheese.

The "cinder city" was pretty well crowded, with troops, going up, & coming down the line. There were Imperials, Australian, & some American Marines – some of the first American troops in France.

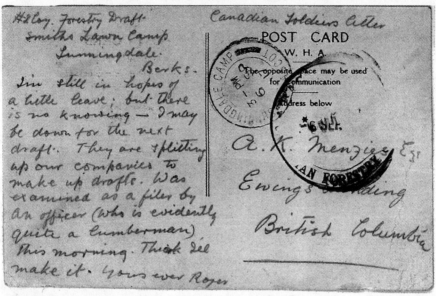

Postcard to A.K. Sept. 1917, Smiths Lawn Camp, England

Postcard photo of Egham, England.

They put us twelve to sixteen to a tent for the first night; it would have plenty of room between heads, but feet were stacked up in a great pile around the tent pole. If you tried to move a foot, it would disturb everybody in the tent.

The next day they moved ourselves & 75 Coy. down to the Gare Maritime.

Here we camped for a week, horses & men all exhausted in the big freight sheds. There was plenty of room: horses occupied one end of the shed, & men the other.

The floor was of square cobble stones, & on these we slept, with one blanket a ground sheet, & a greatcoat. The little yard engines whistled & clanked up & down day & night, outside, & the horses stamped & screamed within, yet none of us slept better before or since. We lived entirely on bully beef & hard tack, augmented, now & then by jam & biscuits bought at the Expeditionary Forces Canteen. We could not get out of the Gare Maritime without a pass, there being an Imperial red cap at every gate. I secured a pass one evening, & went down to Havre on a street car. I had been there before (when we first went to Canada in 1905) but hardly recognised the town. It is a picturesque old town, but like most other French towns, must not be scrutinised too closely.

There were all kinds of unreliable rumours as to where we were going and when. However we got a rough idea of "where" we were going when, one day day they issued us with steel helmets & gas masks! The next day they instructed us in the use of the masks, & put us up through the tear-gas & poison-gas chambers. The latter completely discoloured all brass buttons.

We brought our full quota of horses with us, but they said we would not need them, so we turned them into the remount stables; then they said we would need them, so we took them out of the remount stables; then they said, we would only need a few so we, again, turned most of them into the remount stables. This last order, was, strange to say, final! We had a few fatigues & a bath parade (much needed, though several tried to dodge it) one morning I worked in the A.S.C. feed depot, never have I seen such mountainous stacks of grain & baled hay as there were in those mighty sheds.

About noon, on Saturday the 29th Sept. 75 & 76 Coys. entrained at some station in the town of Havre. It was a real troop train this time, no comfortable passenger coaches, but box-cars, bare of everything except dirt, & all bearing the sign which became so hatefully familiar later on, "Cheveaux 8, Hommes 32-40"

Fortunately, in my experience, I never travelled with more than about 25 "hommes", & then there was only just enough room to lie down, carefully packed, head to feet, like sardines. With 40 in a car they would have to stand up or lie on top of each other.

We were given 48 hours rations & no clue as to where we were going. We rolled along all that afternoon up the Seine valley, as many of us as possible sitting in the wide doorways of the boxcars, with out feet dangling out. We did not make much speed: we passed Rouen sometime that afternoon. Late in the night we pulled up in the yards of Noisy le Sec 6 or 7 miles out of Paris. We discovered a Red Cross canteen here, where they handed out free coffee. After we left Noisy our train seemed to bump along pretty steadily for the remainder of the night. Any how it bumped sufficiently to bring down a steel hat that was hanging on a nail in the roof of a car; it passed within six inches of MY face & landed, edge first on the eyebrow of the man sleeping next to me, & opened up a pretty gash.

The train stopped early in the morning. We looked out in the twilight of the dawn. It was bitter cold, & at first nothing could be seen except the white fog which enveloped everything. We got out, & discovered the remains of a burnt station. Through the fog we could just see a ruined house & some barbed wire entanglements, also an apple orchard. We concluded that we were somewhere on the Western front!

We felt most dejected.

There were a few "poilus" about & they told us we were near Noyon & about 23 Kilometres from the line. I seemed to remember the name Noyon in connection with desperate fighting or something. They also told us quite cheerfully that the battle of the Somme was going on not very far north of us.

After an hour or so the train rattled on again for five or six miles until we came to a little place called Appilly – the rail head.

75 Coy. had been switched off during the night, & we afterwards learned that they had gone to Villers Cotterets, south west of Soissons. We descended from our box-cars at Appilly, & disposed ourselves along the gravel beside the track.

By this time the fog had cleared & the sun was shining, which improved matters a lot. The scenery was typical of Northern France, swampy looking fields, divided by rows of poplars.

There were a lot of board & tar paper shacks where the station had once been; the village of Appilly lay back a little from the track. There was an Algerian labour outfit working on the latter. A few fatigue parties were detailed to unload the waggons etc from our train. This done, a field-kitchen was set up & a meal cooked – bully-beef "mulligan" & tea. All the time we could hear the disquieting sound of the guns rumbling & booming, away to the Eastward. Once we heard "pom, pom" a dozen times or so in succession, right overhead.

All eyes were directed heavenward, & there, far up in the blue, was a string of little white puffs like so many balls of cottonwool. This was our first sight of anti-aircraft shrapnel, with which we were to become very familiar in the next 3 or 4 months.

Sometime, just after noon, we got squared around & marched off. All the officers (except one, who led the Company on horseback) went ahead in the Sunbeam car. We marched with our full equipment (except kit-bags, which went in the waggons) the first 20 men – the "guard" – with rifles & bayonets. (I avoided this section!) At first we walked <u>away</u> from the sound of the artillery, but only for a short distance, then we turned <u>parallel</u> to it, & very soon we turned <u>again</u>, into a long, white, straight road, with the inevitable avenue of poplars. This was the main highway to the front in the Cousy le Chateau Sector.

It was a hot afternoon & it was a long weary march up that white road, which led to No Mans Land. We kept to that road for 4 or 5 hours, & the booming of the guns grew ever louder.

Soon we saw 5 or 6 of the sausage shaped observation balloons, anchored at intervals of several miles along the horizon, ahead of us. We passed several villages in partial ruin – Baboeuf & Ognes.

We had 10 minutes rest every hour, which didn't seem enough. About 3.30 we reached the one-time City of Chauny which was dynamited & blown to bits by the Huns in the spring of '17. We passed on & went through Marizelle, Autreville, & Pierremande. A couple of miles further on we reached our destination, at 5 p.m. We were just inside the fringe of the lower forest of Coucy, & 3 miles this side of Coucy le Chateau, & about 2 miles from the French front line trenches.

At that time, this was supposed to be a "quiet sector", but it sounded noisy enough to us, poor greenhorns.

Our camp was already built – two big French huts, one for a bunkhouse & the other for eating in. Another forestry Company (51 Coy.) had erected these huts; 51 company had been in the Coucy woods 3 months ahead of us; they had a mill & were logging. This was "No. 10 District C.F.C." & consisted of 4 companies - 51 & 76 within two miles of each other on the edge of the Coucy woods; 55 Coy 20 miles west, near Noyon, & 75 Coy 30 or 40 miles South-West, at Villers- Cotterets. We were some distance South of the British Front, & were attached to the 3rd French Army, & most of our work was under their supervision. Our postal address was "Secteur Postal 164, Armée Francaise". We were practically independent of the Canadian Corps.

When the Germans swept through these woods they cut much timber, & left many logs, & tops & litter scattered through the forest. 51 Coy. were hauling all these logs & saving them up at their mill. Our work, we were instructed would be to clean up all the tops & limbs, & chop & saw them into fire wood, to help relieve the fuel shortage which was then in France. Much had to be done in the camp, before the bush work really started. There were barns to be built, huts for the officers & sergeants, Q.M. stores, wash- house & a hundred & one other things. Then every building had to be camouflaged with brush, for we were right under the eye of the German planes. Our camp was situated in a small clearing in the woods, right beside the Noyon-Coucy "grande route", & we used to see all the traffic of war passing up & down the line, - infantry, cavalry, artillery, - guns from the 75s up to 9 & 10 inch naval guns – ambulances, strings of motor trucks, companies of "Genie", despatch riders on bicycles, motor cycles & horses.

For handsome men, I never saw anything to equal a French cavalry regiment.

This was the Forest of St. Gobain, & the lower Forest of Coucy, in which we were, is but a small portion of the former. At that time, the greater part of the St. Gobain forest lay within the Boche lines.

Nevertheless we had a good many square miles of woods in which to work.

The forest was intersected by straight roads which usually cut the woods into triangular sections – 4, 6, & 8 roads would meet in places, & these cross roads were favourite objects for Fritzie to shell – the woods consisted mainly of oak & beech, the largest of which had already been cut down by the Huns.

There were, also, trees of ash, basswood, alder, poplar & hornbeam.

To the westward, the country was open & level until you reached the queer string of wooded topped hills near Noyon, & Guiseard Eastward, the woods rose to a fairly high ridge, on the crest of which was Coucy le Chateau Just over the ridge were the German lines. Halfway between our camp & the Chateau (or Castle) & nestling close under the ridge was a romantic & melancholy village named Folembray.

Folembray was under almost constant shellfire, & its houses, its gardens & chateaux, & its church were all ruined. There were no civilians in Folembray, only soldiers who mostly lived in the old railway tunnel. In, & around Folembray were located many batteries of Artillery. Also there was the "Cantine Coopérative Militaire" which sold much "Vin rouge" No place ever gave me such a feeling of depression & brooding disaster as did this Folembray.

But what a picturesque , peaceful spot it must have been before the war. Three times I attempted to reach Coucy le Chateau & each time I got cold feet & retreated. Each Sunday I tried to get there, the Boche shelled it particularly heavily.

The last time I got right up under the Castle & had a good view of it; but its towers & battlements were little more than a pile of stones.

It is said to be about 900 years old. Westward of us, on the Noyon road, lay Pierremande, Autreville, Marizelle (all ruined villages) & the one time city of Chauny There were huge glass, china, pot & tile factories in Chauny, all completely wrecked. There was one street in Chauny which was not demolished, & here lived a few Civilians, who kept little stores. Here also was a big hospital with huge red crosses painted on the roof. Chauny had not only been shelled, but dynamited also. The bridges across the Oise river had all been blown up.

One of the weirdest sights I have ever seen was the ruined streets of Chauny, by moonlight & under snow.

Here & there you would see a house undamaged except for the fact that the front wall was completely gone, leaving the rooms, furniture & all, exposed to the world.

All manner of loot there was to be had in the shape of furniture & household goods: Our officers had their quarters completely fitted out & furnished with loot from Chauny. They had two 6 foot mirrors, tables, chairs, baths, basins & all kinds of china, & pots & pans. Major Carman – our adjutant – spent most of his time in the Sunbeam car, collecting loot & souvenirs. He, with the other officers had the time of their lives; nothing to do & plenty of men to do it for them.

The constant, though never very heavy, shelling, kept us somewhat on edge; otherwise we had quite a good time at Coucy.

We worked about 7 hours a day in the forest, sawing & chopping wood; No work on wet days, & perfect freedom, to go where you liked & dressed as you like, out of working hours.

It was usual to stroll out to the Pierremande, or Folembray canteens in the evening The booze artists went for "Vin" & the others for candles, matches & food. Our feeding was not good; there was plenty, but it was badly cooked, & deadly monotonous – greasy mulligan, boiled potatoes (skins, dirt & all) rice, cheese, jam, porridge, & bread, also margarine.

We had double-decker bunks in the big hut; which by the way was very draughty & only had 3 stoves. The first time we had a real scare from shells was on the 29th of October. We were working out in a big clearing of the woods; & a Boche airman evidently spotted us. Anyhow, they shelled that clearing; they landed several right amongst us, & never hurt a soul; we then beat a hasty retreat, but Fritzy continued to bombard the clearing for an hour or more.

The trouble was the French had many concealed batteries all through the woods & the Huns were forever searching them out, & They were just as likely to hit a party of harmless foresters as a battery of seventy-fives.

Day & night, the shells were dropping intermittently all through the forest, heavy shells & light shells, ground shrapnel, & now & then gas shells.

Yet in the the four months we were up there not a man of our Company was hurt, nor was the camp hit though shells dropped within 50 yards of it. Frenchmen were killed, & French waggons on the road were hit, but we all got off scot free!

Some nights we could not sleep.

Sometimes it was a single German gun that kept you awake. You would hear its muffled boom away off in the night. Then a few seconds later;- whee oo-oo-oo WUMP! That one was safely landed & exploded, but what about the next one? In five minutes or so you heard the boom again – here she comes! here she comes! Where's she going to land? Ah! a sigh of relief as you hear it explode safely somewhere in the woods nearby. After a bit, you got weary of listening & fell asleep.

There again, sometimes it was a barrage being put down, a mile or so away. Its continuous, crashing, thunder made sleep impossible, so you usually went outside, & watched the glare of the gunflashes & star shells.

One quiet night, we were awakened by the most terrific & earth shaking explosion imaginable. A German plane was droning overhead, so we knew it was a bomb - or rather an aerial torpedo.

Two more of these terrible detonations & then the plane went away. Many of us were prepared to gamble our last franc that those bombs landed right in the camp yard, but next day we found they had dropped half a mile away!

This bombing business happened to us several times.

While working out in the woods our chief danger was from French anti-aircraft shrapnel. They were everlastingly shooting at Boche planes, & what goes up must come down. Whenever the shrapnel puffs were overhead we used to take shelter under big trees & listen to the stuff whizzing down.

Altogether we were about 4 months in Coucy, during which time we cut 20,000 metres of wood (equivalent to about 27,000 cords) & 160000 barbed-wire entanglement stakes. All of this was done by hand - axes & cross cut saws – no machinery whatever. Still, it was not much work for nearly 200 men to do in four months! Early in November a section of the Company (I among them) were detailed to shift camp to the Flavy woods, about 12 miles North of Chauny & 15 South of St. Quentin. We went up there for 3 days & lived in an old German camp, & partially built a camp for ourselves It was just a picnic – a wine & champagne picnic! The two sergeants that were with us, were dead to the world the greater part of the time, & we had a good time!

On the third day the S.M. & the O.C. arrived from Coucy with orders to cease operations & return as soon as we could tear the huts down & pack them up again.

So we went back to Coucy & remained there till the 25th of January 1918.

We had about 3 weeks of exceedingly cold weather that winter. In fact I have never suffered from the cold so much before or since. We slept cold, ate cold, & worked cold.

One Saturday night, (the 22nd of Dec. 1917) I & another fellow decided to visit Noyon – the nearest town which still retained the attractions of civilization – It was 23 Kilometres to Noyon, but a good road & a beautiful night – bright moonlight, a little snow & bitter cold. It took us from 5.30 to 10 o'clock to make it, & when we got to Noyon everything was in darkness & silence – like a grave yard in the moonlight. We located a ruin with 3 walls & a roof, & a little straw on the ground. Here we passed away a few hours of the night, & such agonies of cold I never endured the like of.

About 5 we got out & ran up & down the deserted streets to get warm It was below zero that morning I think & the wind was like a knife.

About 6 we saw a light in a hut, & got admitted into what appeared to be a sort of powerhouse with a couple of sleepy French soldiers in it! They had no food to offer us & they told us nothing would be open in the town before 8 or half past!

However the hut was warm & we soon felt quite feeble & stupid as people do when they get warmed up after being thoroughly chilled for hours.

About 7.30 we roamed out into the old ville in search of "eats". We finally landed up at the Hotel du Nord, & went into the dining room (which looked as though it had not been dined in for years)

Not a bad looking red haired girl appeared after an eternity: we ordered breakfast – half a Kilometre of "pain" & black coffee, <u>pas chaud</u>. We protested, so after a third eternity she returned with more coffee (chaud this time) & a poached egg apiece!

We then went out & inspected the city, an ancient, picturesque, but gloomy old burg, damaged here & there by bombs. We purchased a few articles, drank cognac & coffee at various cafés, & had a fairly good dinner.

About 2 0'clock we hit the road for Coucy. We got rides in various conveyances most of the way, & reached camp about six o'clock (Sunday 23 Dec. '17) The historic town of Noyon which changed hands no less than six times in this war. The last time the Huns went through it, in the great spring drive of 1918, they levelled it to the ground.

This jaunt was merely a French leave - we had no passes: but so long as we turned up for work on Monday morning it mattered not. We did not have much Military discipline at Coucy.

There was some talk of sending us to Italy, also to Bordeaux, the Jura, the Vosges & various other places, but when we did move we knew not where we were going. They chose my 21st birthday (25th Jan. 1918) to prepare for departure. Most of the heavy stuff had already been packed & shipped to Appilly (our railhead) That 25th was a turmoil of a day: every one was overjoyed at the prospect of a move. About 50% of the Company were drunk that night. We had no sleep, & at 2 a.m. of the 26th we fell in & marched to Appilly (about 12 miles)

It was a damp, raw, foggy night. We straggled into the village of Appilly about daylight.

We entrained into boxcars & pulled out about 2 o'clock that afternoon, having been issued with 2 or 3 days rations of bully & hard tack.

We passed Compiegne, & bumped on down to Noisy-le-Sec, outside Paris, where we were sidetracked for the night We bummed a lot of coffee here from a Red Cross canteen.

The next morning we turned eastwards again, & pulled up in Chateau Thierry in the afternoon. We lay there nearly all night.

We were enjoying ourselves immensely nothing to do but dangle our feet out of the boxcar doors & watch the country Slide by, but, God, wasn't it cold at nights!

We nearly always had plenty of time to visit the buffets & canteens at the principal stations. About day light on the 28th we arrived at Chalons- sur-Marne; where we remained until 2.30 in the afternoon. We all strayed off into the town for the whole morning & bought meals drinks & souvenirs.

In all these war-zone towns you could see soldiers of almost every nationality under the Sun. In one of these towns (St. Dizier) I have seen soldiers of all the Allied Nations & their colonies with exception of, perhaps, Australia, New Zealand, Japan & Serbia. But in Paris you could see them all.

About 10 that night we pulled up in a Village called Eclaron in the Haute Marne This, we were told, was our destination We slept (or tried to sleep) in the train that night. The next day (Jan. 29. 18) we unloaded the train, & moved up to where our new camp was to be – In the Forét du Der & about 4 miles from the Village of Eclaron. this was a peaceful, rural district where the Huns had never been, & about 25 miles from the line. Like all Northern France it was flat, low-lying & damp.

Our camp was to be right alongside two other companies of Canadian Forestry (31 & 33 Coys.) They had two mills & were logging oak out of the Forest of the Der.

We picked a good muddy spot to pitch our tents on.

We lived in those tents during the following 3 weeks in which time we had snow, frost & rain. First of all, we built the sergeants quarters, then the Q.M. stores, then the barn, then the officers quarters (the officers were living in a neighbouring chateau meanwhile) & last of all we built the mens huts! Our commander always thought of the comforts of his men first.

Yes, for three weeks we lived in those tents & ate our meals in the open! Just through our half dead O.C. not caring a damn one way or the other.

We were to help the other two companies wherever they needed us. After a couple of months this was found very unsatisfactory; so an arrangement was arrived at – 31 & 33 Coys. were to cut & deck all the logs, & run the mills, while 76 Coy. was to take charge of the light railway & the loading & transporting of the logs to the mills. So for the first two months or so I was building huts & cutting saw logs in the woods. After that I was given a cant hook & put on a loading crew as a right hand sender. This was what I liked. I am happy with a cant hook, to "throw the crooked steel" is the best work I know.

Most of the timber was oak, with a little beech or basswood.

The logs could not be hauled on sleighs as they are in Canada, so we built several miles of narrow gauge railroad with many branches & spurs through the woods. We loaded onto cars, with 8 foot bunks, 1000 to 2500 feet or so to a load. On the down grades the cars would run of their own weight, with a brakesman aboard (a dangerous job as the cars often jumped the track) On the level they were usually pulled by horses (The poor horses wading in mud up to their knees beside the track) On the last lap into the mills we had a couple of "dinky" steam engines which could handle 4 or 5 loaded cars at once. The mills were turning out about 25,000 feet of sawn lumber, per day, apiece.

A couple of miles away from us, there were several companies of American Forestry engineers: they had a single mill which turned out 10,000 feet per day! (double shift) The Yanks had us all beat for a system. The American Forestry consisted of millmen & lumberjacks: 50% of our bunch had never seen the woods before!

I went up & top loaded from the skidways for about 10 months steady.

Most of the lumber was cut into railroad ties & heavy ship timbers, & was shipped away by the French as fast as it was cut.

(All the fire wood we cut up at Coucy was left piled in the bush; the following spring the Germans swept all through that country, retook Chauny, Noyon & all the other Villages on the road & presumably our wood!)

All that spring & the following fall, the mud on the roads, in the woods & every- where was absolutely beyond words. We were supplied with knee-high larrigan oil skin suits, sou'westers & cowboy hats, but in the spring fall & winter we were always wet & plastered with mud.

The huts were cold & draughty, & the food was always badly cooked. Otherwise we had a good time. We were free to wander pretty well where we liked, on Sundays, so long as we were properly dressed & had a belt on!

I visited all the villages & towns within walking distance &

was familiar with all their estaminets; but it was always the safe same fare:- drinks; beer rum, cognac, vin rouge, blanc et gris, byrrh, benedictine eau de vie & various other poisons; food; des oeufs et pommes de terre frites, toujours!

The towns within "hiking" distance of us were; St. Dizier a fair sized military centre with many aerodromes & foundries. This was about 8 miles away.

Wassy was an ancient sleepy town 15 miles distant. In the church at Wassy were many interesting tomb tablets on one of which I noticed the date 1423! Montier-en-der was a similar town about 12 miles away. Nearer at hand were various villages; Champaubert St. Liviere, Grand Côtes, Landricourt, Braucourt, Frampas, Voillecomte, & half a dozen others. 75 miles away was the large town of Troyes in the department of Aube. We could occasionally get week end passes to go there by train. (It usually took 4 hours to go from Eclaron to Troyes.) Altogether, I must have visited Troyes about 7 times.

For amusement at "home", we had a wet canteen, liberty to gamble, & a Y.M.C.A. at which we had some excellent concerts (by American & London concert parties) & moving pictures.

The Y.M.C.A. by the way was only running for about the last 5 months we were in France. The only things that any Y.M.C.A. gave away free, in my experience, were amusement & note paper, food, drink, & tobacco had to be well paid for.

Just at the end of March 1918 it was announced that general leave would be open in April, so they put up a list of the names of men who were to proceed on 14 days leave to the U.K. during the first week in April. My name was, I think, the fifth down the list! Yes, I was actually going to Blighty within the next week. Oh joy! it was what I had hoped & longed for ever since I set foot in France.

Then the Germans opened up a drive – the biggest drive they ever made. All general leave was cancelled! Every available reserve was being rushed to the front They told us, we should be sent to the front within the next two weeks.

We could hear the great guns thundering day & night for

weeks. Haig said we were "fighting with our backs against the wall". But we (the old C.F.C.) carried on with our logging & we could not get transferred to a fighting unit if we wanted to. The summer wore on; the drive was checked, & we never went "up the line" after all!

In September, General leave to the U.K. was opened again. Transports of joy again; but tempered with mistrust & a preparedness for disappointment, this time However the luck was running our way & if we had only known it, the war was nearly over.

My turn came on September 5th, 1918.

I left Eclaron with all my leave warrants "Ordres de transports" etc. by the 5 p.m. train for Troyes. Five men from the other Coys. were also with me.

We reached Troyes at 10 p.m. & waited there till 2.45 a.m. for the Paris train. We pulled up in the Gare de l'Est at 7 in the morning of the 6th. Our leave did not begin till the 8th, but we were supposed to go straight through to Boulogne & wait there in the rest camp for our boat. However, Paris looked better than rest camps so we decided to put in the surplus two days there.

So we spent the 6th & 7th "seeing" Paris, making the British Army & Navy Leave Club (Hotel Moderne, Place de la Republique) our headquarters. Joy rides in taxies occupied most of our time. We felt like Kings driving down such places as the Avenues des Champs Elysées as though we owned the damned place.

She is a "great little town", Paris, as the Yanks say of New York. Fine buildings splendid boulevards, & plenty of trees; but just get off the boulevards & try a "Rue" & you will soon find out what a dirty, smelly town Paris really is.

Of course it was chock-a-block with soldiers of almost every nation under the sun. And what of the fair Parisiennes? Oh, I fell for them, same as the rest.

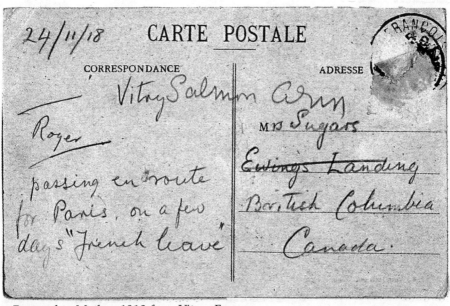

Postcard to Mother, 1918 from Vitny, France

Postcard photo of Vitny, France

On the evening of the 7th we went down to the Gare du Nord, ignored the R.T.O., & boarded the 8.15 train for Boulogne. It took the whole of that night to make the trip. All the way from Beauvais to Etaples we could see the gun flashes on the horizon to our right. The train just crawled & landed us in Boulogne at 6 a.m.

They marched us up to an awful dump called Tetard's Billet, & left several hundred of us penned up in there till about 11 o'clock. They then marched us down to the docks where they deprived us of part of our leave warrants, & gave us a couple of stale currant buns apiece. (These were evidently to insure seasickness) Eventually we got packed aboard one of the little paddle boats, & about noon we moved out into the channel. There were anywhere from a 1000 to 50000 men on that little paddle steamer! Our life belts were black & greasy with many applications of spew! The channel was very rough & a driving rain came on Inside of half an hour nearly everyone seemed to be seasick. Below decks was a seething mass of Rifles, equipment spew & groaning & puking humanity.

And the stench -! On deck was the same, only the drenching waves kept things a bit cleaner. I stood on deck wedged in the crowd, & swallowed hard & managed to keep it down. It only took two hours to reach Folkestone, but two hours of the worst misery I have ever experienced or seen. Lord! how thankful I was to get off that boat & into a comfortable railway coach once more, soaked to the skin & shivering, but happy. We were really in Blighty now, & say, didn't Folkestone look a sweet, homely place with Notices, advertisements & everything in English once more. Instead of "Dubonnet – Vin tonique Quinquina" it was "Whitbread's Ales & Stout".

We arrived at Victoria Station at about 6.30 p.m. (Sept. 8. 18), the first day of our leave gone already!

A motor car took us up to the Maple Leaf Club where we got tickets for supper bed, breakfast, all for 2 shillings, I think it was. Good, wholesome meals, & comfortable, spotlessly clean beds in dormitories, with sheets & pyjamas.

I took that evening pretty easy; I bought a new pair of Foxe's puttees, some shoulder badges, & got all slicked up at the Club barber shop.

The next day I spent in London with old Hepburn (the saw hammerer from 33 mill). First of all we visited the Canadian pay office. On leaving France I had drawn a cheque for £20, this, I had cashed at the Maple Leaf Club. I still had £10 of available pay which I could draw at the pay office, but the officials at this place made a hideous mistake & gave me £30 instead of £10, making £50 in all! A nice little wad to go away on 14 days leave with - $250.

However, it put me in debt for months after I got back to France, & they cut my field allowance down by two thirds, but I didn't care, I always seemed to have from 50 to 500 francs in my purse, somehow.

Well, we dined & supped at the Strand Corner House, to the strains of the orchestra, as nonchalantly as possible. We had rides in taxis, & buses, drank Bass's & whisky (not mixed!) & went to a couple of shows ("The purple Mask" & "Yes, Uncle") .

About midnight we found ourselves out on the streets in a drizzling rain with nothing to do & nowhere to go.

We had an idea that London would be a blaze of light & gaiety all night, but about midnight the streets seemed to be almost deserted, but for a few Bobbys. The only thing left to us was to go back to the Maple Leaf Club for another night, which we did. The next morning I rose early & caught the 9 something train from Euston to Liverpool. Strange to say I had the carriage to myself most of the way, so I reclined at full length on the cushions, & enjoyed myself (I love train journeys).

It was a fine day & the soft, English scenery looked very comforting & peaceful from the windows of the train.

I detrained at Edge hill (Oh, what a God-forsaken dump!) & enquired for transportation to Huyton.

The quickest way, they told me, was by the No 6A Tram from the Corner of Edge Lane to a place called Bowring Park, whence I could walk to Huyton Village. I located the right corner, & I located the right tram, & boarded her & rode her to Bowring Park. Now, the last time I had visited this part of the country, was when I was about 5 or 6 years old, but the minute I got off that tram everything was perfectly familiar. I was on the Broad Green Road & about 15 minutes walk would take me through the Village of Roby, & into Huyton.

I guess it was about 3 o'clock when I arrived at the Cottage at Blacklow Brow, Bessie & Fanny (my aunts) were both at home (I had written them I was coming). After about 5 minutes awkwardness we were perfectly at ease, & I was absolutely "at home", which was not so bad considering they had not seen me since I was 7 years old.

I took to my aunts at once, & I think they took to me. I was pampered terribly during my stay with them – aired sheets, hot water bottles, pyjamas & things, - but I'll admit, I enjoyed being pampered. That evening, my Uncle George arrived from his boat which was luckily in dock at Liverpool.

He, a man of nearly 60, & I, a kid of 21 got along famously. I liked him immensely.

The next afternoon Bessie Michell arrived from Nottingham (specially to meet me, you understand) . A tall handsome dark girl of my own age, she was. Hum, I thought, when we met her at the station, here's where Little Willie falls in love inside of another hour or so! And sure enough that is what happened.

I am apt to fall in love with every nice looking girl I see; but this time it got me badly. I was in deadly earnest. I soon discovered, to my joy, that she was "stuck" on me also.

Whether my aunts had suspicions I know not; if they didn't they must have been pretty blind! In any case they gave Bessie & I plenty of freedom to be together. We went to the theatre in Liverpool; we went to New Brighton, & we took walks in the country. Oh, we had a glorious time!

After a week, Bessie had to return to Nottingham, so I decided I would also go & see Nottingham, en route for London. So on the afternoon of the 17th Sept, we said goodbye at Huyton &

proceeded to Nottingham via Manchester, 1st Class too! (No private soldiers are considered good enough to travel in any thing better than a 3rd class coach, in England!)

Bessie was at a Dancing school in Nottingham. On arrival, I was introduced to some of the inmates; I then went out in search of a "flop"; I located a Y.M.C.A. & booked a bed for sixpence.

I spent 3 days in Nottingham. In the mornings I wandered aimlessly about the town by myself. The afternoons & evenings I spent with <u>her.</u>

We had teas & dinners at "King's" & "Boots", we saw all the sights of the town, & we took Tram & bus rides out to the Trent Bridge & other places

One evening we were sitting on the asphalt steps beside the Trent River thinking only, of each other. She was telling me about her childhood days in Peru, I of mine in British Columbia.

Somewhere about midnight it was time to go: I attempted to rise from my seat on the asphalt, but found that I was glued to the tar! (That tar remained, a souvenir of a happy evening, on the seat of my pants until I finally discarded the garments in favour of a pair of American breeches which I found at Verdun 3 months later!)

Each evening we went to some theatre. One night, Bessie undertook to take me to see: "Henry of Navarre". There were two theatres in one building, & of course she took me into the wrong one, & the evenings entertainment turned out to be a variety show called "Stunts". But we didn't care, "Stunts" was quite good anyway, & the next evening we went to see "Some Boy" at the same house.

My measly 14 days were nearly all gone now, & the prospect of returning to France was almost unthinkable. I still had to visit Flo & Willie Ellis who were having their holiday near Eastbourne.

So on the 19th Sept. I caught the 4.24 p.m. from Nottingham to London.

Bessie saw me off, of course, & it was a most heart wrenching parting!

I reached Marylebone about 8 p.m. & took the tube to Victoria.

I "dossed" that night in a Salvation Army Hostel.

The next morning I took a train to Eastbourne, where I was met by my aunt & uncle, Flo & Willie. Of course I had not seen them since I was 6 or 7 but I spotted them in the crowd on the platform without the least hesitation They entered my heart then & there.

They were staying at a Cottage at Birling Gap, a wee village out on the downs about 4 miles from Eastbourne. After a light lunch at a restaurant we walked out there. Beautiful country those downs; great, rolling, grassy sweeps & snug hollows; but the wind, the sea breeze, blew so you could hardly walk.

Birling Gap was a little grey stone Village in a sort of gully which ran right out to the Gap where the chalk cliffs were quite low. We walked down to the Gap that afternoon & descended to the beach by means of a ladder which was placed at the lowest point of the cliffs. We walked along under the great white cliffs as far as Beachy Head. What an interesting place the seashore is with all its souvenirs thrown up by the waves. There was a wrecked steamer lying up under the cliffs close to the Gap. We had some tea in a cottage near the top of the cliffs, & then walked back to Birling Gap (about 2 miles) We went to bed fairly late that night; there were many things to be talked about. The next morning we took another ramble over the downs & returned to an excellent dinner. (Willie got some beer in my honour) This was the last day of my leave & I had to return to London that night.

I never felt more completely at home (except in my own home) anywhere as I did with Flo & Willie, nor did I ever receive more kindness & consideration. I was more than sorry to say goodbye to them at Eastbourne Station, & very depressed at the thought that the morrow would see me on my way to France.

But that was a great 14 days; I enjoyed every minute of it! I slept that night in another Salvation Army Hostel – in a great dormitory with hundreds of snoring men in it. Hung about in various places were cheering messages to this effect:- "Do not worry, we will wake you in plenty of time to catch the boat train. Good- night, & God Bless you."

They did wake us in plenty of time to catch the boat train, which left Victoria at 6.30 a.m. packed with returning leave men; Imperials, Canadians, New Zealanders & "Aussies" We reached Folkestone at 8.30 Sept 22. We were to have crossed the channel that day, but it was too rough, so they held us over for 24 hours in No. 3 Rest Camp (several blocks of seaside houses fenced in, formed the "camp"). We were allowed out in the town for the afternoon & evening which was pretty lucky as our leave was really over that morning.

Not a bad little town Folkestone: full of soldiers & W.A.A.C's & W.R.E.N.'s The W.A.A.C.s wore a most becoming uniform I thought. If they had been in "civvies" many of them, no doubt, would have been dressed atrociously, but a nice looking little girl in her khaki outfit looked "jake".

About 10 the next morning (Sept. 23) we boarded a transport & said Adios to Blighty. What a lot of glum faces, & small wonder! The channel was pretty choppy but not as bad as last time. We reached the accursed Boulogne about noon, & were met by a band & a cordon of Military Police!

They at once marched us off through the town & up to the Dublin Rest Camp which is away up on a bald hill, well exposed for air raids, with a wireless station, to make it more tempting for the Hun bomber! We were issued with meal tickets & introduced to some tents. a parade soon followed; an officer with a mighty voice announced what time, men for the different sectors, should fall in.

"All of the so & so division without artillery, will fall in at such & such a time" "All men for St. Omer" "All of the Australian Corps" "All of the Canadian Corps" He mentioned 101 different corps, divisions, & sectors. "All men for Marseille & Italy; all men for Paris & beyond" That was me! Paris & beyond. I was among the stragglers, there were not very many for "Paris & beyond", & we did not pull out till 8.30 the following night! (Sept. 24.)

So we put in a day & a half & a night in the Dublin Rest Camp. It was a big camp with the usual Expeditionary Force Canteens, Y.M.C.A.s Church Army, Salvation Army & other huts. The E.F.C. is the best of these, they sell groceries, refreshments, clothing, tobacco, souvenirs, beer & soft drinks.

Just behind the tents was a zig zag line of trenches, dug about 4 feet deep & two feet wide - air raid shelters!

We wondered if we should have to use them; it was not likely, as they had not had a raid on Boulogne for three weeks. However, I had not been asleep very long that night when I was awakened by some explosions & a commotion in the tent.

We all tumbled out & got into the trenches. You had to squat right down to keep your head & shoulders below the top of the trench, then of course there was not room enough for all the men. Those who could not get into the trench lay flat on the ground.

It was a raid alright, the sky was cross barred with searchlights, & we could hear the drone of one or more Boche planes

After a few minutes the barrage started, a continuous, crashing thunder which lasted 10 or 15 minutes. It seemed as though the Air must be full of shrapnel; we could hear it singing down all around us, yet no one was hit. And it sounded as though the Universe was falling to pieces. Nobody seemed in the least frightened, just a-tremble with suppressed excitement.

After a while the barrage died down & all was quiet once more, so we returned to our tents & rolled into our dirty old blankets.

I was just dozing off, when I was aroused again. It was another performance like the first, with, if possible, a more appalling barrage.

Fritz was driven off again & we once more went to bed, & this time, were not disturbed till morning. It seemed as if it was just a gentle reminder that our leave was over & we were really back in France!

I left Boulogne at 8:30 the following evening (Sept. 24) in a crowded, 3rd class wooden seat troop coach with no glass in the windows. I descended at the Gare du Nord, Paris, early the next morning (Sept. 25). I could not leave Paris till 8 that night, so I still had one whole day of pleasure before me! I made the most of it! I picked up with Charlie Staples (one of M.T. men) who was also coming back from leave & spent part of the day with him.

We determined to have a really good dinner – an expensive dinner, & Charlie had an idea that the restaurant in the Bon Marché stores would be a good place. So we took the Metro to that part of Paris where the Bon Marché is situated (I don't know just <u>what</u> part) We wandered through the various departments of these palatial stores, & finally ascended to the big, glass, salle a manger which is up on the roof.

A handsome waitress met us at the entrance to the dining room. "What do you want, Messieurs?" she asked in good English. "We want something to eat". "But you cannot eat 'ere unless you are accompanied by a young lady!"

We looked at each other in amazement This sure had everything beat!

"Go out on ze boulevard" she said "& you soon find someone; one girl, she do for ze two of you"

We went out & soon found a high class, expensive looking restaurant, where we had an excellent dinner; but it only cost 15 francs for the two of us!

About every other shop in Paris is a Café & you do not walk very far on a sunny September day without getting a thirst. So, you do not need to walk very far & <u>remain</u> thirsty!

Intoxicating liquors are almost as common as water in France, but you hardly ever see a Frenchman drunk; you may see them happy - "feeling good" - but never <u>beastly</u> drunk.

We took the Troyes train out of the Gare de l'Est at 8 o'clock that night.

We reached Troyes somewhere in the small hours, & after a considerable waiting, got into the train for Eclaron (oh accursed name!) At ten a.m. Sept. 26. I reached Eclaron, & the absolute end of a most enjoyable 3 weeks.

Back to the routine, back to my working clothes & the log-piles.

But the war news was always good now, the Allies were steadily, though slowly, gaining. Truly the end was near & yet the damned pessimists <u>insisted</u> on another year or two's war: some even prophesied ten & twenty years!

The next two months were fairly monotonous My visits to St. Dizier became more frequent; I used to go there nearly every Sunday, sometimes I would sneak out on Saturday night & come back Sunday night.

Once in a while I'd get drunk, just to break the monotony & to ease the suspense . . .

Then the END came – the 11th of November 1918. We were out working in the woods as usual. Of course we were waiting for it, hoping for it, & fearing it would not be; but sure enough, somewhere about 11 a.m. all the bells of the Village churches around, started to toll.

And that miserable O.C. of ours did not have the common decency to come out & tell his men that the War was over!

He never told us. We got the official news from a French newspaper, when we got in from work that night!

The news was received very quietly & somewhat suspiciously; it seemed almost impossible; why, the War was a business, a permanent habit!

When we were really convinced that the war was over, then came the awful, burning impatience to quit, to leave France & get home. But it appeared probable that we should have to carry on for 3 or 4 months, perhaps longer. We did: we carried on just as if there was no Armistice for nearly 3 months. All the logs that were out in the woods had to be brought in, - there were probably some millions of feet - & all the light railway steel was to be torn up & shipped. The mills were to be gutted & the machinery sent away. The camps, alone, were to be left intact.

I became intolerably restless. On Nov. 23 I & another lad secured a week end pass to Troyes, this entitled us to be away from Saturday noon till Sunday midnight.

Postcard photo at Folkestone, England

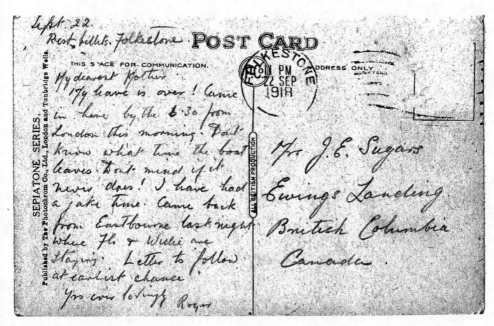

Postcard to Mother, Sept. 22, 1918

Saturday was a beautiful sunny day – perfect weather for travelling - so I armed myself with maps, & we agreed not to return to camp for 8 days. We planned our route & proceeded accordingly. We rode an American truck into St. Dizier, & were just in time to catch the 3.30 p.m. train for Vitry-le-Francois. We resolved to pay no railway fares on this trip, so we never entered a town through the station & the "Sortie". We always used the stations on leaving, but <u>never</u> on <u>arriving</u>. We used to arrive over the railway fence somewhere up the track!

We got into Vitry about dusk & at once hunted up a place to eat. We found a Café Restaurant – "English spoken", near the station. The proprietoress asked us what we would have; knowing we couldn't get what we wanted:- "I am good feesh & potatoes" So we had fish & potatoes.

She let us have a bedroom for 5 francs, & produced her hotel register, & said "you must sign your name in 'ere, I do not weesh it, eet ees ze law, you know" So we signed fictitious names – Brown & Smith! The old girl laughed & remarked knowingly: "Ah, eet ees always Brown!" The next morning we rose early & explored the town of Vitry-le-Francois.

A picturesque & ancient looking place – like all other French towns.

We dined in the big, fantasticly decorated, French Canteen at the Station. All these canteens are run on the ticket system: you have to buy a ticket or tag in order to get the use of a knife & fork or a tin cup even.

We fell in with some Russian soldiers in the canteen: they were very amiable & wanted to talk, but they knew no English & not much French, & of course we knew no Russian & as little French as they did. However, we managed to make each other understood in French! I thought they had about the smartest uniform I had seen, & made of the best cloth.

A little after noon we boarded a first class carriage of a train going west. About 1 o'clock we got out at Chalons-sur-Marne.

This was my second visit to Chalons, so I knew the town a

little. We promenaded for a while, inspected a tank that was on one of the streets, & tried to talk to some of the refugees. The town was full of refugees who were coming down from the towns evacuated by the Germans since the Armistice.

They seemed to be all homeless & didn't know what they were going to do. They certainly looked pitiful, straggling in with all kinds of old wagons & carts, laden with household goods.

They all had hard-luck stories which no doubt were true enough.

We had originally intended to stay overnight in Chalons, but about 4 o'clock we decided to move on, & take a run up to Riems via Epernay. We went down to the station, & I enquired: "A quel heure parti le train pour Epernay" "Ah, toute suite, toute suite!" So we made a run & dived into a "premier classe" coach. It was nearly always thus. No matter what time we took the notion to leave a town, there was a train just about to leave for the place we wanted to go to! If I remember rightly, it was about 5 p.m. when we furtively got out of the wrong side of the train at Epernay. As usual, we skirted round the freight yard & went into the station by the <u>street</u> entrance, to find out what time the train left for Reims.

They told us it would leave at about "Sept heure" which just gave us nice time to go & have supper. We had to ride second class to Reims. I think it was about 8.30 when we alighted in the great skeleton of Reims station. It was a very dark night & there were hardly any lights, but we could see the station was in ruins:- roofless, littered with débris, & all scarred & pitted with shellfire & shrapnel. We had some trouble finding a place to 'flop'. Finally we discovered a portion of one of the platforms, walled off with canvas (evidently it had been used as a hospital) We rooted around in the dark & found a couple of blood stained stretchers, a brazier & a pile of coal. With this material we proceeded to make ourselves comfortable for the night. We set the stretchers in a "V" & put the brazier within the angle thus formed, & got a good fire going with the help of old boards. While out foraging on the platforms for these boards, I stepped off the platform in the darkness; it was a drop of only about 4 feet, but I thought I had stepped into a bottomless pit!

We managed to get a little sleep: the fire in our brazier would burn down about every 2 hours, & we would at once wake with the cold. Of course we had no blankets, not even greatcoats! Some old sacks helped a little.

We did not lie abed very late the following morning, but were abroad in search of nourishment. There were no hotels, cafés, canteens or any other of the usual eating places. After a time we found a "Foyer du Soldat" where they gave us (free of charge) a hunk of bread & a cup of hot "café noir". Of course it was not enough, but it had to do; there was no prospect of getting a square meal until we got back to Epernay. We then proceeded to see the town – the "Martyred Town" which had been under shell fire for four years.

It was weird, it was terrible. It was almost inconceivable that this desolation had once been like other cities. – full of people, traffic, industry, & noise. Now it was as sombre & gruesome as ten thousand graveyards. After the mangling & pounding of four years war it was at rest, & silent.

Oh, the feeling it gave one is beyond description. My chief emotion, I think, was pity; it seemed so terribly sad.

Streets were there(some of them must have been almost like the boulevards of Paris) & buildings were there, but in the most awful state of wreckage. Nothing was undamaged.

Every here & there was a great shell hole in the street, with the tram line metals torn up & twisted like bits of wire, in the air.

Everywhere, the ground was strewn with fragments of shells, shrapnel bullets & "duds."

The famous cathedral is still standing though all battered & scarred, with several great shell holes clean through the roof.

In spite of all this, it still looked magnificent & almost defiant. You could imagine it thinking: "I have stood here through the ages, & here I will stand, though I be almost wrecked." And indeed, though it was terribly battered, yet it was not nearly so completely ruined as the other buildings of the town.

The cathedral was fenced off with barbed wire, & the doors were blocked with sandbags. We got through the fence into the yard, but we could not get into the cathedral itself.

There were hardly any human beings about, only a few French soldiers.

We were seeing many strange sights in Reims; & we were filled with wonder & interest, but we could not forget our stomachs: they were so terribly empty! Somewhere about noon we could stand it no longer, & jumped a train for Epernay. For ten or twelve miles back of Reims, there were intermediate rows of trenches & barbed wire, stretching on either side of the railway as far as the eye could see. We were in the heart of the Champagne country now, a dismal, rolling country it looked in winter. After we passed the trench & wire region, we entered the Vineyards, mile after after mile of them – thousands of acres of vines each supported by little stakes like hairs on a brush. We were very thankful to get to Epernay, & get a good feed in a café-restaurant.

Not only were we hungry, but pretty well "all in" After dinner we went to the best hotel we could find in Epernay, & booked a room for the night; they said we could pay in the morning. We went up to our room & ordered water, soap, & towels. We had a good wash & then went to bed & got a couple of hours sleep.

We felt better for this, so went out & promenaded the streets of Epernay till perhaps 8 o'clock. It seemed a fairly lively burg: - it ought to be, since it is the home of the worlds most famous champagne -!

We went down to the station & had some supper in the buffet. We never returned to our hotel, but boarded a westbound train which we rode as far as Chateau- Thierry. We were just in time to get a bed in a hotel near the station.

The next day we explored Chateau Thierry. This was the scene of desperate fighting not many months before. It was here that the Americans saved the day, in the extremity of the last great German drive. When we passed through Chateau Thierry in January , it was much battle scarred. Considerable damage was done in the town, chiefly by allied fire, I believe. Both the bridges across the Marne had been blown up by the Americans, to prevent the Germans getting over.

It was said that the old Marne river was literally dammed with corpses, & ran red with blood. It is a beautiful town, built on the slopes on both sides of the river. The North side is the steepest, & therefore the most picturesque.

Also it was on the North side where most of the street fighting took place. There were hundreds of "doughboys" about, & they all had wonderful stories to tell, though many of those who were in Chateau Thierry then, had not been there at the time of the fighting. We got into the tower of the church & mounted upward; it was a spiral staircase of 326 steps; we examined the bellfry & then climbed to the top. There were several shellholes clear through the walls of the tower. There was no spire, so we stepped out on the lead at the top, which was flat & walled with low battlements. On the top of the little "super" tower the flag of France was flying. There must have been a wonderful view, but as luck would have it, it was a misty morning, & we could scarcely see as far as the river.

Later, we walked out on the hills to the North of the town. Here, indeed had been a battle- ground. Everything was left just as it was on the day of the battle except that the dead had been buried. The slopes were pitted all over with great shell craters, & every tree was blasted & splintered. Nothing had been salvaged; the hillsides were littered with great German "duds" – unexploded 9-2s – fragments of big shells, of whizz bangs. There were broken rifles, German & French gas- masks, shreds of clothing, old boots, clips of machine gun cartridges, French & German helmets, water-bottles, & 101 other gruesome relics. But most conspicuous of all were the too numerous graves, each with its little wooden cross.

Most of the crosses on the French graves bore, simply, the inscription; "died for France July – 18" On top of the cross, the dead poilu's helmet was usually hung, & sometimes his rifle was laid on the grave. The French are big- hearted enough to erect crosses even on the graves of their enemies: there were plenty of German graves, & each cross was labelled "Un Soldat Allemend."

We came across one poor Fritzie who had been overlooked; his body was buried in a shellhole, but his arm was reaching upward out of the ground. The shrivelled fingers were bent like claws & the sleeve of his tunic was almost rotted away. My partner, who was a hardened specimen – took hold of the arm, & it broke off: the flesh was about the same consistency as fried fish! I felt a little sick; I couldn't have touched the blessed thing myself. There was a fine view of Chateau-Thierry & the Marne from those ghastly hills.

We returned to the town, washed the heavy mud from our boots under a pump, & went down to the station where we rested in the big canteen for an hour or so, & talked to some doughboys. It was getting fairly late in the afternoon, so we decided to beat it on the next train. I forget what time it rolled in, but it was somewhere about dusk.

We boarded her & were soon speeding Westward again, in a first class carriage, in company with a couple of American Flying Corps Officers. It was unusual to do much speeding in French trains, but this time, it seems, we had boarded the Paris-Nancy Express. This worried us a little; you see, Paris was to be our next stop, & we planned on entering Paris via Noisy-le-Sec in order to avoid the Military Police who infest the Gare de l'Est. The question was; would an Express stop at Noisy?

Right from the outset of the trip, Paris had been my main objective; Paris had many attractions, & not the least of these, was the fact that it was pretty hard to enter the Gay City & get out again without being nabbed by the British M.P.s. Hitherto, we had been travelling in safe territory, the French seldom, if ever, asked questions, & of course it was no affair of the Americans whether we had passes or not, but now we were going to try our luck in Paris which was full of British M.P.s whose business it was to arrest soldiers going around without passes

Well, our express rumbled through Noisy- le-Sec at top speed! That was surely our last chance gone, there would be no stop now till we had run into the Gare de l'Est. But the luck was running our way; the train stopped for about two minutes somewhere in the freight yards outside the Station, we were out in a twinkling & swallowed up in the darkness & smoke of the yards

They were huge freight yards, a maze of tracks & switches, & full of standing freight trains & busy yard engines.

There seemed to be a high wall on either side of the yards & we had some difficulty finding our way out onto the street. We had a good supper in a second rate restaurant, & then went out to locate ourselves. We were, of course somewhere on the North Eastern edge of Paris. I had a map of the city & a compass. We struck off, taking all the Rues & Boulevards that led in a Westerly direction, steering by the compass. We started at the Magasins du Butte Chaussant. It was not long before we came onto a broad Boulevard which I seemed to recognise; I looked up at the name-plate on the corner & saw it was the Boulevard Magenta. "Let's get to hell out of here toute suite" I exclaimed; We were only five minutes walk from the British Army & Navy Leave Club!

The Boulevard Magenta cut our route at right angles, so we went straight across it & took the first Rue leading Westward. After half an hour or so of walking across boulevards, & along rues & alleys, we came onto a great street which could not be mistaken anywhere; it was the Avenue des Champs Elysées. Since I had been in Paris before, the Armistice had taken place, & the city was gaily decorated with flags & captured guns & aeroplanes. Down both sides of the Champs Elysées for its entire leg length, there were German field guns standing hub to hub, & the Arc de Triomphe was surrounded with captured Artillery. The town was not brilliantly lit, but it was very different to the darkness of the war days.

We got a 7 franc room, in a small hotel, on a Rue somewhere off the Madeleine Church.

Before starting out on the trip we had agreed to go on no drunks, for there is nothing more fatal to the soldier who is A.W.L. than getting his senses fuddled with booze. He is sure to get into some trouble, & be arrested.

Therefore we conducted ourselves very soberly & only drank in moderation.

The next morning we breakfasted in an American Y.M.C.A. hotel, which we found not far from our room. The thing I remember most about that breakfast was the cornmeal porridge, served with milk <u>and</u> <u>sugar</u>! I laid in a supply of Camel cigarettes (3 packs $1.20 cents) & we then set out on the days adventures. The first thing we did was to get a shave.

It was somewhere near the Trocadero that we boarded a train, & rode it out to the end, at Auteuil – a suburb, right in the South-Western corner of Paris & on the river –

We walked back along the bank of the Seine (on the North side) It was a lovely sunny day, & the river with all its barges looked beautiful. Half a mile or so up the river we came on a Bleriot aeroplane factory, & were permitted to be shown through. Our guide took us into every department of the factory: it was interesting on entering the shop where they stretch the canvas onto the planes we were greeted by a chorus of "Oh, la, la", this shop was full of girls, & they seemed astonished to see us; "Anglais, non? Ah, Canada"! I passed round my Camel cigarettes which pleased them greatly, & we then went into the last shop – the painting & varnishing department. We thanked our guide & he asked us to come again.

We walked on up the river until we were opposite the Eiffel Tower, & then turned into the city past the Trocadero. We took a street car to the Boulevard de la Madeleine [*Madeleine Sugars was named after this street*], & had lunch at our Y.M. After dinner we held a council of War. We came to this conclusion; that we were fairly safe out in the suburbs, but there was nothing doing there, while in the city, the constant vigilance spoiled one's pleasure. Of course we had seen hundreds of British soldiers & officers, & not a few M.P.s, the latter, however, we had given a wide berth, & had met none face to face.

We had passed the gates of Pepinéne Barracks in a street car.

Pepinéne Barracks appeared to be the head- quarters of the British in Paris, anyhow they had a jail there, where they treated their military offenders like animals. The Peep-in- éne (no thank you) Barracks they were sometimes called.

If I remember rightly, they were located in the Place St. Augustine.

Well, we thought, under the existing circumstances, there was much to stay in Paris for, & if we left that day we should have accomplished the coveted deed, - entered the town & got out again - So we decided to beat it – not hurriedly, but gradually, via Noisy-le- Sec. We walked Eastward along the Rue de Rivoli for some distance, & then fairly bribed a taxi-driver to take us out to Vincennes. We played about there for an hour or so & went through the old Fort which is just outside the Port du Vincennes – We had a weary wait, in a dreary street, for our tram. At O la la (it was pronounced like that; I don't know how it was spelt!) we changed into another tram, packed chock a block, which finally landed us at Noisy, sometime after dark. Noisy was safe enough – no British soldiers to be seen – We went to the station & I enquired for the Troyes train; "Sept heure quarante-neuf, troisieme quai, change a Gretz".

This gave us plenty of time to have supper & look round a bit.

At half past seven we were waiting for our train, she was pretty well on time & we secured a first class carriage to ourselves as usual. I think it was about an hour's run to Gretz, where we were to change. When we got there, my partner got a crazy idea into his head that he would travel no further that night, but stop in Gretz.

We found that Gretz was just a Village & there was absolutely no place to stay. We waked up most of the inhabitants & asked for "un chambre", but they shoved us off in the most hostile manner!

In the end we had to jump a train back towards Paris. We got out at Nogent le-Perreux-Bry, a fair sized town about 20 miles out of Paris. We were too late to get into any hotel, but we found a first class waiting room with some velvet lounges & a glorious coke fire,

& there passed a comfortable night. About 5 o'clock the next morning we got a first class compartment in the Troyes train. We changed at Longue Ville & had breakfast. It was quite a long run to Troyes, & I think we got there about 11 a.m. At Romilly, I think it was, a French Military Policeman got into our carriage. He was all silver braid & revolvers & asked for our "Permissions"!

Now we're up a tree, we thought; as a last resource I handed him my out of date Troyes Pass. He could see the word "PASS" & the official stamp, but evidently could not read the rest! Anyhow, he was satisfied; "Ah, ces bon, merci Messieurs" & he went out, leaving us very much relieved. We stayed in Troyes till six o'clock that evening, when we took the familiar old train for St. Dizier. We got into St. Dizier about 11 p.m. & just in time to secure a room in a hotel. We were only 7 miles from camp now, & we didn't know when we might bump into some of our own officers.

(They were always in St. Dizier when they weren't in Paris, or Dijon, or Nancy, or some place!) The next morning we took our stand on the Bar-le-Duc Road, just on the edge of the town. It was not long before we saw what we wanted – an American motor lorry. He stopped at the railway crossing to let a train go by; on seeing us, he called out "Hey, Tommy come here a minute" We went over to him & he passed us a bottle of cognac, "Where you fellers headed for?" he asked "Bar-le-Duc, eh, well you'd better pile in, that's where I'm going'" He turned out to be the driver of the tail end lorry of a convoy that was plying between Chaumont & Verdun – evacuating troops from the latter, into Chaumont, which was American G.H.Q.

We soon caught up with some more of the convoy, & we shifted into the next lorry which was driven by a fine young lad named Moody. We rode on the driving seat with him, all that day.

All the lorries seemed well supplied with beer cognac & cigarettes.

They never offered you a drink or a cigarette, these Yanks; they just handed you a bottle, or a packet.

It was this young Moody who unbuckled the Colt's Automatic

from about his waist & gave it to us – either of us that wanted it; (it became mine in the end) He also gave us 25 francs in case we might need it.

The Yanks liked the Canadians & they would do anything to help a Canadian who was A.W.L.

The idea of a soldier being absent without leave appealed to them. (The American army had about 20 000 absentees at the time of the Armistice)

We got into Bar-le-Duc about noon. (It is the usual style of French town, of fair size) we spent an hour there, in a joint with which the lorry drivers seemed very familiar There was a "Gold Brick" guarding the entrance but we went in via a stone wall, a portion of roof, & a jump down to a back door!

Poor young Moody went in with some hundreds of francs, & came out practically "bust."

He asked us where we thought of going from Bar-le-Duc, we told him Verdun; Well, he was going to Verdun & we'd better come along. So away we went, through Bar-le-Duc & on into the hilly country of the Meuse. Moody was about half pickled by this time, but he drove straight & fast. We munched biscuits smoked cigarettes, & drank beer, almost continually It was a very cold day, & sitting for hours in that lorry would certainly have been torture but for a little booze.

The Verdun road passes through a rather wild, bleak, hilly country, very different from the flat country of the Haute Marne.

About dusk we arrived at a big American camp, just a few miles South of Verdun. We got supper here, & then said goodbye to our friend Moody, & took another truck right up into the front of Verdun.

It was pitch dark when we got there; our lorry driver said; "you fellers'll likely get a flop over there in the quarters of the So & So division, but look out you don't fall into the trenches in the dark; a guy broke his leg there last night" With that he left us. We couldn't get a flop with the outfit he mentioned; their "barracks" were plumb full of men who were going to leave early in the morning. After some groping round we entered another building. In one room in the upper storey we found 3 doughboys toasting themselves before an open fire, which they had built of old furniture & boxes. They made us welcome as usual, gave us a packet of Camel cigarettes each, & told us to take a seat (on the floor) before the fire.

We yarned with them for a little, but soon got sleepy, so they fixed us up in the next room with a couple of old cots & mattresses & some blankets. There was an open-fire place in this room also, & we soon had a roaring fire going, & were comfortable for the night. The next morning we fell in line with so & so Coy of the --- Division for breakfast which they were taking round a field-kitchen, outside just before departure.

We then hiked off to explore the famous fort of Verdun. To all appearances, the fort is just a hill braced with a wall of masonry about it. The top is intersected with trenches & earthworks, grown over in the most natural manner with turf & bushes.

In the centre is a group of store buildings (in one of which we had slept) surrounding a sort of square. But in reality, this hill is like an ant's nest. Every here & there around the edge of the hill, you would see, on top of some grassy mound, a little, steel, sort of pill-box, in which a machine gun could evidently be placed, from below, & in many of the deeper trenches you would come on a passage way with steps leading down into the bowels of the hill. All these entrances were guarded by French soldiers & they would not let us go into the underground part of the fort at all. Of course there is a beautiful view from the hill in every direction

It was a fine sunny morning, & we felt much impressed as we looked down on the grey & battered old town & the Meuse river sparkling in the Sunshine.

The fort was battered about quite a bit but nothing to what I had expected; it was the town, as usual, which had suffered the worst; it was wrecked – just like Riems.

When we had got our fill of exploring outside, we turned our attention on the buildings in the centre. These had evidently been used as barracks by the Americans for some time. Every room was just littered with American equipment of all kinds & in any quantity; clothing, hats, caps, boots, belts, gas-masks, "tin-hats", bully-beef, hard tack, & bull Durham tobacco. The fort was deserted; the last of the Yanks, with the exception of a few stragglers, had gone that morning.

In one of the buildings I found a French bayonet in good condition; I wrapt an American puttee around it, hung on my belt &, -- took it back to Canada with me!

I also found a pair of American breeches, almost new, I put these on & left my tar-stained trousers behind!

I wish I could have brought home a few Springfield rifles; I could have got a wagon-load of them, if I had had any means of carrying them.

We intended to make camp that night, & as we had about 100 miles to go, we decided to start early, so about 10 o'clock we left Verdun, & walked out on the Bar-le-Duc road. Pretty soon we jumped a truck which carried us as far as Souilly, from there we got another for a few miles, then we had to walk a mile or so. Several cars & trucks passed us too fast to jump, then one decent fellow slowed down a little for us, & after a 20 yard run we got aboard. This lorry took us all the way to Bar-le-Duc. We were back on the railway now so didn't have to bother about any "lorry hopping". –

We had dinner in the big station canteen (it being 1 p.m. now), & about 3 o'clock we boarded a train for Blesme.

For the first, & only time on the whole trip a ticket collector tackled us. We said we had "pas tickets", & told him to "go jump in the lake". He went off, finally, muttering threats about "beaucoup police".

We left this hostile train at Blesme about 4 p.m. After an hour's wait, we got the St. Dizier train, which landed us at that city about 6 o'clock.

We went up to the Hotel du Soleil d'Or & had a 4 or 5 course dinner, which we did not pay for. (We had an old score to pay off on the Hotel du Soleil d'Or.)

We then proceeded across country on foot, along the well-known canal & the familiar fields, to camp – detested hole! –

It was about 9 p.m. Nov. 30th, when we reported ourselves in, to the Sergeant Major. He ordered us to shift our blankets into the "clink" & sleep there that night. The next day we loafed round camp, under "open arrest", & in the evening we got our trial, & sentence, - "7 days No.1field punishment, & 6 days pay forfeited by Royal Warrant" –

This was easy, it had been a cheap trip; we had expected at least 14 days. " F.P. No. 1" in No. 10 district C.F.C., consisted merely of eating & sleeping in the "clink" & carrying on as usual, with the days work. The "clink" was warmer, less noisy, & generally more comfortable than the huts; also we got more than we could eat there. There were three or four other jail birds, most of whom were in for the same offence as ourselves.

I was sorry when my 7 days was over & I had to forsake the comfort & privacy of the jail.

Another blank!

Christmas & New Year passed uneventfully Bracey, our hut orderly, bet his hut a pail of beer we would be on the move by the 20th of January; the 20th came but no move, Bracey bought the pail of beer for the boys! About that time, I & Bob Bradbury, got a week end pass to Troyes That was the last jaunt I had in France, & I made the most of it. Troyes was Paris on a very small scale.

Several of the boys got 4 days passes, & went into Germany; I would have done so, only my funds had almost given out. For the last two or three weeks we did practically no work, but just stood over gangs of German prisoners while they lifted & loaded narrow guage railway steel. The poor "P.G.s" were very willing & would work their heads off for a little food or tobacco.

Our neighbours, 31 & 33 Coys. had already gone about 10 days when our turn came February 1st 1919 we said goodbye to the Forêt du Der. About noon we were all packed up & ready to travel. I don't think any body had any regrets as we marched out of the old camp where we had lived for a year. Anyhow the boys sang most of the way to Eclaron!

We entrained into the good old boxcars once more & about 2 p.m. our old freight, (which was about a mile long – 76 Coy only occupied a few coaches of it) pulled out of Eclaron on the Southwestern route.

We had now, really started on that wonderful process – demobilization - "Demobilization" – what a beautiful word it was!

There were about 18 of us in the car I was in. We had plenty of straw, & "Micky" Fraser, had had the foresight to fix up a little tin stove, & carry it down from camp; thus our chief misery, cold, was considerably allayed.

There was an accordion & mandolin, & a concert- ina in our car, also a couple of good singers! We were, dirty & cramped but happy as maggots in a grease-pot.

Our train crawled away down the familiar route to Troyes, through Montier-en-Der, Brienne le Chateau, Mathaux & Piney. We got into Troyes after dark & lay some time in the yards. After she got started again we fell asleep.

There is nothing like rhythmic, "bump, bump, bumpity, bump" of a train, to make you sleep.

We slept, scientifically fitted in like sardines head to feet. When your sleeping partner stirred in his sleep he would dig you in the chest or under the chin with his toes!

We woke at dawn the next morning to find the train standing in a siding with no engine! It was an unfamiliar looking, dreary place, with hills on either side.

We walked up to the station & found it was a small town called Sens. On looking at the map I found that we were in the department of Yonne; We had strayed far to the south of the usual Troyes-Paris route; we had left the Chemin de Fer d l'Est & were now on the Paris, Lyons, Marsailles line.

It appeared that we had got side tracked here & forgotten. Leut. Schmechl (our old S.M.) went to the Chef de Gare & made a fuss, & after a time an engine came along & towed us out.

We didn't care, we were seeing a part of France we had never been through before.

We rolled North Westwards all that day (with frequent, more or less short stops, of course) We passed through Pont-sur-Yonne Monteriau, Fontainebleau, & Melun.

I thought the Forest of Fontainbleau with it's little towns, such as Thomery, & Bois- le-Roi, was the prettiest part of France I had seen. We side-tracked that night, as usual, somewhere beyond Melun – probably at Corbeil --. The next day we travelled on, through Noisy-le-Sec, & the Northern suburbs of Paris, & on down the Seine Valley. We made good time that afternoon; we passed Rouen, & came to a halt late in the night, a few miles out of Havre. this was a remarkable distance to cover in one day, & carried us, practically, to the end of our box-car journey.

We lay in that yard till 10 or 11 the next morning. Micky Fraser & I made the most of our time in getting rid of the left over rations. In our car, we had about 30 cans of bully beef & pork & beans left over, also a hunk of cheese. Micky & I sold the canned stuff to the French railway men for a franc a tin, & the hunk of cheese we disposed of for 5 francs.

The proceeds were divided up amongst the occupants of the car; it came to one franc apiece & a few centimes over which Micky & I kept as "wages" for our labour!

The day before, every man had been given 200 "Camel" cigarettes (dividends of the old canteen funds) I was well supplied with tobacco but almost broke, so I sold my cigarettes for 10 francs.

I think it was about 11.30 when our train pulled into the No. 2 Rest Camp, Havre. This was February. 4th – 3 days since we had left Eclaron.

No. 2 Rest Camp – the old "Cinder city" looked much the same as it did when we were going "up the line" a year & a half before, but it was now called the "Canadian Embarkation Camp."

Two men of our Coy. (Harry White & Watts) had thought of a much better way of travelling to Havre than in the boxcars with the rest of the bunch. They left camp two days before the Coy., & travelled by passenger train to Paris to where they put in two or three days, & then went on to Havre, & reported in to the "Cinder City"! Their case was overlooked, anyway, they got no punishment. Several men were left behind at Bois- le-Roi, but they jumped the next train & overtook us at Melun!

We spent four days at Havre, & there was always something going on. The camp was crowded with men; the 3rd Division was demobilizing & there were 3 or 4 battalions going through while we were there, among them, the 49th the 16th & the R.C.R.s

The latter were a "classy" bunch with more polished metal on them than any other unit. They certainly made our scratch Forestry crowd look like a lot of hoboes!

We were billited in long, corrugated-iron huts, with cobble stone floors; it was frosty weather & they were terribly cold; no heating at all, of course. There were two E.F.C.s a Salvation army & a Y.M.C.A.

One evening at the Y. we were entertained by the "Dumbells" (the 3rd Division troupe) & a splendid performance it was too. The Y. provided free tea, & biscuits at 50 centimes, & the Salvation army, tea at a penny a cup & biscuits at 60 centimes! The feeding was the worst feature, the food itself was alright, but at mealtimes there were two double line-ups to each cook house, anywhere from 100 to 200 yards long.

I bumped into Arthur Stocks one after- noon . He was a 49th Batt. reinforcement & had been in France under a year, but had seen a little fighting & had marched into Belgium.

A few Americans used to visit our camp; I sold a belt I had to one of them for 10 francs. This, with the ten francs I got for my cigarettes raised my capital to about 25 francs. I was thus enabled to go down to Havre almost every evening. I "went with" Micky Fraser while at Havre, & though we hadn't much money we had a pretty good time. I was always able to pay for my supper, carefare & a few drinks of cognac; with such slim pockets we had to carefully avoid madamoiselles.

It was about a 10 minute tram ride from the Cinder City to Havre; we could go down town any time we liked, without passes.

The trams were all double ones – a trailer hooked on behind. Going back at night it was usually impossible to get standing room, let alone a seat. One night, after letting two or three trams go by, crowded to overflowing, I had to ride to camp standing on the couplings between the two cars!

On the evening of the 8th February, we fell in for embarkation, together with the 49th Batt. & some stragglers.

We had a mile & a half to march down to the boat. It was a comfortable boat for a troop ship, but of course overcrowded.

I managed to find just enough floor space to stretch my carcass on, & got a little sleep during the night. The next morning we found ourselves anchored in Portland Harbour, Dorset. France was no more, it had passed out of our lives, probably for good.

We disembarked somewhere about 1 p.m. The 49th entrained & went to Bramshot, while we marched across to the mainland to the camp of the 3rd Dorsets.

It was a fine sunny day, & Blighty looked good; the villages on the island of Portland & the mainland looked homely, comfortable, & so wonderfully <u>clean.</u>

We passed the night at the 3rd Dorset camps. Of all the military camps I have been in, this was the most comfortable & clean. The huts were of the usual type, but on entering we were astonished at the dazzling cleanliness of the interior. The walls were washed pale blue, & the floors were scrubbed; in the corner was a stack of bed- boards, & snow-white palliasses, filled with fresh straw. It was a "home from home".

The next morning we were on the road to Weymouth before daylight. We entrained into 3rd class passenger coaches & travelled Northwards all day, through Dorchester, Bath, Bristol, Monmouth, Hereford, Shrewsbury, & Chester. At Chester we changed for Rhyl, N. Wales, where we arrived about 11.30 p.m. Half an hour in the Military Camp Railway took us to Kinmel Park. We could not understand why we had come to Kinmel & not to our Base (Smiths Lawn). Kinmel was the final Canadian Embarkation Camp, & we hoped that we might get away without going to the Base.

However, it turned out that we had been shipped to Kinmel by some mistake!

On February. 15. having been 5 days at Kinmel, doing absolutely nothing, they gave us £8 & 8 days leave with orders to report in to the Base Depot C.F.C. Smiths Lawn! This £8 was the first money we had received since leaving Eclaron, & most of us were bust.

I proceeded to Huyton & spent two, quiet, pleasant days with my aunts. On the 17th they accompanied me to Manchester, where we had dinner & spent a few hours.

Fanny took me through the Exhibition, where several of her own pictures were hung. About 3 o'clock they saw me off to Nottingham. We said goodbye as that was likely to be my last leave before sailing for Canada. That was the last time I saw them. I was very sorry I had not seen George again. They had certainly done all in their power to make me welcome while I was in England.

I descended at Nottingham about dark, in the midst of a sloppy snowstorm, & went up to the "Gilmer School of Dancing".

I was able to see Bessie for about 20 minutes that evening; they were terribly busy; half the staff were down with flu or something, & she was taking the place of two or three. However, she promised me the whole of the next evening, & part of the afternoon so I had to go away contented. I went down to King's Restaurant & lingered over a supper there till after 10 o'clock. An artisticly fitted up place it was, warm & comfortable & almost empty that night. And there were some pretty & amiable waitresses – when the joint closed I escorted one of them home.

This act proved very decidedly that I was no longer in love with Bessie. It was a fact, as soon as I saw her this time, I knew I loved no more; I don't know why; she was just the same in every way. I could not help it. I liked her ever so much but I did not love her. Oh, I guess my head gets turned pretty easy!

I have never told her to this day, but I hope & rather think, she feels the same. She is back in Arequipa now, & writes me "chummy" letters – not love letters!

On the afternoon of the 20th I left Nottingham, for London, to visit Flo & Willie. I got into Marylebone about 8 p.m. , & made my way by buses & trams to Nether Street, North Finchley. I received a hearty welcome, as before. It didn't matter what time of day or night I turned up, or under what circumstances I could be sure of a welcome from Flo & Willie.

I had wired to the Base from Nottingham for 48 hours extension, & on the eve of the expiry of my 8 days, the reply arrived; "48 hrs. extension granted", so I had 5 days altogether at Finchley, & I thoroughly enjoyed them, it was a "home from home" know what I mean! On the visit, Flo presented me with Jack's camera *[Jack Semple]*– a beautiful post card size Kodak. Jack, who was Flo's only boy & my cousin, died of wounds in the spring of '15. He is buried at Rouen. On the morning of the 25th Feb. I went to Waterloo & took the train for Egham. On arrival, I & another lad hired a car to take us up to Smiths Lawn (about 2 miles), it cost us seven shillings each!

The Base Depot of the C.F.C. had not altered much since the Summer of '17, the mud was just as deep, & the huts just as draughty.

The greater part of the process of demobilization was done at Smiths Lawn, that is all the 101 necessary (?) papers were prepared here. They put us through 4 or 5 different Coys, each Coy., attending to a different set of papers. The first was the "receiving" & Q.M. the next, Medical Board, the "Leave" (for exceptional cases) "Dispersal Area" etc. & finally "draft". There were many fatigues, almost every day you would be detailed for a fatigue party.

I always gave them the slip, however; out of the many fatigues I was detailed for I only took part in one – a trip on a motor lorry! One morning I was put on a mud shovelling gang close to the hut I was living in, so when the corporal wasn't looking I dropped my shovel & stepped into the hut. I sat on my blankets & read all the morning, & I could hear the wretched party shovelling mud just outside! By taking advantage of opportunities it was always possible to escape from a fatigue-party, because the idiots never took your name!

You could sleep in any hut you had a mind to, so as long you fell in on your proper Coy. parade ground. I found most of the one-time 76 Coy. scattered all through the camp.

One evening in the beer canteen I discovered my old friend Charley de Chastelain. He had been with 78 Coy away down near Dax on the Bay of Biscay.

Charley was over 50 but we got on well together. He had a blank piece of floor beside him so I shifted my blankets into his hut. We stuck together for the rest of our army lives (about 6 weeks) While at Smiths Lawn, he & I used to go out nearly every evening to Englefield Green. This place was about a mile & a half away, & though only a small Village, it had at least half a dozen homely, comfortable little pubs. We usually patronized the "Happy Man" or the "Holly Tree"

We spent some very pleasant evenings, sitting by the open fire, yarning, & absorbing vast quantities of stout. We always drank stout when we could get it; it is the finest drink I know, pleasing & satisfying to the palate, it is just intoxicating enough to make you feel good, it never gives you a "head" the next morning, & it fattens you like cream. We used to get back to the camp about 11 o'clock, roll in our blankets on the hard floor & sleep like logs, to wake up in the morning feeling nourished & stimulated.

The old fashioned Village pub is one of the best things England possesses. God guide her safely through the prohibition campaign!

I could never induce old Charley to walk any distance, so when I went to Egham or further it was usually alone or with Ed. Hewlett. One afternoon I headed out for Windsor (alone). About 6 miles it was, but good walking, most of the way on the "Long Walk." I had dinner & supper in Windsor & went all through the exterior of the Castle. It was most interesting & there were many beautiful views from the Terraces The town itself is very picturesque & quaint.

It seemed to be populated mainly with Eton boys, Coldstream Guards & Waacs.

I returned across country through the Park to Englefield Green which I reached about dusk. Charley was waiting for me at the "Happy Man".

By March 5th I had progressed as far as the Company which was said to give leave. The Sergeant told us in the morning there would be a parade for leave, but that it was useless for any men to apply who had had leave since Christmas. It was only about 10 days since I had come off leave but I determined to try for it again, so I fell in line with my paybook the last entry in which was; "Feb. 15. Kinmel Park Leave 8 days, £8." I handed the officer the tell tale pay book; he looked at it & started to hand it back to me, saying;"But you've only just had leave from Kinmel!" "Yes Sir" I said, declining to take back the pay- book, "I know, but my brother is in London now & I haven't seen him for 3 years – " "I'm afraid it's no use" he said turning to the next man, & shoving the pay book toward me. As a last I hope I hurriedly said, "Couldn't you give me 48 hours, Sir?" sick of me, he snapped "alright" & gave me two pounds! The lie carried me through & the next morning I proceeded on my 48 hour pass to London.

This was my last visit to Flo & Willie On the evening of March 9th I returned, having overstayed my leave by 36 hours. I said goodbye to Flo at the Lodge, & Willie accompanied me to Waterloo & saw me off. I got into Smiths Lawn about 11 p.m. got some blankets from the Q.M. & went to my hut. Charley had succeeded in reserving my place beside him. I lit a candle, spread my blankets & then waked up Charley for a smoke. He was always ready for a smoke day or night. He gave me a cigar, & said he was glad to see me back - he had been lonesome!

On March 19th we left Smiths Lawn with a large draft for Rhyl. We were now sorted out into "Military Districts"; ours was M.D. 11 (British Columbia). M.D. 11 was again divided into 3 dispersal stations or areas; "U" (Victoria etc.) "T" (Vancouver etc." & "T.1" (Revelstoke) This last was mine, Revelstoke being only 60 miles from Salmon Arm.

The pipe-band played us down to Egham, where we entrained

at 10 a.m.

About 7.30 that evening we arrived at Abergele (near Rhyl) & had to walk up to Kinmel Park Camp, a distance of about 4 miles. Kinmel is a vast camp, covering about 2 square miles, & said to be large enough to accommodate 40,000 men. It is scientifically built & laid out. The frame huts are lined, roofed with slate, & set on cement blocks; the streets are all properly built & drained

It really consists of about a dozen camps, each one representing a Military District, & each having its own parade ground, guard room, Q.M., Canteen, cook- houses etc. Each camp had a Navy & Army Canteen Board hut. The N.A.C.B. is one of the best canteens I have struck; the huts are large, & well fitted & decorated, one end handles general supplies, while the other sells beer The wet canteens were always crammed full of an evening, & much gambling went on, cards were not allowed so they played "House" ("Keeno"). In addition to the numerous N.A.C.B.s there were 3 Y.M.C.A.s, 2 or 3 Salvation Army Huts, a Church Army Hut a Wesleyan Soldiers' Institute, & a camp theatre.

On the road outside the camp gates was a row of civilian buildings, rushed up to get the trade of the camp; this was called "Tin Town", most of the shacks being built of corrugated iron. It consisted of a movie house, several refreshment rooms, a photographers & Tatooers, & a number of shops that sold the usual "military supplies" – badges, buttons, caps, breeches chevrons etc. There was a Military Camp railway with 2 or 3 trains a day to Rhyl (about 5 miles) also many "jitneys" & a motor bus. Since I had been in Kinmel before there had been some rioting, evidence of which could be seen in the numerous broken windows in the canteens, & the almost wrecked condition of Tin Town.

The cause of the rioting was that the troops were not being drafted off to Canada fast enough; they were often held there as long as six weeks, & were constantly being put on sailings & then taken off again.

The authorities said that the shipping was short & the men were being sent to Canada as quickly as was possible. However, after the riots, the sailings increased in some mysterious way, & they seldom kept men in Kinmel longer than ten days. Of course everybody except the rank & file condemned the rioters as Bolshevists & rebels; anyhow, I felt like shaking hands with them, they had done a good work.

We were ten days at Kinmel. – a pretty easy time, a short & to-the-point parade every morning & afternoon, & one or two fatigues (which could not be dodged as at Smiths Lawn). Charley & I used to go down to Rhyl nearly every evening, have supper & drink stout, beer & gin-vermouth till about 10 o'clock, when we usually took the train back to camp. We were pretty tight sometimes, but we never failed once to find our hut, which wasn't bad considering there were some thousands of them all exactly alike!

Not a bad little town, Rhyl, but too much overrun with Canadian Troops.

There was a little tobacconist on Bodfor Street that Charley & I used to visit quite a lot to buy "Warlock" Navy cut & little cigars. There was a little girl of about 16 or 17 in there, whom I almost fell in love with. She wrote to me once or twice & it seems she did fall in love with me. I guess she would soon get over it, same as Bessie Michell (By the way I have just heard that Bessie is engaged to be married!) On the morning of the 29th of March 1919, we were drafted out of Kinmel!

We marched to Abergele, & entrained there for Liverpool, we embarked that afternoon on the R.M.S. "Coronia" a big Cunarder. At 5.30 we drew out from the Riverside Landing Stage, & moved slowly down the Mersey. That was my last day in the old World. I never had such a feeling of suppressed emotion as when that great liner started moving out of Liverpool. A band was playing on the landing stage, & of course the cheering was deafening. I was overjoyed to be going, & yet I was a little sorry too. It is quite a place, England, after all, & I wondered if I would ever see it again.

If I remember rightly, there were 3,000 "other ranks" on board, & 800 officers, bound for all parts of Canada & the U.S.; (Charley, of course, was going to California, after getting his discharge in

Vancouver).

The saloon deck (where the officers lived) was in its' condition, but on the lower decks all the cabin partitions had been knocked out to make room for troops.

The hammocks were hung on the roof with about 6 inches of play between each, the long messing tables were directly underneath: you stepped out of your hammock onto the table.

Charley & I were lucky enough to get our hammocks slung right beside a port hole on "E" deck (the top deck was "A"!"). We thus had light to read by, & fresh air. The greatest blessing you can have in the bowels of a great ship.

There is not much comfort on a big troopship, but I don't think anybody minded: we were going home & that was all that mattered. The food was not very good but there was plenty of it – in fact, too much.

I lived almost exclusively on hard tack, apples & oranges, & slept & read most of the time in my hammock. We had a good quiet crossing & the weather was warm. Nothing exciting or unusual happened.

We steamed into Halifax at 5.30 p.m. April 5th 1919, having been seven days on the Atlantic. Every ship in the harbour blew its siren to welcome the troopship. M.D. 11 was second for disembarkation. We marched into the dock- side station at 7 p.m. We were welcomed by Red Cross & Salvation Army outfits who shook hands with every man, & passed round refreshments. By 8 p.m. we were entrained – in the big, comfortable C.P.R. coaches. No, crowding; blankets, mattresses & pillows provided, lavatory & ice-water! Some luxury! A bit different to our train journeys of two months before. No messing about for hours & days, either; at 9 o'clock we were rolling Westward.

The next morning we stopped at St. John, New Brunswick, & dropped a small draft of troops there. We passed on through N.B. & into the State of Maine. The State of Maine – never have I seen such a wild & desolate country as that part through which the C.P. passes; a chaos of rocky hills, burnt timber, scrub spruce & little lakes, all ice & snow bound.

I asked the Station agent at the Divisional point of Holeb, what they did in that country; "Jest as little as we can" he said "a little lumberin', a little fishin', an' that's about all". Holeb was just a station in the heart of this winter-bound wilderness.

That evening, we recrossed the Canadian line & stopped for a short time in Megantic, Quebec.

Early next morning we arrived at Smith Falls, Ontario; we were making rapid time, we had left Halifax 12 hours behind the "Imperial Limited" & were already overhauling it. That night we got as far as Sudbury: after that we once more enter- ed the wilderness. The following morning (the 8th) we got to White River, a little town on the North Shore. Most of the snow had gone here, but the temperature was down near zero. All the Bays of Lake Superior were still frozen up.

At Nipigon there was no sign of spring. The snow still lay thick, it was bitter cold & snow was falling. Nipigon seems to be just a trading post for the North Shore. The C.P. passes through, east & west, but to the south is the Lake & to the North, the woods, clear to James Bay. That evening we arrived at Port Arthur – the "GateWay of the Great West". The most conspicuous objects in Port Arthur & Fort William are the many huge grain elevators. In the small hours of the 9th we made Winnipeg. We were on the prairie now & we sure travelled some.

The next day we made Calgary. The journey was getting near the finish now, for me anyhow; there were only a handful of men for Revelstoke, the bulk of them were going to Vancouver & Victoria. We were due into Revelstoke sometime that night. It was a picnic, that trip, the grub was A1 & plenty. All the principal towns met the train, presented cards of welcome to every man, & plied us with refreshments & smokes.

That journey seemed to be just one long meal. The effects of it & the stout drinking days in Blighty made me so soft & fat I could hardly move. Well, we left Calgary, crossed the Rocky Mountains got held up for an hour with a fallen Rock in the Connaught Tunnel in the Selkirks, & got into Revelstoke at midnight, April 10th, 5 days since leaving Halifax.

I said goodbye to a few of my friends, Charley de Chastelain, & old Griffiths of the Yukon, in particular.

Ed. Hewlett had missed that draft at Smiths Lawn (through no fault of his own) & did not get to Canada till 10 days later.

By 2 a.m. of the 11th I had my discharge certificate, service button, & a ticket to Salmon Arm. I was free, I was a Civilian! But I still had a uniform on & I didn't feel any physical change!

I didn't bother about sleep that night, I had an early 2.30 a.m. breakfast in a chink joint, & then went to the Y.M. & had a bath, change of underwear & general clean up.

About 7 o'clock I boarded the West bound, had a good breakfast in the dining car, & arrived at Salmon Arm about 9 a.m. April 11th 1919.

Here ends the story of my adventures in the Canadian Expeditionary Force.

My people had sold the old place in the Okanagan to Godwin, for $1,000 & had come to Salmon Arm in November 1918, with the intention of trying a photography business with A.K.

They rented a shack on Lyman Hill, just outside the town for $6.00 per month. they soon found that photography was not going to be a success, so they took to the ordinary manual jobs again, & Mother started giving music lessons. She was most successful & now has about 20 pupils. I was very disappointed, on my return, to find Mother laid up, with the after effects of a bad attack of tonsilitis. Two weeks later she went to hospital & had the tonsils removed: the operation was successful, but one of the fool nurses left an uncovered hot- water-bottle against her foot while she was under the anaesthetic. It burned the entire sole of her foot very badly indeed, & of course she was unable to walk for 3 weeks; also she suffered much pain. I was thankful I was at home to help take care of her.

Very soon after my return, I decided to get a ranch through the Soldier Settlement Board, & thereby secure a home, & possibly a living for us all.

I was getting $70 a month War Service Gratuity, for 3 months, & this enabled me to abstain from work for a while.

I looked at many places, & finally chose the place we are now living on, which then belonged to "Gene" Timpany.

I will not detail all the proceedings with the Soldier Settlement Board – all the signing & filling out of hundreds of documents, the feverish letter writing & telegraphing.

Suffice it to say that about the middle of April I put in my application, & on the 13th of August I took up residence on the ranch!

The place cost $5,500, $500. of which we paid ourselves. The loan of $5000 from the S.S.B. is to be paid back in 25 equal, annual instalments [sic], with interest at 5%.

I secured a further loan of $1250. for the purchase of stock, equipment etc. This is to be paid back in 4 equal annual instalments, with interest at 5%.

My first payment falls due on October 1st 1920.

Fortunately for me, my uncle in Arequipa, Willie Sugars [*Arequipa, Peru, S. America*] has undertaken to help me out with the payments. A.K. also, is in on a third share basis.

The place itself is situated on what is known as, the "Limit", a bench about 2 miles North of the Village of Salmon Arm. It consists of 40 acres of almost level land only about 2 acres of this is unfit for cultivation At present there are about 17 acres under cultivation; 4 acres in 7 year old apple & cherry trees. There are also about 10 acres all cleared but the stumps. The balance – 13 acres – is still in timber. the house is small & plain, but well finished & warm; it consists of 5 rooms & a summer kitchen (which we recently added) The barn is of logs, & will accommodate from 4 to 5 head, the loft will hold 5 or 6 tons of hay.

There is also a chicken house, pig pen, grain-room, woodshed, & tool shed. There is enough small fruit for our own use. City water is piped in: school is only 1/2 mile away & telephone line 500 yards.

The soil is a heavyish clay loam, & will grow stuff to beat the band.

At the time I am writing – May 22nd – is just 9 months since we came on the ranch.

Last fall I spent in ploughing & slashing. During the winter we cut wood – I hauled about 160 cords of rick-wood to town last winter, on sleighs & on wheels, & sold it for $6.00 per cord. We have about 75 cords on hand for next winter.

This spring we have built 500 yards of "A" rail fence. Seeded 5 acres to alfalfa, 3 acres to clover (with wheat which was planted last fall) 1/2 an acre in field roots, & cucumber & 1/2 of an acre to potatoes. We have also set out 550 raspberry plants, & put in a kitchen garden.

We blasted about 2-1/2 acres of stumps & have got about an acre of that cleaned up & ploughed.

So the greater part of our spring work is done. We have still got 1000 tomato plants to set out & the remainder of the blasted stump field to clean up.

After that it will be a case of "carrying on" – cultivating & so forth, till harvest time. Expenses, of course, are very heavy. Hay is now $60 per ton, oats about $85, & stumping powder $8.90 per case. 75 lbs. of alfalfa seed cost us $41.00! The clover seed was 75 cents a lb., & seed potatoes are 5 & $6.00 per hundred. (We fortunately had nearly enough left over from last year.)

For the first few years I expect it will be a bit of a struggle, but 'ça ne fait rien' if you weren't struggling on a farm you would be struggling somewhere else!

Anyhow, I have acquired a home & an interest. Of course I am not perfectly contented – no man ever was, I guess – but I'm as near it as might be expected.

I am 23 years of age, & I think my character is about set. My ideas & beliefs will never be set. The older I grow the more perplexed I become. When I was 16 or 17 I had quite a decent religion framed up for myself, & some cut & dried ideas on social & political matters: but those are all at sixes & sevens now.

Religious beliefs do not worry me a great deal, but the more I think about them the more tangled up I become. I am still decidedly Socialistic but my notions in that line are not nearly so neat & complete as they were.

The more I know, the more I realize how little I know.

* * *

Roger Sugars recounted his entire Army and war experience from June 4, 1917 to April 11, 1919 from memory. He never missed a word, sentence, an experience or anecdote. He told it as it happened.

– John Sugars, 2004

*Roger and wife Margaret
"Honeymoon Hotel" 1923*

*Below: "Old" Kennard, and
Margaret Okanagan Centre
1923*

Margaret Sugars
Sugars' family photos.

Edmund feeding chickadees

Lilian in soapbox

Clockwise from top:
Roger and Margaret's children Edmund, Lilian, John, Madeleine
Sugars' family photos.

John among the hollyhocks

Maggie and Pluto the pup.

Clockwise from top:
Edmund, Lillian,
John, Madeleine

From left: John, Lillian, Madeleine, Edmund

CHARACTERS IN ROGER'S LIFE

By John Sugars, Editor, 2005

H.B. KENNARD: "Old Kennard" was a brewmaster in England who emigrated to Canada (and Fintry) in the late 19th Century. At that time, Fintry was known as Shorts Point, named after Captain T.D. Shorts who owned the point and later sold it to James Dun-Waters. "Old Kennard" ran the General Store and Post Office at Nahun (Nay-hun) for many years, Nahun actually being 3 or 4 miles south of Fintry. As children growing up, our parents often spoke of "Old Kennard" – not by his first name(s) and we thought he must have been *born* "Old Kennard." We don't think he practised his trade (professionally) in Canada, but he had the space and equipment to make a mean batch of beer for his friends. He moved from Nahun to Okanagan Centre about 1918 and died there in the 1930's.

A.K. MENZIES (Mingees) was born in England and emigrated to Canada a year or two before the Sugars. He convinced the Sugars to emigrate to Canada also – "The Land of Milk and Honey." Certainly Shorts Point was worlds apart from London, England! A.K. had little or no money, but lodged with the family at Shorts Point for several years. He was a good hunter and often provided a deer to the Sugars, which assisted greatly in feeding these new pioneers. Menzies eventually moved to Salmon Arm where he started an insurance business. He married and had a daughter, Hillary. Now I think of it, they never mentioned Menzies first names - just A.K., but they never called him "Old." *Ed. Note: Found on the Internet April 2005 - A.K. Menzies names were Allan Keith.*

DUN-WATERS: Much has been written about this man of great wealth. He changed the name of Shorts Point to Fintry to commemorate his home in Scotland, built a hydro electric system and a complete water supply for his house, barns etc. at Fintry – all from Shorts Creek Falls. Although a bit eccentric, he was very kind, having invited my father to his home to read books from his massive library.

Dun-Water became known as the "Laird of Fintry" and has been known as such ever since. He died in Fintry on October 16, 1939 at age 75 years. His wife predeceased him and is buried on the property.

ALBERT HOLLICK-KENYON: Although not mentioned in Roger's diaries, he had been a playmate who had a real bent to the military. He became a flyer and flew a plane to Antartica in the 1930's to rescue a stranded explorer. He became chief flying instructor for C.P. Air and his name and fame have gone into the Candian Pilots' Hall of Fame in Ottawa. Albert's sister Patty, mentioned in the diaries, at 16 years of age married Wallace Colquahoun (Age 30) in1914. They took over Mr. Fox's store at Ewing's Landing, where the latter died.

HERCULES LOVE: After working his "gold mine" for many years, Mr. Love packed up and left Fintry, moving to Washing State to live with his sister. No one heard from him again.

CONTRIBUTION TO THE 50TH ANNIVERSARY REPORT OF THE OKANAGAN HISTORICAL SOCIETY (1975)

Editor's Note: Retrospective Reproduced with Permission of the
Okanagan Historical Society

By Roger Sugars

As I grew up in the Shorts Point area I feel I am in a position to relate, as accurately as possible, what happened there from Capt. Shorts' time up to the Dun Waters' era when the property became known as Fintry. Nor is it my intention to confine my remarks entirely to Shorts' Point or Fintry but rather to the West side of Okanagan Lake in this vicinity. I think, also, I should explain how and why my parents came to be pioneers on a remote bush ranch in B.C. We lived on the edge of Clapham Common, London, which at that time (1904) was almost rural. My father was an M.A. in classics, Oxon, and had a comfortable living as a tutor coaching young men for Oxford and Cambridge.

My mother, however, was a restless type who became "fed up" with the humdrum life in suburban London. She became obsessed with the urge to go and seek a new life in Canada. My father being a gentle and non-aggressive man, soon gave in and agreed to pull up roots. So on the 24th of March 1905 we sailed from the Port of London on the S.S. Sarmatian (An Allan line converted cattle boat) bound for Montreal, where we arrived on April 13th. What a voyage! I was only 8 years old but I shall never forget it. To me it was like pictures of the arctic. Dense fog and icebergs along the Grand Banks of Newfoundland; then days of grinding at "dead slow" through floe ice which covered the sea beyond the horizon in every direction. The old Sarmatian was a sturdy ship and several other steamers followed in our wake. We finally docked at Montreal where we stayed about 3 days at the "Turkish Baths Hotel"; a very nice, quiet and comfortable place. I can't remember what street it was on nor have I been able to find anybody who remembers it. We thought Montreal was a beautiful City, especially when viewed from the cable car which was running up Mount Royal in those days. Our next stop-over was Toronto for two days pf which I recall very little; it evidently did not impress me too much.

From here we went on to Winnipeg where my parents had arranged to meet a friend by the name of A.K. Menzies (hereinafter referred to as "A.K.") He had been "out West" for some months and was to give us some guidance as he was supposed to "know the ropes". My parents had no idea where they were going and were depending on his advice while he, I suspect, was depending on them for some financial assistance. He was practically broke and had no really constructive ideas as to what to do or where to go. However, he understood that the Okanagan Valley in B.C. was a veritable land of promise; full of opportunities with a glorious climate and an easy life (anything to get out of Manitoba!) The decision was made! After about 5 days at the Winnipeg Hotel we left for the Far West via C.P.R. tourist class.

While in Winnipeg my father rescued me on two occasions. He had foolishly presented me with a "Daisy" air rifle. From the second floor balcony of our hotel I was tempted to test my skill as a marksman with my new air rifle. I was watching the traffic going by Portage Avenue and there on the opposite side of the street (Portage is quite wide) was a farmer perched on the box seat of his wagon wearing a jaunty bowler hat - it was too good a target to miss I guess; anyway, I drew a bead on that bowler hat and to my amazement I heard the B B pellet go "pop" when it struck the hard crown. The farmer immediately drew his team to the curb. He then came straight over to the hotel and up to the second floor where I was huddled in mortal fear. My father had no trouble appeasing his anger with a 5 dollar bill and that was the end of my first adventure in the Wild West! Then, like a typical small boy, I had to explore around an old boat house and fell into the Red River over my

shoulders in the muddy water. My father was at hand and promptly pulled me out to safety, otherwise I'm sure I would have
drowned. This was my second rescue. While in Winnipeg we visited Fort Garry and Silver Heights, where I recall, was an unfortunate brown bear chained to a post. He was known as the "Pop
drinking marvel" - All the visiting tourists brought him a bottle of
pop which he eagerly consumed and cast the empty bottles aside -
he was literally surrounded with empties - I would think the poor
thing must have finally died of kidney trouble!

And so we crossed the prairies and somewhere - probably
Saskatchewan - I was thrilled to see, from the train window, real
Indians wrapped in coloured blankets and their real tepees. I think
the southern prairies were briefly known as the territories of
"Assiniboia" and Alberta. I recall that we stopped briefly at a small
town called "Calgary,"

The main things that come to mind in connection with the
Rocky Mountains was a small station called "Laggan" (now Lake
Louise) and the tremendous climb up and along the almost per-
pendicular face of Cathedral Mountain with two great steam
engines and a "pusher". The spiral tunnels and the Connaught tunnel were yet to be built. Our long train journey ended at the jumping off place for the Okanagan - Sicamous Junction on the 29th day
of April 1905. We stayed overnight at the Sicamous Hotel and the
following day proceeded south on the "Shuswap and Okanagan"
branch line 50 miles to Vernon. Here we remained for two weeks at
the Coldstream Hotel. The plan was to use this as headquarters
while seeking a suitable place to buy land and settle. Real Estate
Agents were ready and willing to provide transportation by horse
and buggy to take us out to see the fabulous orchard lands just cry-
ing out to be cultivated and planted to apples and pears and peaches which in no time would be yielding a bountiful and highly prof-
itable harvest. However, even in those early years, the boom had
started and the price of good (and not so good) orchard land was
far beyond my parents' somewhat meager capital.

In the interests of economy we checked out of the Coldstream Hotel; we purchased a couple of tents and some camping equipment, a shaky old rowboat and some grub and were ready for anything! We camped on the shore of Long Lake - a beautiful spot, with a sandy beach and a grove of aspen trees about 2 miles from Vernon on a very hot and dusty road on foot. Another thing which added to the sense of adventure was the presence of rattlesnakes, which were fairly common. My father ruined a perfectly good bag of sugar while attempting to kill a rattlesnake which had got itself into a box of groceries in our tent. Indeed there must've been a guardian angel who looked after children and greenhorns; I ran around with bare feet most of the time; no one was bitten during our summer in that camp on Long Lake (now called Kalamalka). This was 1905, about 10 years later the C.N. & C.P. joint tracks ran right through the site of our old camp and along the lakeshore to Oyama where they crossed the lake to the east side on the isthmus which divided Long Lake from Woods Lake. For some reason this isthmus was known as "the Railroad" long before the actual railroad was built. This branch line proceeded on to Kelowna where boxcars were loaded on barges which carried up to 16 cars and were pushed back and forth to and from Penticton by powerful Tugs - "Castlegar", "Naramata" and later C.N. No. 5 and the "Pentowna" - The last of these tugs went to its final berth only last year, 1974.

THE BUSH RANCH

The camping season was drawing to a close and we seemed no nearer to finding a permanent location and in desperation my father purchased a 160 acre pre-emption from Fred Stedham., the original pre-emptor, for the sum of $500.00. This comprised 1/2 a mile of frontage on the west side of Okanagan Lake adjoining the south boundary of the Shorts Point Ranch. It was completely wild land with no improvements other than an ancient log cabin and a tent on wood frame and floor. The natural assets were pine parkland of virgin Ponderosa pine and some Douglas fir. The land was steep, rocky and totally unsuited to farming or fruit growing. There was however, a large cedar swamp near the lake, fed by crystal clear ice cold springs which bubbled and gurgled all the year round and never froze in the coldest weather. The area was a dense jungle of willow, osier, dogwood, birch and other deciduous bush which formed an undergrowth to large cedars. There was no road save the old Hudson Bay Trail which was the route of the early Fur Brigades and later the prospectors and miners bound for the gold fields of the Cariboo. in order to reach this destination it was necessary to move our effects from the Long Lake camp to the end of the road at the head of Long Lake by rowboat and hence by hired wagon to Okanagan Landing where it was loaded on the SS York - a small screw steamer under Capt. Weeks. This was an auxiliary vessel to the larger stern wheeler SS Aberdeen under Capt. Estabrooks which made the regular runs up and down the lake. The York unloaded ourselves and our effects on the wharf at Shorts Point. We got no further than perhaps a 1/4 mile round the Point with an overloaded rowboat when we were met by the full force of a south wind and a very rough lake. Everything including the boat was piled in the bush on the upper part of the beach and was picked up piece meal in the next few days. We then proceeded to walk some 2 miles to our "bush ranch" along the Hudson Bay Trail which we located with some difficulty only to lose it again at the Cedar Swamp. A.K. lost one of his boots while I, up to my ankles in wet moss and ooze, refused to move any further! My father and mother bravely struggled on and urged me to follow. We finally located the log cabin and tent in the dusk of evening , thoroughly exhausted and discouraged. We had fortunately packed in a few blankets and some grub. This was Sept. 1905. So here we were really out in the wilderness.

Our Mr. Stedham evidently felt we were a "soft touch" for a grubstake and had all sorts of progressive ideas including some elaborate plans for a house he was going to build for us. In the meantime the fall was rapidly approaching and my mother's patience had run out. She told Mr. Stedham to pack it up and she went to Kelowna and engaged two carpenters - a Mr. Creighton and an assistant by the name of Clement (of an old Kelowna family). Lumber was ordered and delivered on a small scow to the beach. Some of the lumber was hauled up from the beach with a single horse while much of it was carried by hand, piece by piece, mainly by my father. Eventually a small two storey frame house was built. The inside walls were never properly finished but we moved in anyway - two stove pipe chimneys served a cook stove and an "airtight" heater. It was the coldest and hottest house I've ever had the misfortune to live in. Water had to be hauled up from a catch basin of one of the springs by means of a bucket on a pulley which ran on a steeply inclined tight wire about 150 feet long. (In later years we built a good warm log house with spring water piped in).

Our nearest civilization was Shorts Point P.O. where we called for mail once a week. Shorts Point, even then, was a beautiful property with many acres of orchard and hayfields all irrigated from Shorts Creek. It consisted of two ranches, the larger of which was owned by a Mr. McMullin who, apparently was a bachelor; he lived alone, save for his Chinese cook, in a large frame house. He was an aloof man, and nobody seemed to know much about him.

The C.P.R. wharf was on the Dundas property and they ran the Post Office. All supplies had to come via Okanagan Landing on the stern wheeler Aberdeen which was the only vessel on the Lake at that time except the York, a small screw steamer. The Aberdeen rendered regular service south to Penticton - returning the following day. The Dundas family were fine people, and our first real neighbors. Bob was a tall handsome man. A great horseman, he made a striking figure in his high crowned Western hat and black angora chaps. He taught me how to pack a horse and throw a "diamond hitch". As a little boy he was my hero. The Dundas' arranged with my father to give their children lessons; Nita, a very pretty little girl about 8 and Duncan about 7. Jenny was too young for lessons. I joined in these classes and my father and I walked over to their place twice a week. At that time (1906) there were no schools nearer than Kelowna, and, I might add that with the exception of my mother and Mrs. Dundas and her "lady help", Miss Hayne, there were no white women in some 25 miles of Westside Okanagan Lake.

Our first saddle horse - Ginger - was purchased from Bob Dundas for $25.00 and to a great extent became my charge. I picketed him out in the best bunch grass and learned to ride him bare back or with a saddle. Our men folk were not interested in riding so my mother and I made many trips taking turns in the saddle and occasionally doubling up - the two of us weighed no more than a good sized man - Ginger was also an excellent pack pony and many a load of groceries and other supplies have I packed home 4 miles from our nearest store at Nahun. Another somewhat colourful neighbour was Tom Hamilton a soft spoken Englishman who quite often dropped in while riding the range "looking for horses". He owned a horse ranch about 3 miles up Shorts Creek, known to his friends as "Rum Jug Canyon" where he lived in an old log cabin. He usually wore a pair of greasy old fringed leather chaps and a battered Stetson of the old style. A most likeable character with a fondness for Hudson Bay overproof rum which was much favoured by the early settlers; I can recall seeing him bringing home from Ewings Landing a supply of this beverage with 3 pack horses each with a gallon jug hung around its neck with a bell strap. About 1908 or 9 Tom left for the Old Country. Evidently he had inherited a legacy as he returned to Rum Jug Canyon in a few months with a change of name to Attenborough, a wife, a hackney stallion named Agitator, and a thoroughbred stallion named Brockhampton and a string of blood mares. He proceeded to have a large log house built close by his old log cabin and a good bunk house which was soon filled with hired men. Mr. Attenborough now wore riding breeches instead of beat up old chaps but he still liked his Hudson

Bay rum and so did most of his hired men. His most reliable employee was, probably, Erland Okerblad, a magnificent Viking-like Swede who was reputed to be the son of a Swedish Ambassador to somewhere or other! Erland's job was traveling the stud horse and he became quite well known from Vernon to Kelowna. He was quite a dandy and always rode the stallion in full cowboy regalia. He liked to have a bit of fun on these trips - on one of which the police advised him to stay out of the City of Vernon for 6 months!

Old timers of the Okanagan might recall the names of some of the other "characters" who worked for Old Tom (as Attenborough was affectionately known) such as Billy Rylands, Red Marshall, Jack O'Mahoney, Jos. Woods. Woods later became a Forest Ranger; O'Mahoney committed suicide, while Erland became manager of a cattle ranch in Paraguay. Old Tom and his charming but plain little English wife sold out some years later to Dun Waters, who named it Fintry High Farm.

The only other settler of the upper Shorts Creek area was "Old Man Love" who had been drilling a tunnel in the base of Goat Mountain since the 1890's. Hercules Love was a Civil War Veteran and had been an Indian fighter and plainsman before coming to B.C. to prospect. He was a small wiry old man with a long white beard and as I remember him he seemed a bundle of energy, probably in his late 70's. With unflagging optimism he was always on the verge of striking the "pay lode" though he was already 200 feet or more into the mountain. How he handled his rock drill and sledge hammer alone I'll never know. He spent a large part of his American Army pension on dynamite and coal for his small forge and lived in a tiny log dugout where he could sit on his bunk and reach everything else in the cabin. About once a week he hiked down the Creek trail to Tom's ranch some 3 miles to pick up his mail and supplies and back-packed it to his cabin. Tom occasionally helped with a pack horse to take in dynamite and coal. With people he knew he loved to yarn about early days on the plains, but with strangers he became shy and reticent, punctuating his brief remarks with profanity. The following is, in part, quoted from my old diary - "Sept. 6, 1914. Not a drop of rain has fallen since Aug. 16th. Two forest rangers (E. McCluskey and W. Ryan) who had been fighting a big fire at the headwaters of Shorts Creek were on their way out and found another fire near Love's. Old man Love was in a desperate state, having fought the fire all night alone. He saw he was beat, so moved his stuff across the Creek. The two rangers remained a week to make sure there was not a fresh outbreak." About 1915, Love's "Golden Dream" mine became flooded. This was too much for the old man, so he packed up and left for his old sister's place in Kittitas County, Washington. There, no doubt, he cashed in the last of his U.S. Army pension cheques.

Sometime in 1906, the Dundas family sold their Shorts Point property to a Mr. Ludovic Lailavoix. (A property registration gave his name as Louis). Mr. Lailavoix was perhaps thirty-five years of age, while his wife was undoubtedly many years his senior. An air of mystery surrounded this suave young Frenchman, with his imperial beard and moustache, as he had no knowledge of farming or fruit growing. It seemed there was no apparent motive for settling in this somewhat remote area of Western Canada, unless he was seeking a hideout.

By a strange coincidence, however, our Mr. A.K. Menzies, who had lived some years in British Guiana, knew that Mrs. Lailavoix had been a wealthy widow there, with a grown-up family, prior to her marriage to Mr. Lailavoix. Also, it was rumoured that she was reputed to have a weakness for alcohol. In any event, one cold night in the winter of 1907, one of the Shorts Point ranch hands by the name of Harry Howis (who later settled in Summerland) arrived at our place on horseback and leading a spare horse. "Would Mrs. Sugars please come with me to the Lailavoix house as Mrs. Lailavoix is very ill." No doctors or telephones, so of course, my mother dressed in warm clothes and her heavy riding skirt and went with Mr. Howis. She found Mrs. Lailavoix to be unconscious and after a few simple tests she decided Mrs. Lailavoix was obviously dead. She reeked of alcohol and the remains of a bottle of wood alcohol was in evidence. Mr. Lailavoix explained that his wife had been drinking and run out of whiskey (or brandy) had found the bottle of wood alcohol and evidently swallowed most of it. Sometime the next day a doctor arrived from Kelowna or Vernon and rendered a verdict of death by alcohol poisoning. As simple as that! However, Mrs. Lailavoix's will was in favour of her husband and it was quite substantial. Her grown up family in South America fought the Will through the courts and won the case. Not long after, Monsieur Lailavoix left the country and has never, to my knowledge, been heard of since. There is a story that the old ranch house is haunted; perhaps Mrs. Lailavoix is still looking for the brandy bottle! The property was, apparently, heavily mortgaged in favour of Mr. McDonnell of the B X Ranch in Vernon, who foreclosed as soon as Lailavoix departed. Was a bizarre crime involved or what? I leave it to you.

In the meantime, Mr. McMullin's house had burned to the ground and all these events culminated in the sale of the entire Shorts Point property to Jas. Dunsmuir, Lt. Gov. of B.C., who bought it for his son-in-law Major Audain in 1908. The Audain's evidently did not care to live there so the property was up for sale again. The next purchaser was Jas. C. Dun Waters and Dave Falconer actually picks up the story at this point 1909 "Dun Waters of Fintry" 38th Report O.H.S.

As my report is intended to cover the history of Shorts Point up to the time of Dun Waters arrival in 1909 I feel that the various registrations of ownership should be recorded here. Capt. Thomas Dolman Shorts who operated the first steamboat on Okanagan Lake was the original pre-emptor in July 1883. He obtained a Crown Grant in Jan. 1890 and at the same time conveyed the property to the Hon. John Scott Montague (Viscount Ennismore) and G. Hare. In 1892 these people conveyed the property to John Poynder Dickson Poynder. In 1903 Poynder conveyed part of the property to

Murray McMullin and in 1904 the remaining 19.80 acres to Robt. Napier Dundas. In 1906 Dundas conveyed to Louis Lailavoix. In July 1907 the Lailavoix 29.80 acres together with the balance of the land, which belonged to McMullin, was conveyed in its entirety to the Hon. Jas. Dunsmuir* who, in October of that year, conveyed to Laura Miller Dunsmuir. In November 1908 she conveyed to her daughter Sarah Boyd Audain (wife of Major Audain). On October 5, 1909 the entire property was finally conveyed to Jas. Cameron Dun Waters. I should think that very few properties anywhere have had so many owners in such a short space of time.

NOTE: *Jas. Dunsmuir was Lt. Gov. of B.C. at that time.

THE WESTSIDE NORTH OF SHORTS

Before taking leave of the Shorts Point area entirely I would like to make some mention of the adjacent districts - Ewing's Landing to Whiteman's Creek on the north and Nahun to Bear Creek on the south. A few names of the earlier settlers may "ring a bell" with some of the oldtimers who are still surviving. Robt. Leckie-Ewing was amongst the earliest - "Bob" ran the Post Office for many years. His brother George had a small orchard nearby and sold to the Kenyon family about 1911. "Bert" Kenyon was then a teenager and later became Commodore Herbert Hollick-Kenyon who distinguished himself during and after World War I. (See Footnote)

Other names such as Teddy Haynes, Andrews, Muirhead, Hodges, Tangue, Pease, have all gone except some of their offspring who are settled all over the world. In 1907 or 8 a Mr. and Mrs. Boyd came out from Scotland to Ewings' with two pretty daughters. For sometime they ran a sort of Tea Shop which they called the "Clachan Inn."

A few miles further north was Indian Reserve which stretched from Whiteman's Creek to the head of the lake at the O'Keefe Ranch. Near the reserve on the south was a large acreage owned by the Willet family who came to Canada at the same time and on the same ship (the S.S. Sarmatian) as ourselves. Mr. & Mrs. Victor Willet with 3 sons and one daughter. On, or near, the reserve I recall such names as Dave Cameron - a "bad man" who was reputed to have "held up" the Hudson Bay store in Vernon; he had a handsome Indian wife. Harry Tronson, a son or nephew of one of Vernon's pioneers E.J. Tronson. Tommy Struthers, Lou Everett, George Smith, construction men and loggers.

Now let's take a look at the oldtimers who lived in the country south of Shorts Creek north to south in that order. Most were single, young and middle aged, who lived in shacks of varying types, some excellent, others somewhat crude, but all cosy homes in their way. Many of these men married later; some remained confirmed bachelors. John McNair, a big rawboned Scotsman who built beautiful rowing and sail boats but held power boats in contempt. He sold out to Chas. Durant about 1911. The "Colonel", a nickname for John Brixton a Boer War Veteran and originally from London, England. A great hunter who always got his "Mowich" (deer) when the larder was getting low - died in his 80's at Okanagan Centre. H.B. Kennard, Postmaster and store keeper at Nahun; a remarkable man who remained single all his life; an Englishman educated at Marlborough, he came to the States as a young man. He sold Nahun to Bernard Biggin about 1919 and moved to Okanagan Centre where he built himself a charming little house on the lakeshore where he lived until his death. He lived at Nahun probably 25 years; his cabin was never locked and anyone was welcome, whether he was at home or not, to help themselves to a meal - (meat in the meat safe, bread and butter in the bread box). Mail days (Monday and Friday) were quite an event at Nahun. Most of the settlers for miles around foregathered, some on horseback or boat, others on foot. The mail, freight and sometimes, a passenger was delivered at the wharf by the SS Aberdeen and later by the Okanagan and still later by the Sicamous, which is permanently beached at Penticton. Stripped of her boilers and machinery, she is well preserved as a tourist attraction and museum.

A couple of miles south of Nahun was Caesar's Landing. Walter Legge lived there for a number of years but lost his life while flying in England in 1917. In the meantime the property had been purchased by Herbert and Percy Leney, who developed the place considerably but later gave up and left the district. Following the lakeshore southward was a large pre-emption purchased by two young Englishmen about 1907 from the original pre-emptor who had the romantic name of "Fishhead Hanson" or "Two Bit Hanson" as a polite alternative.. Roy Bachelor and Percy Seeley built a large log house which burned to the ground and was replaced by a good frame house. Roy was killed in World War I. Seeley distinguished himself in assisting R.D. Ramsay in the capture at gun point of two desperadoes, Boyd James and Frank Wilson in the summer of 1912. (A full account of this may be found in the Police Gazette). James died on the gallows for the murders of Constable Aston. Wilson was found "not guilty", I believe. This was near Wilson's Landing, named for Ex Private Wilson, known better as the "Major" - another Boer War Veteran and a close friend of "Colonel" Brixton. The Major was a handsome bachelor who affected the neatly trimmed imperial beard which was so popular in those days. He also favoured simplicity of apparel and in summer wore nothing but a sort of "Nightie" which he made himself of flour sacks. This, with a big "two-bit" straw hat was ideal for the hot summer days. Allan Brooks, the well known artist and naturalist, was a popular and frequent visitor to the bachelors of the West side. Brooks, who lived at Okanagan Landing, painted most of the beautiful illustrations in "Birds of Western Canada."

About 2000 feet above the lake and west of Nahun was a broad bench known as Bighorn Flats, covered with dense forest of lodge pole and spruce interspersed with wild hay meadows and bulrush sloughs. Bald Range Creek meandered through this area and finally emptied into Bear Creek opposite Kelowna. This became the site of a group of pre-emptions mostly filed by young Englishmen. One of the first was Alfred Stocks who, about 1909, together with W.R. "John" Tozer cleared some land and built a good cabin of jackpine logs. All supplies and material (except the logs themselves) had to be transported by pack horses up the mountain on a tedious zig zag trail. They were soon followed by other adventurous young men; some names I recall were MacAllister and Horner, Sam Lister, Charlie Critchley, Mark Ellis and Somerset Brothers. All built cabins and cleared an acre or so of land. Stocks was joined by his younger brother Arthur and soon after by another brother Lumb, two sisters and father and mother. These members of the Stocks family did not settle at the pre-emption, but all got married and went to live in Penticton and Kelowna. The exception was the father - The Rev. Phillip Stocks who was buried at the old pre-emption which they named "Stocksmoor". Tozer opted out fairly early in the story; got married to a Miss Surtees and became father of Tony, Hugh and Geoff Tozer. World War I took most of the young men from the neighbourhood, and few survive today. All the pre-emptions are abandoned, but the loggers moved in in the 30's or 40's and cleaned out some beautiful stands of spruce. Shortly after building a fine log home for their mother and sister, who came out from England, the two Somerset boys died in the War, there upon the mother and sister left the country.

The Coldstream Ranch near Vernon grew many acres of hops in those days and Indians were employed for the harvest (there was a brewery in Vernon). Among these, was the entire Nez Percé tribe, who came all the way from their reservation in Washington State about the middle of September each year and returned sometime in October. The last of these "migrations" took place in 1908. To us this was one of the highlights of the year. They were about 300 in all, men, women and children all mounted with several hundred pack horses. The Nez Percé are of the Plains Indians type, tall and handsome. In those days their dress was almost traditional; buckskin shirts, leggings and moccasins; much fine bead work was in evidence, also on gloves, gun scabbards and cradle boards slung from the saddle horns. Some of the young bucks were more modern and affected leather and angora chaps, cowboy boots and Mexican spurs. All wore the type of cowboy hat that was fashionable at the time with wide stiff brims and high crowns of black or fawn felt with fancy beadwork or metal studded bands. Their hair was worn in long braids and bright coloured neckerchiefs were much in favour. The Squaws dressed more simply but were always colourful with their bright head scarves and cotton dresses. Together with multi-coloured saddle blankets and many beautiful horses the cavalcade created a spectacle not easily forgotten. Our house was located close by the old Hudson Bay Trail so we had a real "ring side" seat. One year two or three of the young braves got themselves some "hooch" and became separated from the main column. They camped not far away and spent the night galloping madly up and down the Trail emitting the most blood curdling war whoops. I don't think we slept much that night either! The next day, however, they departed peaceably and presumably, caught up with the rest of the tribe. A noteworthy character to be seen occasionally riding on the Hudson Bay Trail was Chief Tomat of the Shuswaps. A dignified old gentleman with a deeply furrowed copper coloured face, white hair and goatee beard. As symbols, no doubt, of his high station in life he wore a brown bowler hat and a black cutaway coat turning slightly green with age; behind him rode his squaw, an ageless lady with the story of many parching summers and harsh winters written in her face.

We had little in the way of entertainment in those early years; no radio, no gramophone, and no shows or concerts nearer than Vernon or Kelowna. It was a major expedition to either of those places on the sternwheeler Aberdeen and took up at least two days, so we seldom went to "town". My mother was an excellent pianist and one of the sacrifices she had made on leaving England was having to leave her Steinway piano behind. We had no music in our home for 8 years, but in June 1913 we pooled our resources and a second hand piano was purchased in Kelowna from Dayton

Williams. It was a "Steinbach" made by the Mason & Risch people and quite a good instrument. It was delivered at our beach on a small scow. As our house was 2 or 300 feet up a steep bank, a sort of road or grade wide enough to accommodate the piano in its case had to be constructed. I did this job with a pick and shovel and our neighbour, Chas. Durant helped considerably and with block and tackle and skids and rollers we had little trouble in getting the piano up to the house. Of course it required tuning, so a week or so later a tuner by the name of McGeorge made a special trip from Kelowna to tune my mother's piano and also Dun Waters' player piano at Fintry. I was now exposed to "good" music mainly of a classical nature and developed a great love of the music of Beethoven, Chopin, Greig and many others. With the exception of a few of the popular songs and "pieces" of that era, I had little knowledge of "Ragtime" and "Jazz" which came later. The preference for so-called "good music" stayed with me to this day. Our house now was one of the very few that could boast of a piano and someone who could play and so became quite popular with the young people who liked to drop in for a musical evening. Some had excellent voices notably John Tozer and the Stocks boys. Sometimes we had a violin solo by Miss Isabel Somerset or Mrs. Nora Robinson.

In 1909 we had our property surveyed and obtained title to same. On account of the bay in the half mile of lake frontage, the actual acreage was reduced from 160 to 140, more or less. At this time we began to reap some returns from our "bush ranch." Art Dobbin of Westbank took out some fir piling which yielded a few dollars. He was followed by Art Johnson who "summerlogged" the virgin Ponderosa pine and some Douglas fir by means of a heavy two wheeled dolly hauled down the steep hills by a team of big Percherons. The logs were chained on the heavy cross bunk of the dolly with the ends allowed to drag and act as a brake. From 2 to 7 or 8 logs would make a load of up to 2000 ft. B.M. The falling, bucking and swamping was done by young woodsmen; mainly

McDougalls; Urban, Lesime, Amable, Dan and Albert - also 2 relatives - Angus Thompson and Billy Smithson. Albert ran-a-foul of the law and spent several years in jail for murder. Billy Smithson, unfortunately, was thrown from a horse and killed. All the others served in World War I. The Boss was Art Johnson, a handsome young American from Minnesota who had followed construction and lumber camps most of his life. In addition to Johnson's big team, a second one was used for skidding and driven by a little French Canadian by the name of Joe Goodreau. He had an Indian wife known as "Bat eye Mary" (not to be confused with "High tone Mary"). She did some cooking for the crew and tanned deerskins in her spare time.

These people all camped on our place throughout the summer of 1909. People used to ask my mother "aren't you terrified having all those rough characters so close?" Her reply was "No, they all behave like perfect gentlemen." They did, indeed, treat her with the utmost respect. She often rendered little kindnesses such as giving them a loaf of home made bread or a cake. The sale of the timber netted us about $500.00 for nearly a 1/2 a million feet (B.M.) of Ponderosa pine and fir. The area had never been logged before so this was virgin timber. If I remember rightly the logger received $5.00 per thousand feet B.M. yarded on the lakeshore.

When the Dundas family left, the Shorts Point P.O. was closed. We then went to Kennard's at Nahun for our mail - four miles of very rough trail which was about the last remnant of the original Hudson Bay Trail. A narrow wagon road had been punched through from Westbank to Nahun by Jim Silver and his crew from Peachland about 1908. The almost sheer rock bluff at Nahun presented a formidable barrier and it was 7 to 8 years before the remaining 10 or 12 miles of rough and narrow wagon road to Ewing's Landing was completed thus making Vernon accessible without crossing the lake by ferry at Westbank. It is only a secondary road to this day. This was before tractors and bulldozers and the heavy grading was done with 4 horse teams.

My wife and I recently had the pleasure of visiting Major C.H.R. Dain whom I have known as an acquaintance for many years. Charlie, now 87 years of age is one of the few surviving original settlers of the Westside - Bear Creek area. As a young man he came out from England to his uncle's place near Bear Creek in 1906. This was known as the Dain property and was located just north of the McLennan Ranch which was later purchased by R.A. Pease. Charlie Dain leased the Pease property for a number of years and finally purchased it outright about 1925. Thus Charlie has been, practically, a continuous resident of the Westside since 1906, interrupted only by his service in 2 World Wars. Charlie mentioned several old timers of the Bear Creek country whom I could personally recall prior to World War I; Henry Childers owner of Bear Creek ranch and brother of Erskine Childers, author of "The Riddle of the Sands"; "Sully" Sullivan a Game Warden; Fred Stocks, South African War Veteran; Bob Foulis, Browse, Lefroy, Bill McQueen, Art Johnson of Johnson's Crossing of Bear Creek. who logged our place in 1909 and Father Carlisle.

* * *